AQA History

A2
Unit 3

British Monarchy: the Crisis of State, 1642–1689

Exclusively endorsed by AQA

David Farr

Series editor
Sally Waller

Nelson Thorn

D0996032

Text © David Farr 2009
Original illustrations © Nelson Thornes Ltd 2009

The right of David Farr to be identified as author of this work has been asserted by
him in accordance with the Copyright, Designs and Patents Act 1988.

All rights reserved. No part of this publication may be reproduced or transmitted in any form
or by any means, electronic or mechanical, including photocopy, recording or any information
storage and retrieval system, without permission in writing from the publisher or under
licence from the Copyright Licensing Agency Limited, of Saffron House, 6–10 Kirby Street,
London EC1N 8TS.

Any person who commits any unauthorised act in relation to this publication may be liable to
criminal prosecution and civil claims for damages.

Published in 2009 by:
Nelson Thornes Ltd
Delta Place
27 Bath Road
CHELTENHAM
GL53 7TH
United Kingdom

10 11 12 13 / 10 9 8 7 6 5 4 3 2

A catalogue record for this book is available from the British Library

978 1 4085 0554 0

Illustrations by Bob Moulder at Graham-Cameron Illustration, David Russell Illustration and
Trevor Parkin/Linda Rogers Associates

Page make-up by Thomson Digital

Printed in China by 1010 Printing International Ltd

Contents

AQA introduction

Nelson Thornes and AQA

Nelson Thornes has worked in collaboration with AQA to ensure that this book offers you the best support for your AS or A-level course and helps you to prepare for your exams. The partnership means that you can be confident that the range of learning, teaching and assessment practice materials has been checked by the senior examining team at AQA before formal approval, and is closely matched to the requirements of your specification.

How to use this book

This book covers the specification for your course and is arranged in a sequence approved by AQA.

The features in this book include:

Timeline

Key events are outlined at the beginning of the book.

Learning objectives

At the beginning of each section you will find a list of learning objectives that contain targets linked to the requirements of the specification.

Key chronology

A short list of dates usually with a focus on a specific event or legislation.

Key profile

The profile of a key person you should be aware of to fully understand the period in question.

Key terms

A term that you will need to be able to define and understand.

Did you know?

Interesting information to bring the subject under discussion to life.

Exploring the detail

Information to put further context around the subject under discussion.

A closer look

An in-depth look at a theme, person or event to deepen your understanding. Activities around the extra information may be included.

Sources

Sources to reinforce topics or themes and may provide fact or opinion. They may be quotations from historical works, contemporaries of the period or photographs.

Cross-reference

Links to related content within the book that may offer more detail on the subject in question.

Activity

Various activity types to provide you with different challenges and opportunities to demonstrate both the content and skills you are learning. Some can be worked on individually, some as part of group work and some are designed to specifically 'stretch and challenge'.

■ Question

Questions to prompt further discussion on the topic under consideration and are an aid to revision.

■ Summary questions

Summary questions at the end of each chapter to test your knowledge and allow you to demonstrate your understanding.

AQA Examiner's tip

Hints from AQA examiners to help you with your study and to prepare for your exam.

AQA Examination-style questions

Questions at the end of each section in the style that you can expect in your exam.

Learning outcomes

Learning outcomes at the end of each section remind you what you should know having completed the chapters in that section.

■ Web links in the book

Because Nelson Thornes is not responsible for third party content online, there may be some changes to this material that are beyond our control. In order for us to ensure that the links referred to in the book are as up-to-date and stable as possible, the websites provided are usually homepages with supporting instructions on how to reach the relevant pages if necessary.

Please let us know at **webadmin@nelsonthornes. com** if you find a link that doesn't work and we will do our best to correct this at reprint, or to list an alternative site.

Introduction to the History series

When Bruce Bogtrotter in Roald Dahl's *Matilda* was challenged to eat a huge chocolate cake, he just opened his mouth and ploughed in, taking bite after bite and lump after lump until the cake was gone and he was feeling decidedly sick. The picture is not dissimilar to that of some A-level history students. They are attracted to history because of its inherent appeal but, when faced with a bulging file and a forthcoming examination, their enjoyment evaporates. They try desperately to cram their brains with an assortment of random facts and subsequently prove unable to control the outpouring of their ill-digested material in the examination.

The books in this series are designed to help students and teachers avoid this feeling of overload and examination panic by breaking down the AQA history specification in such a way that it is easily absorbed. Above all, they are designed to retain and promote students' enthusiasm for history by avoiding a dreary rehash of dates and events. Each book is divided into sections, closely matched to those given in the specification, and the content is further broken down into chapters that present the historical material in a lively and attractive form, offering guidance on the key terms, events and issues, and blending thought-provoking activities and questions in a way designed to advance students' understanding. By encouraging students to think for themselves and to share their ideas with others, as well as helping them to develop the knowledge and skills they will need to pass their examination, this book should ensure that students' learning remains a pleasure rather than an endurance test.

To make the most of what this book provides, students will need to develop efficient study skills from the start and it is worth spending some time considering what these involve:

- Good organisation of material in a subject-specific file. Organised notes help develop an organised brain and sensible filing ensures time is not wasted hunting for misplaced material. This book uses cross-references to indicate where material in one chapter has relevance to material in another. Students are advised to adopt the same technique.

- A sensible approach to note-making. Students are often too ready to copy large chunks of material from printed books or to download sheaves of printouts from the internet. This series is designed to encourage students to think about the notes they collect and to undertake research with a particular purpose in mind. The activities encourage students to pick out information that is relevant to the issue being addressed and to avoid making notes on material that is not properly understood.

- Taking time to think, which is by far the most important component of study. By encouraging students to think before they write or speak, be it for a written answer, presentation or class debate, students should learn to form opinions and make judgements based on the accumulation of evidence. These are the skills that the examiner will be looking for in the final examination. The beauty of history is that there is rarely a right or wrong answer so, with sufficient evidence, one student's view will count for as much as the next.

Unit 3

The topics chosen for study in Unit 3 are all concerned with the changing relationship between state and people over a period of around 50 years. These topics enable students to build on the skills acquired at AS level, combining breadth (by looking at change and continuity over a period of time) with depth (in analysing specific events and developments). The chosen topics offer plentiful opportunities for an understanding of historical processes, enabling students to realise that history moves forward through the interaction of many different factors, some of which may change in importance over a period of time. Significant individuals, societies, events, developments and issues are explored in an historical context and developments affecting different groups within the societies studied from a range of historical perspectives. Study at Unit 3 will therefore develop full synoptic awareness and enable students to understand the way a professional historian goes about the task of developing a full historical understanding.

Unit 3 is assessed by a 1 hour 30 minute paper containing three essay questions from which students need to select two. Details relating to the style of questions, with additional hints, are given in the table below and helpful tips to enable students to meet the examination demands are given throughout this book. Students should familiarise themselves with both the question demands and the marking criteria that follow before attempting any of the practice examination questions at the end of each section of this book.

Answers will be marked according to a scheme based on 'levels of response'. This means that an essay will be assessed according to which level best matches the historical skills it displays, taking both knowledge

Unit 3 (three essay questions in total)	Question types	Marks	Question stems	Hints for students
Two essay questions	Standard essay questions addressing a part of the Specification content and seeking a judgement based on debate and evaluation	45	These are not prescriptive but likely stems include: To what extent … How far … A quotation followed by 'How valid is this assessment/view?'	All answers should convey an argument. Plan before beginning to write and make the argument clear from the outset. The essay should show an awareness of how factors interlink and students should make some judgement between them (synoptic links). All comments should be supported by secure and precise evidence
One essay question	Standard essay question covering the whole period of the unit or a large part of that period and seeking a judgement based on debate and evaluation	45	As above	Evidence will need to be carefully selected from across the full period to support the argument. It might prove useful to emphasise the situation at the beginning and end of the period, identify key turning points and assess factors promoting change and continuity

and understanding into account. All students should keep a copy of the marking criteria in their files and need to use them wisely.

Marking criteria

Level 1 Answers will display a limited understanding of the demands of the question. They may either contain some descriptive material that is only loosely linked to the focus of the question or they may address only a part of the question. Alternatively, they may contain some explicit comment but will make few, if any, synoptic links and will have limited accurate and relevant historical support. There will be little, if any, awareness of differing historical interpretations. The response will be limited in development and skills of written communication will be weak. *(0–6)*

Level 2 Answers will show some understanding of the demands of the question. They will either be primarily descriptive with few explicit links to the question or they may contain explicit comment but show limited relevant factual support. They will display limited understanding of differing historical interpretations. Historical debate may be described rather than used to illustrate an argument and any synoptic links will be undeveloped. Answers will be coherent but weakly expressed and/or poorly structured. *(7–15)*

Level 3 Answers will show a good understanding of the demands of the question. They will provide some assessment, backed by relevant and appropriately selected evidence, which may, however, lack depth. There will be some synoptic links made between the ideas, arguments and information included, although these may not be highly developed. There will be some understanding of varying historical interpretations. Answers will be clearly expressed and show reasonable organisation in the presentation of material. *(16–25)*

Level 4 Answers will show a very good understanding of the demands of the question. There will be synoptic links made between the ideas, arguments and information included, showing an overall historical understanding. There will be good understanding and use of differing historical interpretations and debate and the answer will show judgement through sustained argument backed by a carefully selected range of precise evidence. Answers will be well organised and display good skills of written communication. *(26–37)*

Level 5 Answers will show a full understanding of the demands of the question. The ideas, arguments and information included will be wide-ranging, carefully chosen and closely interwoven to produce a sustained and convincing answer with a high level of synopticity. Conceptual depth, independent judgement and a mature historical understanding, informed by a well-developed understanding of historical interpretations and debate, will be displayed. Answers will be well structured and fluently written. *(38–45)*

Introduction to this book

Fig. 1 *A contemporary image of the trial of Charles I*

The historian Christopher Hill entitled his general text on the 17th century *The Century of Revolution* (1961). Although Hill's Marxist views led him to view revolution and the nature of revolution in different ways from other historians of the period, there can be little doubt about the political, religious, economic and social turmoil that the multiple-kingdoms of 'Britain' and Ireland went through, even just in the 47 years from 1642 to 1689. Indeed the title of one of Hill's most influential texts, *The World Turned Upside Down* (1972) derived from contemporary reaction to the forces unleashed by the revolutionary years of the 1640s and 1650s that made many at the time feel that everything that they were accustomed to was under threat. Between 1642 and 1689 there was:

- **civil war:** A war between the Crown and Parliament of England, but one that encompassed all three kingdoms, including war between the kingdoms (1642–51). England lost a greater percentage of its population in the civil wars than it did in either of the world wars of the 20th century.

- **regicide (1649):** The most singular act of British history, the public execution of the monarch. On 30 January 1649 King Charles I was taken through his palace of Whitehall and beheaded by axe in front of a large crowd.

- **republican rule (1649–60):** For the period of the Interregnum, England was governed without a monarch. At first this was a formal republican regime, the Rump Parliament. This was followed by a brief-lived godly assembly before Oliver Cromwell became Lord Protector by the terms of Britain's first written constitution, the *Instrument of Government*, and ruled as head of state for the next five years.

- **revolution (1640–60):** Republican rule was established on the back of a revolutionary army, the New Model. The years specifically from 1647 were for many contemporaries 'the world turned upside down'. This army was the prop for all Interregnum regimes, as well as in the short-lived major-generals' experiment, being the closest England has come to direct military rule. The New Model was also the chief vehicle for the explosion and survival of radical religion, through groups like the Quakers.

conquest (1649–60): After the regicide the various English regimes of the Interregnum conquered and ruled Ireland and Scotland. In 1649 Oliver Cromwell led the forces of the New Model Army to crush an Irish Catholic rebellion. His rapid victorious campaign was followed by an occupation and an immense transfer of lands to Protestants.

restoration (1660): In 1660 monarchy returned to England and an attempt was made to reverse the forces unleashed by the English Revolution and construct a viable settlement. Such was the fear of a repeat of the mid-century revolution that the later Stuart monarchy of the 1680s appeared stronger than it had ever been.

revolution (1688): From inheriting a crown that appeared to be developing into an absolutist form, James II, by his aggressive support of Catholicism, provoked his removal by his Dutch son-in-law, who had been invited to invade England by some of the English political elite and was then crowned as William III.

Kishlansky (1996), in one of the most recent general overviews of the century, has re-stressed that the **Stuart Age** witnessed remarkable changes.

> The collapse of an entire system of government; the creation of a revolutionary new one based on zeal and Utopian vision; its failure; the restoration of the older system; yet another collapse, followed by a foreign invasion; still another revolution; and finally Britain's absorption into and domination of the European state system.

1
*M. Kishlansky, **A Monarchy Transformed: Britain 1603–1714** (1996)*

Some change was driven by forces beyond the control of the governments and individuals of the time.

> Whilst kings and generals toiled and failed, however, a fundamental change was taking place in English economy and society, largely unheeded and certainly unfashioned by the will of government. In fact, the most obvious revolution in seventeenth-century England was the consequence of a decline of the birth-rate.

2
*J. Morrill, **The Tudors and Stuarts** (1992)*

For the majority of the population, in a hierarchical society where they had little real power, it was probably the consequences of this unseen force – the decline of the birth rate – that had more impact on life than who ran the state and local government. The decline of the birth rate in the later 17th century clearly improved, in general terms, conditions for much of the population, whereas economic pressures in the period 1550–1640, specifically the consequences of inflation and population growth, made life more difficult and pressures on the **early modern** state greater.

As a consequence of population growth in the period 1550–1640, there were:

- food shortages and periods of localised starvation
- price inflation, particularly with regard to food
- land shortage
- unemployment
- greater reliance on the state for poor relief.

Key terms

Stuart Age: a phrase for the period 1603–1714 during which the Stuarts were monarchs of England, Scotland and Ireland.

Early modern: the period in British history c.1485–1750.

Fig. 2 *The Great Chain of Being: the contemporary idea that everyone's place in society was ordained and that all were linked together in an order*

In contrast, a declining population after 1650 saw the gradual disappearance of these problems. Indeed, increased agricultural productivity, the emergence of a national economy – rather than a localised one – and the emergence of a newly defined aristocracy were all signs of a changed economy and society. This made a repeat of 1640–60 less likely as there was a stronger and thriving conservative centre. Increasingly the post-1689 elite were men who had power other than from their estates. They had money from trade and government, business and professions, and lived in the town and the country. They had an interest in protecting their position and, at a time when those at the other end of society were in less economic distress and therefore less likely to rebel, there appeared no need for the vast majority of this conservative centre to consider radical political solutions.

All of these economic changes happened, however, in the context of the politics of the 17th century and both were interlinked in the long-term development of the early modern state into something more like a true modern state. These changing economic conditions were a subtext for the political narrative that is the focus of this study.

Under Cromwell in the 1650s there was resolution of some of the long-term structural problems that faced the first Stuart English king, James I (1603–25). The regime of the 1650s was essentially military based. This **fiscal-military state** was only developed further in the 1690s and it was then that the problems of 1603 (religious division across and within the multiple kingdoms and the financial limits of the early modern English state) were more permanently addressed as the British state emerged as a world power.

Despite the upheavals, there were elements of continuity across the 17th century. These elements of continuity meant that in 1689:

- monarchs still had a great deal of personal political power
- the main forum of politics was still the royal court
- local areas were still run by a few powerful men: the landed elite
- religion was still central to daily life and politics.

Apart from the years 1649–60, the institution of monarchy remained the most important constant throughout this period. The position of the monarch may have been different in 1689 from that in 1642 but in a system of **Personal Monarchy** the characters of each monarch did much to shape the period in which they ruled.

Whatever the balance between unseen impersonal forces, such as economic change over the period and the role of the Stuart monarchs, their individual approaches were significant. It was the two Stuarts who most tried to shape their reigns – Charles I and James II – who triggered revolutions. James I was pragmatic, understanding the art of the politically possible. In the context of the failure of the Stuarts as a dynasty, recent assessments of James I, particularly in the light of his son Charles I (1625–49) and grandson James II (1685–8), have shown that for early modern Britain he was a successful king. Charles I's absolutist style of rule and religious policies exacerbated all the structural problems of early modern Britain to the point where he faced rebellion, civil war and his own public execution.

That Charles I was, by nature, unsuited to rule in a time of Personal Monarchy seems, with hindsight, all too apparent when considering his reign up to the outbreak of the English Civil War in 1642. Charles's reign before 1642 can be viewed in three phases. The period 1625 to

■ **Key terms**

Fiscal-military state: a state financially organised for war with a supporting administration. Through the 17th century the state developed in 'Britain' towards one more financially and militarily capable to wage war.

Personal Monarchy: the power of the Crown in this period was theoretically absolute and this was supported by the concept of the divine right of kings. In such a framework the monarch was government and expected to rule actively. Therefore his or her personality and aims shaped policy.

Key terms

Prerogative: the power of the Crown in theory derived from God as divine right. From divine right the powers of the Crown were referred to as the prerogative. Such prerogative powers included the right to call and dissolve parliament. The monarch could also declare war. Theoretically the monarch still holds such powers today.

Exploring the detail

Calvinism

Named after John Calvin (1509–64), an influential Protestant reformer. Central to Calvinism was predestination and the discipline imposed on members of the Church by the elders who ran the Church. Calvinism became the branch of Protestantism predominant in the Church of England. The anti-Calvinists were those Protestant conservatives who did not wish the Reformation to go any further; indeed they wanted elements of the pre-Reformation Church brought back. They put ceremonies above sermons and, unlike the majority of English Protestants, did not regard the Catholic Church as evil but as the 'mother church' that had gone off track.

Exploring the detail

Laudianism

Laudianism was the term for the anti-Calvinists under Charles who were allowed to dominate the Church of England during the 1630s. They derived their name from the Archbishop of Canterbury, William Laud. Laudianism placed more stress on ceremony and outward forms of religion and was thus regarded by some as too close to Catholicism.

1629 witnessed a rapid deterioration in Charles's relationship with the parliamentary class. The consequence of this was that Charles ruled without parliament for the next 11 years, the Personal Rule. A growing discontent with the financial, but particularly the religious, policies of the Personal Rule brought about a rebellion to his rule in Scotland that triggered a crisis of rule in England, forcing Charles to recall parliament in 1640. The increasing division of the political nation over the next two years, particularly in reaction to a Catholic rebellion in Ireland in October 1641, made civil war in England possible.

Before Charles came to the throne, he aligned himself with Parliament's opposition to James I's refusal to accept war against Spain. Charles's superficial popularity soon disintegrated. The years 1625 to 1629 saw Charles provoke war against both Spain and France and fail on both fronts. He antagonised the parliamentary class by resorting to **prerogative** means to fund his disastrous foreign policy and heightened their distrust by supporting a gradual anti-Calvinist dominance in the Church.

Charles's style of rule further underpinned the deterioration in Crown–Parliament relations in the years 1625 to 1629. Charles would not accept criticism and subverted the accepted constitutional norms in his relations with the three parliaments of this period.

The years of Personal Rule (1629–40) were, on the surface, ones of calm and peace. Charles quickly signed peace treaties with both Spain and France and further ensured he would not need to resort to another parliament by exploiting his means of raising finance through his prerogative. What was more antagonistic to the political nation

Fig. 3 *Prince Charles in 1624 at the time of his alliance with MPs against his father's peaceful foreign policy*

was the consolidation of the anti-Calvinists, or Laudians, in the Church of England.

While the 1630s witnessed large-scale emigration of Puritans to North America and some individuals opposed Charles on religious and financial grounds, there was no widespread open discontent until after 1637. In 1637, as a result of Charles imposing an English Laudian prayer book on Scotland and refusing to compromise, the Presbyterian Scots rebelled. The underlying discontent that Charles's policies had engendered saw the collapse of his financial position and his authority in England in response to his failure to defeat the Scots militarily in 1638–40. Charles's military failure against the Scots, who occupied Newcastle in 1640, forced him to call an English parliament.

The MPs of 1640 to 1642 could generally agree on what they did not like about Charles's Personal Rule, but when it came to considering what should be put in its place, particularly with regard to religion, division began to emerge. As those who considered more radical solutions, like John Pym, became more influential, a growing reaction of Constitutional Royalists saw the political nation divide.

It was the rebellion of Irish Catholics in October 1641, however, that transformed the political situation. MPs could agree that an army needed to be raised to crush the rebellion, but could Charles be trusted with it? This fundamental questioning of the prerogative alongside other signs of a breakdown of order enabled a royalist party, rather than supporters of Charles, to form and meant that there were two sides to fight a civil war. Although most still wished to avoid conflict, a minority of activists, chiefly motivated by religion, seized the initiative in spring and early summer of 1642, and conflict escalated into civil war.

After the experience of his father and his own years of exile on the continent (1649–60), Charles II was determined to stay on his throne and was, until his later years, too lazy and lacking ideals to initiate reform or to seek a fundamental political change. James II, by contrast, inherited a stronger monarchy in 1685, but his aggressive promotion of Catholicism alienated the anti-Catholic English elite. In both cases, however, it is clear that it took a lot of provocation for the English elite to even consider rebellion. Essentially conservative and with a vested interest in maintaining their social position, the English elite did what they could to avoid revolution both in the 1640s and 1680s. The difference in the 1680s was that they, with the context of the mid-century revolution, remained in control and ensured that the revolution was their conservative revolution. In the Revolution Settlement of 1688–9, there was an adjustment of the relationship between the ruler, the elite and the ruled.

Even during the 1640s and 1650s many of the revolutionaries, like Oliver Cromwell himself, were politically conservative. They sought 'healing and settling', which they recognised could only be achieved through compromise with the traditional gentry elite. Such were the conservative forces, even at the heart of the Protectorate, that Cromwell was offered the Crown in 1657 as a means to secure the support of the political nation. Despite such conservative political impulses, religious radicalism drove the revolution to be radical and prevented the traditional elite from accepting regimes that relied on the New Model Army. In ruling the three kingdoms, the regimes of the Interregnum developed a stronger state financially and militarily that was, in many ways, the forerunner of the one that established Britain as the world power in the 18th century in providing models for post-1689 regimes.

The consequence of the Revolutions of 1640–60, and more fully that of 1688–9, was the resolution to varying degrees of the problems that beset the early Stuart rulers:

- **Post 1689:** Saw the formation of the fiscal-military state and through this the increasing influence of Parliament by controlling the finances of the state.
- **Post 1689:** The role of religion became less politically problematic. Spurred on by Renaissance humanism and contacts with more of the wider world, there was a more rational approach, scepticism and a distrust of religious enthusiasm.
- **Post 1689:** Britain became a world power.
- **Post 1689:** The threat of **absolutism** had been removed by the two revolutions of 1640–60 and 1688–9.

To get to this point, however, the three kingdoms went through civil war, revolution, regicide, republican rule, restoration and further revolution.

Exploring the detail

Constitutional Royalism

This was a reaction by moderates who, although they may have been concerned or even opposed to Charles's policies in the 1630s, were more worried by the development of parliamentary radicalism since 1640, exemplified by Pym, and the apparent growing threat of social order across the country. In the face of radical Puritanism, Parliament taking over the prerogative of the Crown and the power of the mob, many nobles and gentry looked to monarchy, rather than Charles, as the best protection for a moderate Protestant church, law, order and their continued influence.

Key terms

Absolutism: a monarch with unlimited powers, specifically one able to make law and raise taxes without the need for Parliament's agreement. The main examples were Spain and France. As both were also Catholic, most English equated Catholicism with absolutism.

■ Timeline

1642	1643	1644	1645	1646	1647	1648
Outbreak of civil war	Solemn League and Covenant	Battle of Marston Moor	Creation of the New Model Army Battle of Naseby	Charles I surrenders to the Scots	Army's Heads of the Proposals Putney debates Charles's engagement with the Scots	Second Civil War Battle of Preston *Remonstrance of the Army* Pride's Purge

1656	1657	1658	1659	1660	1661	1662
Second Protectorate Parliament Nayler Crisis	Cromwell offered the Crown	Death of Oliver Cromwell Richard Cromwell becomes Lord Protector	Third Protectorate Parliament Rump Parliament reinstated Army dissolves Rump	Monck and Scottish New Model Army intervene in England Long Parliament re-established Convention Parliament Charles II enters London	Cavalier Parliament	Act of Uniformity

1672	1673	1674	1675	1676	1677	1678
Stop of the Exchequer Third Anglo-Dutch War	Test Act Duke of York's Catholicism becomes public knowledge	End of Third Dutch War	Attempt to impeach Danby Secret financial funding of Charles II by Louis XIV	Further secret financial funding of Charles II by Louis XIV	Marriage of Princess Mary to William of Orange Anglo-Dutch Treaty against France	Further secret agreement between Charles II and Louis XIV Peace of Nijmegen Popish plot unveiled Exclusion crisis begins

1686	1687	1688	1689	1690
Godden v. Hales Commission for Ecclesiastical Causes	Declarations of Indulgence Parliament dissolved	Mary of Modena gives birth to a son Invasion of William of Orange James flees to France	Convention Parliament Coronation of William and Mary Bill of Rights	Battle of the Boyne

1649	1650	1651	1652	1653	1654	1655
Trial and execution of Charles I

Monarchy and the House of Lords abolished as England becomes a republic

Cromwell leads the New Model Army to Ireland | Cromwell leads the New Model Army to Scotland | Cromwell defeats Charles Stuart and Scots at Worcester

Incorporation of Scotland into the Commonwealth with England | First Anglo-Dutch war | Cromwell dissolves Rump

Nominated Assembly

Protectorate established with Cromwell as Lord Protector | End of Dutch War

First Protectorate Parliament

Western Design | Major-generals established |

1663	1664	1665	1666	1667	1668	1670
Charles withdraws Declaration of Indulgence	Triennial Act	Second Anglo-Dutch War

Plague in London | Great Fire of London | End of Dutch War

Fall of Clarendon | Triple Alliance | Secret treaty of Dover |

1679	1680	1681	1683	1684	1685
Charles dissolves Cavalier Parliament

Danby resigns

Exclusion Bill receives first reading in First Exclusion Parliament

Charles dissolves Parliament | Petitioning campaign supporting Exclusion

Second Exclusion Parliament

Exclusion Bill passes Commons but defeated in Lords | Second Exclusion Parliament dissolved

Further secret funding of Charles by Louis XIV

Third Exclusion Parliament dissolved after one week

Tory reaction | Rye House Plot | Charles II violates Triennial Act | Death of Charles II and accession of James II

James II's first Parliament

Monmouth's rebellion |

1

The Defeat of Charles I, 1642–6

In this chapter you will learn about:

■ the personality of Charles I

■ the policies of Charles I at war

■ the reasons for the defeat of the royalist cause, 1642–6.

Key terms

Conspiracy theory: a belief, in any period, that the explanation for events or actions is more sinister than the official explanation. Charles believed there were some radicals, many of whom were motivated by Puritanism, whose agenda was to undermine his power. In contrast there were some, especially Puritans, who believed Charles intended to establish absolutism and Catholicism in England.

Ancient constitution: during this period there was no 'written constitution' and England was said to be governed by the 'ancient constitution': a system that had evolved over time. Part of this constitution were documents like the Magna Carta, but the working of the constitution depended upon trust between Crown and Parliament and the balance of the prerogative and privilege.

Feudal/feudalism: a system introduced into England by the Normans after the conquest of 1066. The King owned all the land and distributed it among his followers. In turn they attended court but also owed military service to the King and administered central and local government.

On 5 January 1642, Charles marched with troops into Parliament in the hope of arresting the five men he regarded as his leading opponents. The failure of this attempted coup to re-establish his authority precipitated Charles's departure from London. On 22 August 1642, Charles I's royal standard, the symbol of his authority, was planted in the ground in Nottingham, marking the official start of the English Civil War. He was the first and last monarch to declare war on his own Parliament. A few days later a high wind blew the royal standard to the ground, which some took as an omen. By 1646 Charles had been militarily defeated, his armies in England decimated. Charles fled from Oxford and surrendered to the Scots. They promptly handed him back to the English Parliament who placed him under guarded house arrest. In 1648, for the first time since 1642, Charles returned to London, but this time under an armed guard for his trial and execution.

■ The personality and policies of Charles I

Charles's personality

In a time of Personal Monarchy, the personality of the monarchy was central, and shaped policy. Charles's personality was the root of his problems. In contrast with his outgoing father, James I, Charles I was shy and hampered by a speech defect. Both led to his being unapproachable and uncommunicative, especially with Parliament. Here his intentions and actions often went unexplained, leaving others to interpret them. Charles had an inferiority complex that made him overstress his prerogative. Charles, because of his insecurity, had none of James's political shrewdness or flexibility; he did not know the meaning of compromise. He seemed unable to understand viewpoints that differed from his own. It could be argued that Charles had a **conspiracy theory** mentality.

Charles would not countenance even the slightest criticism, believing that it was a deliberate attempt to undermine his prerogative.

In the period up to the outbreak of civil war in England in 1642, Charles's actions and others' perceptions of his motivation invariably added to the political tensions of the period. Many of his subjects came to question whether he was a monarch who could be trusted to rule within the ambiguous bounds of the unwritten **ancient constitution**.

Charles did not have the personality or political skill that invited loyalty. This meant he was a weak king, would be a poor leader in war and was unwilling to compromise to achieve settlement once defeated.

The policies of Charles I at war

Charles as a war leader was, initially, in a strong position. As King he naturally had greater political sway for those deciding their allegiance because he was the central recognised authority. Charles called for military support through commissions of array, a **feudal** call for troops from each county.

In contrast, the position of Parliament was less sure.

Fig. 1 *A later depiction of Charles I rallying his troops*

Exploring the detail

Charles I's policies 1625–40

- Foreign policy: Failed wars against Spain and France between 1625 and 1629.
- Religion: Allowed the Laudians to dominate the Church.
- Parliament: Three failed parliaments in the first four years of the reign.
- Personal Rule: Eleven years (1629–40) of ruling without parliament.
- Finance: Exploited his prerogative forms of income to enable him to rule without parliament.
- In 1637 the Scots rebelled against Charles's imposition of Laudianism on them. They defeated Charles, occupied the north of England and thereby forced Charles to recall parliament in 1640.

Did you know?

Parliament

Before 1640 Parliament's main function was still to support the monarch as a 'Greater Council'. It did not meet regularly; only sitting when called by monarchs, usually when they needed finance. Parliament only met on average about three weeks a year during the 45-year reign of Elizabeth I. Thus revisionist historians referred to Parliament in this period as more of 'an event' rather than 'an institution'.

Parliament's call for troops was on the novel basis of the Militia Ordinance, the first piece of legislation passed by Parliament without the royal assent. To counter the novelty of their position, Parliament, through propaganda pamphleteers like Henry Parker in his *Observations* (1642), argued that Parliament as a representative of the people was a legitimate authority, especially when the current monarch had relied too much on dubious 'private' advice rather than the 'public' counsel of his Great Council, Parliament.

■ Reasons for the defeat of the Royalist Cause, 1642–6

There were a number of the reasons for royalist failure:

Military failures

Charles I failed to take advantage of the early strength of his position. After the stalemate of Edgehill, Charles had the opportunity to advance on London. After slow progress the royal army was forced back at Turnham Green.

In 1643, however, there were a number of royalist victories:

- ■ **30 June:** Adwalton Moor.
- ■ **5 July:** Lansdown.
- ■ **13 July:** Roundway Down.
- ■ **26 July:** Bristol.

In September 1643, at the first Battle of Newbury, Charles's advance on London was once again halted and the civil war descended into stalemate. Charles's war-effort was hampered by a series of royalist military mistakes, in particular the weak coordination of their forces. Some of this was due to the divided nature of royalist councils. The Earl of Newcastle's failure to march his northern royalist army south in 1643 stopped a royalist attack on London when it might have been successful. Charles made crucial mistakes. After Edgehill he fell back to Oxford rather than proceed to London. He then chose an engagement at Naseby (1645) against the newly formed New Model Army of whom royalist commanders were dismissive. Defeat at Naseby destroyed Charles's military capabilities in England.

Charles also suffered military defeat in Scotland. Montrose led royalist forces north of the border against the Covenanters. After some initial successes Montrose was defeated.

Fig. 2 *The religious motivation of parliamentary troops*

Royalist strengths	Royalist weaknesses
Led by the recognised lawful ruler	Problems with organisation of war effort
More support from aristocracy and higher gentry, more of whom had financial reserves and military experience	Charles I was a poor commander-in-chief
Focused strategic objective: the taking of London	Areas under royalist control generally poorer
Military aid from abroad, notably Princes Rupert and Maurice	Clubmen as an example of increasing failure of local communities to support royalists
	Commissions of array of dubious legality
	Charles's willingness to use troops from Ireland reinforced the impression of his favour to Catholics

As well as defeat in the field there are a number of areas that contributed to royalist military failures:

- **Administration:** The royalist council of war at Oxford was an effective organisation, particularly in contrast, initially, to the tensions between the parliamentary commanders in the field and the direction of the MPs through the Committee of Both Kingdoms, which managed the war. It suffered, however, from the limited range of its authority, with the royalist commanders in the north and west in effect being independent. Added to this problem was Charles's decision to set up a separate council at Bristol that removed men as capable as Clarendon. Charles was a poor war leader. Richard Cust (2006), in the most recent study of Charles I, argued that the King was unable to provide the strong leadership that was needed as his cause disintegrated.

- **Indecisiveness:** Charles and the royalists proved indecisive through failing to follow through their initial promising start to the war. This was not only in terms of strategic considerations, but also in taking advantage of the resources at his disposal. Charles was not decisive enough to take control of his early advantage of the greater experience of his generals, as well as greater support from the aristocracy.

- **Generals:** In the early months of the war, Charles used influential local men as lieutenant generals in their local areas in the hope that they would rally support in their locality. They weakened the royalist war effort, however, and Charles began to appoint men with military experience; notably his two nephews, Princes Maurice and Rupert. While this was sound militarily, it further provoked division in royalist councils.

Key profile

Prince Rupert (1619–82)

Rupert was Charles I's nephew who, with his brother Maurice, rallied to his uncle's cause. With some experience from the Thirty Years War, Rupert was Charles's General of the Horse, but eventually became commander-in-chief. Rupert proved himself to be one of Charles's chief military assets, if lacking discipline. After the fall of Bristol in 1645, Charles sent Rupert into exile. Charles was angered by Rupert's claim following his defeat at Naseby that a settlement with Parliament was needed. In the period 1648 to 1652, Rupert undertook naval action against the Rump Parliament. Rupert returned to England at the Restoration and undertook naval command in Charles II's wars against the Dutch.

Key dates

War in Scotland 1642–6

1644

September Royalist forces under Montrose defeat Covenanters at Tippermuir

1645

May Royalist Montrose defeats Covenanters at Inverlochy

May Montrose defeats Covenanters at Alford

September Crushing defeat of Montrose forces at Philiphaugh

Fig. 3 *A London newsbook image of Prince Rupert. Birmingham is shown burning in the background as a reference to the destruction of 80 houses in the town by Rupert's troops in 1643*

Fig. 4 *Queen Henrietta Maria (1609–69)*

Key dates

War in Ireland, 1642–6

1642

April Anti-Catholic Scottish army of 10,000 lands in Ireland

1643

September Agreement between Charles and Irish Catholic confederacy

1646

March Ormond, leader of royalists in Ireland, signs peace with Catholic confederates

June Irish confederate victory over Monro's Scots at Benburb

Activity

Revision exercise

Write a paragraph explaining which factor you think was the most important in weakening Charles's position.

Division: In the royalist councils the different views put forward by individuals (like the Queen Henrietta Maria and Edward Hyde, first Earl of Clarendon and adviser to the King) led to incoherent policy because of the lack of leadership from Charles, as well as his failure to recognise or select the best advice. Hyde advised continuing attempts to settle with parliament, whereas Henrietta Maria counselled a continued war until total victory was achieved. She, even when in exile, held most sway with Charles. Lord Digby and Prince Rupert also opposed a negotiated settlement, although the two carried on a running feud. While the influence of all three was affected by absences, either in exile or on campaign, Henrietta Maria repeatedly stressed in her letters to Charles that it would be a diminution of his honour to negotiate. Henrietta Maria's return to Oxford in 1643 saw the appointment of her supporters to key positions in Charles's administration. Henrietta Maria did, however, in her time at Oxford up to 1644, prevent much faction and allow Charles to stand above the competing groups. When she went back to France it left Charles exposed to men such as Digby and Rupert.

Charles as a military leader: Charles made himself commander-in-chief. While this may have strengthened his position if he could provide strong leadership and bring his generals and politicians together, it also meant he became more responsible for defeat. While he clearly did consult his council of war, Charles did not listen to nor act on the best advice.

Charles's agreement with Catholics: In September 1643 Charles signed a truce with the Catholic Irish rebels who had rebelled against Protestant rule in October 1641. The troops that were brought over from Ireland proved ineffective. Furthermore, many of Charles's supporters were disturbed by his willingness to use Catholics in arms in England. Out of the 603 officers he had as colonels during the war, 117 were Catholics. Charles repeated this mistake by trying to negotiate a second peace treaty with the Irish Catholic rebels in 1645.

Reliance on foreign aid: Charles's use of Rupert and Maurice left him open to attack. More seriously, his captured correspondence, which showed that Charles was negotiating with the French and the Pope, was wonderful propaganda for Parliament when they published some of the letters in *The King's Cabinet Opened*.

The royalist weaknesses and mistakes were matched by Parliament's growing strengths. As the war became one of attrition, Parliament was more flexible and brutal in its response, enabling it to fight the war more effectively. In particular, Parliament was able to finance its war effort more efficiently.

Parliament's financial management of the war

It was not just royalist failures but also parliamentary successes that enabled them to win the civil war. At Westminster, John Pym played a key role in laying the foundations of parliament's wartime administration. After the outbreak of civil war, Parliament combined executive with representative authority and developed methods for running the country without the King. This partly meant creating new structures like the Committee of Both Kingdoms and seeking to control finances.

Key profile

John Pym 1584–1643

While Pym was highly visible in the Parliaments of the 1620s, he was pre-eminent in the Commons of 1640 to 1642, to the extent that from the autumn of 1641 he was referred to as 'King Pym'. Pym emerged in 1640 because most of the other leading MPs of the 1620s were dead. More importantly, the crisis mood of 1640–2 fitted exactly with Pym's strengths. He continued to be the leading figure in the Commons until his death.

Fig. 5 *John Pym, one of the leading MPs of the early 1640s*

Parliamentary methods of raising finance

General method	Specific effect
Weekly/monthly assessments	Direct tax on income, particularly land
Sequestrations	Confiscation of royalist land
Compulsory loans	Forced loans
Excise	A duty/tax on goods; for example, beer

Through these methods Parliament was able to fund its war effort. The assessment in particular raised substantial amounts of money.

Pym was also vital in keeping Parliament together, despite the different factions within it, especially persuading them to accept a formal alliance – the Solemn League and Covenant – with the Scots in 1643. In return for what they believed was an agreement to establish Presbyterianism, the Scots through the Solemn League and Covenant, a religious agreement and military alliance, sent 21,000 men into England to aid Parliament. Although this army proved to be disappointing, in practice it did force Charles's northern army to remain in the north.

Did you know?

London's population in the 17th century reached 500,000. It has been estimated that one-sixth of all those born in England spent some of their life in London. In 1650 seven per cent of the English population lived in London. The next largest towns were Norwich, Bristol, Exeter and Newcastle. By 1700 London overtook Paris to become Europe's largest city.

Fig. 6 *London in the early 1600s*

The advantages of holding London

Controlling London gave Parliament a number of advantages:

- **Propaganda:** As the centre of printing, Parliament had an advantage in the production of propaganda.
- **Finance:** Access to resources, especially City loans.
- **Manpower:** Trained bands were vital at Turnham Green. London was also home to one out of ten of the English population.
- **Port:** England's largest port.
- **Industry:** England's chief industrial centre and thereby supplier of arms, clothes and shoes.
- **Administration:** Parliament could take advantage of an already established centre of administration.

Local administration and local communities

The organisation of Parliament's war effort not only involved developments at a national level, but also transformed government at a local level through setting up special committees in each county. This, in the counties, led to the employment of local men who were activists dedicated to the cause. Anyone who was not was removed. This led in many places to the replacement of the traditional ruling elite. Parliament showed a much greater willingness to do this, partly out of necessity. Charles was also hampered by the areas under his control being relatively poor in comparison to those under Parliament's control. Both sides encountered the resistance of local communities who resented the cost of war that they had no wish to be part of. Such resistance led to the growth of the 'clubman' movement. These armed groups of men, notably in the west and south, opposed the exactions of both armies, but became more favourable to the New Model as it came closer to winning the war and through Fairfax's willingness to negotiate directly with them. Hutton (1999) has argued, in his consideration of the royalist war effort, that 'it was the local community, not Parliament, which defeated Charles I, not hatred of his cause but from hatred of the war itself'.

Control of the Navy

Parliament, through control of the navy, was also able to supply its forces and strongholds, such as Hull and Plymouth, as well as hamper the supply of royalist areas. It also prevented Charles receiving supplies or men from the continent or Ireland.

All of these factors meant that when the civil war became a war of attrition, Parliament would be in a stronger position.

Despite being in a stronger position, Parliament was hampered by a division over how to pursue the war. From the very outbreak of war there were groups more inclined to make peace and groups more determined to negotiate only from a position of military strength, in order to force concessions from Charles. This was most memorably portrayed in an account of the words of the Earl of Manchester, Commander of Parliament's Eastern Association Army, to a council of war.

> Gentlemen, I beseech you let's consider what we do; the King need not care how oft he fights, but it concerns us to be wary, for in fighting we venture all to nothing. If we fight 100 times and beat him 99 he will be King still, but if he beats us but once, or the last time, we shall be hanged, we shall lose our estates, and our posterities be undone.

1   *Calendar of State Papers Domestic 1644–1645, p.159*

Activity

Revision exercise

Produce a spider diagram of the reasons for the defeat of the royalist cause in the English civil war. Then answer this question: Why did the royalists lose the first civil war? Use the information in this chapter to construct paragraphs for this essay.

Activity

Source analysis

What is Manchester's concern as expressed in Source 1, and how realistic was this?

Such an attitude provoked disgust in Manchester's more radical subordinates, Oliver Cromwell and Henry Ireton. Some in Parliament shared their distaste and the concern that such an attitude as Manchester's prevented the achievement of victory helped push Parliament to remodel its armies and thereby its war effort. In 1644–5 Parliament undertook political and military restructuring. Most significant was the formation of the New Model Army. Regularly paid, professional and motivated, it was never to be defeated in battle.

The defeat at Naseby in 1645 might have all but ended the King's hopes of winning the civil war in England, but he was still king. The next three years indicate that defeat at Naseby did not mean that the King was no longer a threat or that he could not overturn his military defeat.

Fig. 7 *Charles I dictating despatches to Edmund Verney. Verney disapproved of Charles's policies but felt honour bound to support his monarch when war broke out. The royalist standard bearer at Edgehill, Verney was killed after killing 16 parliamentary troops*

The position of Charles I in 1646

Defeated militarily, Charles I was still, however, in a strong position in 1646. As king he was still regarded as essential to a lasting settlement. Charles's realisation of his centrality to the political system was the basis of his approach in the years to 1648. Charles sought to play upon the divisions among the groups who had an interest in the post-war settlement: principally, the English Parliament, the Scots and the New Model Army. That all groups sought to negotiate with Charles merely reinforced his rigid belief in the divine right of kings. Charles was stubborn and failed to negotiate seriously. Over the period Charles's intransigence, while initially politically astute, radicalised some of his opponents to contemplate a settlement without him.

> Charles's bargaining position was stronger than it may appear to us in retrospect. His greatest bargaining chip was the simple fact that he was king. Unless his adversaries wished to do away with monarchy – and most of them still had no such intention – they had no choice but to strike a deal with Charles. Furthermore, those adversaries were far from united, and Charles could hope to exploit their differences. Many shared the King's view that monarchy needed to be maintained as a bulwark against the disintegration of the social order. Rule by Parliament or the army was beginning to look much more alarming than the familiar and traditional rule by the King.

2

*M. Young, **Charles I** (1997)*

Understanding Charles I's approach to settlement is crucial given that he was the centre of the political system, and in 1646 all envisaged settlement based on monarchy. It is also, however, important to understand the role of Parliament.

Activity

Talking point

In pairs, write directives for Charles I as if you were two of his advisers in 1646. One of you should outline the strengths of his position, while the other should highlight the weakness of his position. Each pair should present their lists of strengths and weaknesses to the class with a list of all points raised noted down by everyone.

Activity

Source analysis

From Source 2 note down the reasons given for Charles's continuing influence in 1646.

Summary questions

1 Why was Charles's personality a political issue?

2 How did Parliament fund its war effort?

3 To what extent was the royalist defeat in the civil war due to Charles I?

2 The Failure of Attempts to Reach a Settlement, 1646–9

On 30 January 1649, Charles I was led through the Banqueting House of his Whitehall Palace. Above him on the ceiling were three images of his father James I, constructed by Rubens under commission from Charles, depicting James as the biblical King Solomon. They have been described by Morrill (1988) as representing 'one of the greatest statements of absolute monarchy in Europe'. The Banqueting House was to be the central part of Charles's plans to turn Whitehall into his main palace through a massive building programme. The plans indicate that Whitehall would have been a symbol of Charles's perception of his divine right of kingship. The project was never finished. A deluded Charles was still considering plans in 1647 that would have made Whitehall twice the size of the Escorial, the Spanish royal palace. In 1649 Charles was taken through the palace and out to a specially constructed scaffold where a large crowd was waiting. On this scaffold he was beheaded by axe and became the first English monarch to be publicly executed.

Four key themes are central to understanding 1646–9. The failure of settlement and the eventual execution of the King derive from their interweaving:

■ **Charles:** His failure to accept a settlement.

■ **Parliament:** The role of Parliament; the division between Political Presbyterians and Political Independents.

■ **New Model Army:** The politicisation of the New Model; its relationship with the Levellers, its attempt to settle with Charles, the role of key army figures, its relationship with Parliament.

■ **Radicalism:** The nature and development of religious and political radicalism, particularly in the New Model.

These themes run through 1646–9, which can be broken into four stages:

■ The Political Presbyterians alienated and politicised the New Model who could work with their Political Independent allies in Parliament.

■ Charles's intransigence in refusing to come to settlement forced many in Parliament, but particularly key figures in the New Model, to be more radical in their approach to settlement and towards the King.

■ Charles further radicalised the New Model by refusing their moderate *Heads of Proposals* and starting a second civil war.

■ Political Presbyterians further alienated the army in continuing to try to negotiate with Charles even after his defeat in the Second Civil War. This forced the army to act against their enemies in Parliament to secure the trial of the King.

Fig. 1 *Ruben's painting on the Banqueting Hall ceiling in Whitehall Palace. Commissioned by Charles to glorify his father and the divine right of kings, Charles walked under this ceiling to his execution in 1649*

Parliamentary factionalism

Charles's intransigence was encouraged by the division that had emerged in Parliament about how to fight the civil war: between moderates and radicals, sometimes labelled Peace Party and War Party. By 1646, a division had emerged at Westminster between two broad factions that have been labelled Political Presbyterians and Political Independents. These labels clearly indicate a religious dimension to parliamentary divisions, but this was also a political division. The complexity of this division and the interrelation between political and religious terms has been summarised by the historian of the Second Civil War, Ashton (1994).

> It used to be customary to interpret the parliamentary conflicts between Presbyterians and Independents along largely religious lines. While it was clear that the Independents also took up a politically more radical, and the Presbyterians a politically conservative, stance, this was seen as all of a piece with their religious beliefs. The work of Professor David Underdown and other historians has done away with these comfortable certainties. It is not easy to come to terms with the existence of religious Presbyterians who were Independents in politics or Presbyterians in politics who were Erastian or episcopalian in religion.

1   R. Ashton, *Counter-Revolution: The Second Civil War and its Origins, 1646–8* (1994)

Political divisions became more entangled and religion was also part of approaches to politics. Accepting Ashton's comment on the interrelation of religious and political factors and Morrill's that it 'is important to realise that when used in this sense, nothing should be assumed about the religious views' of those labelled Political Presbyterians or Independents, the following can be used as general definitions of the two main groups in Parliament in 1646:

Political Presbyterians:

- Conservative in social and political matters.
- Opposed to religious toleration.
- Favoured a negotiated peace with the King.
- Increasingly disenchanted with the New Model Army.
- Drew closer to the Scots.
- Support for Presbyterian Church to prevent social revolution.

Political Independents:

- Disliked the authoritarianism of Scottish Presbyterianism.
- Wanted a considerable measure of religious toleration.
- Allied with New Model Army.

The Political Presbyterians were willing to accept settlement with the King on minimal terms. For the Political Independents, Charles had to accept limitations before the New Model – thus security for the settlement – was disbanded. In 1646 the Political Presbyterians were the most influential group in Parliament.

Activity

Thinking points

As you read through the chapter think about the role of Charles I and the different groups in the failure of settlement. You need to ask yourself:

- how important the role of Charles I was
- what other individuals were important in this period
- at what point did the search for settlement with Charles I change to one where some contemplated executing him
- what the role of religious and political factors was.

■ Did you know?

Most bodies after battles did not receive an individual burial. Only those from aristocratic or gentry families might receive a funeral. The risk of disease meant that most bodies were piled into mass graves.

Most of the country would have favoured the Political Presbyterians because of their peace policy. The war, as well as leading to the development of radicalism, had also sparked a conservative reaction to the intrusions of Parliamentary administration, focused on county committees and tax collection for the army, inflation and the rigours of civil war. Between 1643 and 1645, roughly one in eight of the adult male population were in arms in England. There were 190,000 deaths: 3.7 per cent of England's population of around five million: a higher percentage than either of the twentieth century world wars. Six per cent of Scotland's population and 41 per cent of Ireland's population died as a result of the wars.

The country was weary of war and wanted peace. In 1646, if Charles had accepted reasonable terms presented to him by the Political Presbyterians, their rivals in Parliament, the Political Independents, the New Model and the country would have accepted this.

The *Newcastle Propositions*

The Political Presbyterians presented their plan for settlement, the *Newcastle Propositions*, to Charles in July 1646. The main features of the *Newcastle Propositions* were:

■ **religion:** Charles was to accept the establishment of Presbyterianism in England for three years.

■ **militia:** Parliament was to control the militia – the armed forces – for 20 years. This was regarded as the likely remainder of Charles's life.

■ **parliament:** The Triennial Act was to remain, guaranteeing regular parliaments as a limit on the power of the monarch.

■ **royalists:** Only 58 royalists were not to be pardoned, thus hopefully encouraging others to accept defeat.

Charles's response to the *Newcastle Propositions* was to prevaricate. He had no intention of agreeing to them but did not say this directly.

Settlement was also hampered by Parliament's political divisions, which were deepened by religious differences. More importantly, the means by which the Political Presbyterians used their political ascendancy in the winter of 1646–7 created further political instability. They not only sought agreement with the King based on a revision of their *Newcastle Propositions*, but also to implement what in effect amounted to a counter-revolution, consisting of two parts:

■ Demobilise the New Model, but keep a smaller force to go to Ireland.

■ Create an alternative 'safe' army based on London-trained bands.

In attempting to implement this programme the Political Presbyterians brought a new force into the politics of settlement: the New Model.

■ The politicisation of the New Model Army

The New Model was created by Parliament in early 1645 by merging three regional armies with the aim of making the war effort more effective. It was commanded by Thomas Fairfax, with Cromwell as lieutenant general, its principal cavalry commander.

Key profile

Thomas Fairfax 1612–71

General of Parliament's Northern Association Army, commanded by his father Ferdinando Fairfax. In 1645 Fairfax was appointed commander-in-chief of the newly created New Model. An excellent general, Fairfax was less sure of himself in politics, being naturally conservative. With the politicisation of the army, Fairfax increasingly found himself politically sidelined as his subordinates, particularly Cromwell and Henry Ireton, took the lead in the politics of settlement. Nominated a commissioner for the trial of Charles I, Fairfax only attended the first preliminary meeting and thereafter withdrew. Despite the regicide Fairfax remained as commander-in-chief, only retiring in protest at the decision to invade Scotland in 1650. During the 1650s Fairfax lived on his country estate in Yorkshire, Nun Appleton. In 1660 he helped facilitate the return of monarchy.

Fig. 2 *Thomas Fairfax, commander-in-chief of the New Model Army*

Cromwell, a member of the minor gentry, had been spiritually transformed by his acceptance of God's direction in the 1630s into one of the godly. Cromwell was elected an MP in 1640, but it was through war that Cromwell was once more transformed into, in his perception, one of God's agents. Cromwell had been lieutenant general of the Eastern Association Army and became second in command of the New Model as its chief cavalry officer. Cromwell was a godly warrior who, although naturally politically conservative, came to believe, through his experience on the battlefield and as a member of the New Model, that God had judged Charles I.

The army was abused by the Political Presbyterians' leader, Denzil Holles, in a document that the army subsequently referred to as the 'Declaration of Dislike'. This stated that army petitioners were 'enemies to the state and disturbers of the public peace'. The Political Presbyterians' programme was offensive to the New Model. It appeared to them and their allies in Parliament, the Political Independents, that the Political Presbyterians were attempting to construct a rival army through raising a force for Ireland relying on the remaining regional Parliamentary armies in the west and north that were led by sympathetic political allies.

What particularly incensed the New Model, however, were more immediate concerns:

- Their wages were £3 million in arrears. They faced disbandment before this money was paid.
- There was the possibility of being charged with offensives committed during the war, as Parliament had not passed an indemnity act.

Holles' strategy should, however, be set in the context of the problems Parliament faced. They owed the army £3 million, when royal revenues before the war had never amounted to £1 million. Gentles has argued that these material grievances were key in pushing the army into direct political action. These material grievances are now accepted as the dominant motive in mutinies in 1646 and 1647, but radical religious and political demands became bound up with the financial issues and turned the army against the Political Presbyterian's parliamentary ascendancy. Their entry into politics had a significant impact on settlement. From becoming a political force the New Model was central to all that followed until the restoration of monarchy in 1660.

The ideas and influence of the Levellers and Diggers

The Levellers were a predominantly London-based pressure group that sought political, economic and social reform. Crucial in shaping the Leveller movement were its leading figures, particularly John Lilburne.

Key profile

John Lilburne (c.1615–57)

A puritan who suffered persecution in the 1630s, Lilburne was publicly flogged through the streets of London. Lilburne was released from prison in 1640 after Oliver Cromwell pleaded his case in Parliament. Lilburne joined the Eastern Association Army, eventually becoming a lieutenant colonel. Along with Cromwell he became bitter over Manchester's negative tactics, eventually resigning his post in protest at the Solemn League and Covenant. In 1646 he was sent to the Tower for attacking Manchester as a royalist sympathiser. He emerged as a key figure in the development of the Leveller movement and was their leading spokesman, facing Ireton at the Whitehall Debates in December 1648. After he attacked the Rump Parliament in his *England's New Chains Discovered*, Lilburne was charged with treason, but the jury found him not guilty. As part of a long-running dispute with Haselrig, whom he denounced during legal proceedings, Lilburne was forced into exile. He returned in 1653 and, although found not guilty at trial, was imprisoned as a danger to the state. During his imprisonment he converted to Quakerism.

Gaze not upon this Shaddow that is vaine,
But rather raise thy thoughts a higher Straine,
To GOD (I meane) who set this young-man free,
And in like Straits can eke deliuer thee.

Fig. 3 *John Lilburne, one of the leaders of the Levellers*

Key terms

Natural law: a law that is set by nature and therefore has validity everywhere above human laws. Associated with natural rights that limited the power of monarchy.

The development of the Leveller movement was the result of economic distress caused by civil war, especially in London, in a time of political and religious uncertainty. As a reaction to this, and building on an intellectual tradition of dissent and ideas of **natural law** and traditional English freedoms, the Levellers called for economic, political and religious reform.

As with the Levellers, the Diggers, or 'True Levellers', were another response to the political, economic and social effects of the civil wars. Led by Gerard Winstanley, the Diggers established a commune outside London and saw such organisations as a solution to social inequalities. Kishlansky argues that the 'Digger movement appeared more ominous than it actually was'. The reason for this is that the ideas and actions of the Digger movement offered a fundamental challenge to the nature of politics and society at the time, but their influence was limited. Winstanley, who through his writings emerged as the leading Digger, wrote in 1649 that 'Freedom is the man that will turn the world upside down'. Unlike the Levellers, the Diggers believed in total social and political equality. They referred to themselves as the True Levellers and Winstanley's first Digger pamphlet was entitled *The True Levellers Standard Advanced*. In 1652 Winstanley produced a pamphlet, *The Law of Freedom in a Platform*, in which he argued that:

> Every freeman shall have a freedom in the earth to plant or build or fetch from the storehouses any thing he wants, and shall enjoy the fruits of his labours without restraint from any: he shall not pay rent to any landlord.

2

Key profile

Gerrard Winstanley (1609–76)

A Digger and political writer. He supported Parliament but became increasingly radical after 1643, especially anti-clerical. He was never really well off: from 1647 to 1648 Winstanley suffered economic collapse and depression. This seems to have been the trigger for a more radical stance and the production of pamphlets. On 1 April 1650 he began the occupation of St George's Hill. After the collapse of the Digger movement, Winstanley increasingly became part of established society in Cobham parish, although at some point he became a Quaker.

In the case of the Diggers, while they were a reaction to upheaval of the years 1647 to 1648, their moment was really in 1649 after the execution of the King.

The Levellers and the New Model Army: April to November 1647

If the Levellers were to stand any chance of success they would need more support in the army. The Levellers sought to make use of the army's adjutator movement. At the end of April 1647, eight cavalry regiments chose **adjutators**. These were men chosen to represent the regiments and meet with the senior officers.

The army's continued negotiations with Charles over the *Heads of Proposals* provoked concern among the rank and file that their officers might sell them short. This fear was exploited by the Levellers who denounced the leading army officers, particularly Cromwell and Ireton, as 'grandees'. They claimed that 'Wee have labour'd to please a Kinge, and I thinke, except wee goe about to cutt all our throates, wee shall not please him'.

In October new soldiers' representatives, now called 'agents', with close links with Levellers appeared in five cavalry regiments. The pamphlet *The Case of the Army Truly Stated* attacked the army leadership for their continuing attempts to settle with Charles. As division threatened the army it held the Putney debates in October 1647 to discuss with the Levellers their written constitution the *Agreement of the People*, a more radical proposal for settlement.

Key terms

Adjutators: men and junior officers who took a leading role in the politicisation and political life of the army. In the late 1640s, the words adjutator and agitator were used interchangeably. The more modern meaning of the word agitator has more aggressive radical political overtones. In the context of the emergence of the Leveller movement, some historians have seen the 17th century adjutators in such a vein. The actions of the men themselves tend to suggest that, especially initially, the term adjutator is more appropriate for these men as it meant to work with a senior colleague, more in the sense of an adjutant.

Engraved for the Univerfal Magazine.

GENERAL IRETON.

For I. Hinton at the King's Arms in Newgate Street.

Fig. 4 *Commissary General Henry Ireton, the New Model Army's theoretician and the driving force behind the regicide*

■ Exploring the detail

The Levellers' Agreement of the People

The Levellers' constitution proposed that all who wished to be citizens of the state had to sign the document as a sign of their agreement, hence the Agreement of the People. Sovereignty would reside in the people rather than with a king or parliament through making parliament more representative and answerable to the people. The main proposals in the Agreement were:

- MPs should be elected in proportion to the population of their constituencies

- parliaments should be elected biennially

- parliament would consist of one chamber/house.

The Putney debates

At Putney in late October and early November 1647, the General Council of the Army met with adjutators and representatives of the Levellers to debate the nature of settlement. The debates came to focus on the Levellers' ideas for the extension of the franchise which provoked, at times, a heated argument between the two main protagonists, the Leveller John Wildman and Henry Ireton.

■ Key profile

Henry Ireton (1611–51)

Ireton had served in the Eastern Association where he met Cromwell and became his son-in-law. Ireton as commissary general was third in command of the New Model Army. Ireton and Cromwell shared a godly zeal. The experience of war further bound them together as a political partnership that was central to the politics of settlement. Ireton was more politically radical than Cromwell and was responsible for most of the political statements of the army from the *Solemn Engagement*, the *Heads of the Proposals* to the *Remonstrance* that called for the execution of Charles I. He played a leading role in the politics that led to the regicide. After the execution of Charles I, Ireton accompanied Cromwell as second-in-command of the invasion of Ireland. After Cromwell's victories Ireton was left to subdue and control Ireland. He died as a result of the rigours of campaigning in Ireland in 1651.

In the short term, the Levellers succeeded in emphasising to Ireton that he needed to keep them from taking any more direct action if the army was going to deal with Parliament and the King. This need to work with the Levellers, as well as a genuine desire to debate the nature of settlement, led to the Whitehall Debates of December 1648. The greater significance of Putney, and later Whitehall, lies in the realm of political ideas. The very fact that the debates took place was a remarkable sign of what the revolution had unleashed.

In Putney church the army leaders, notably Ireton and Cromwell, sat down with civilians from the Levellers, notably Wildman, as well as army officers who had some sympathy with the Levellers, such as Colonel Thomas Rainsborough, and seriously debated how England should be governed. In the 1630s the voices of these men would have counted for nothing in corridors of power at Charles's court. It is perhaps fair to say that at no other time in England's history has there been such a constitutional debate at such a level, but more importantly, in the context of the ideas being voiced, a debate of ideas that genuinely had a chance of being implemented, if the army supported them. The power of the words of Putney for future generations is most vividly illustrated in Rainsborough's call for an extension of the franchise:

> For really I think that the poorest he that is in England hath a life to live, as the greatest he; and therefore truly, sir, I think it is clear, that every man that is to live under a government ought first by his own consent to put himself under a government; and I do think that the poorest man in England is not at all bound in a strict sense to that government that he hath not had a voice to put himself under.

The Putney debates ended on 5 November with a clash between the Leveller sympathiser Rainsborough and Ireton over the army grandees' attempts to settle with the King. Cromwell and Ireton reinforced their control over the army and prevented the Levellers provoking further discontent in the ranks.

Yet, just at this point, all that Ireton and Cromwell had argued for at Putney was undermined by the escape on 11 November 1647 of Charles I from Hampton Court.

Cross-reference

To read about the repression of the Levellers and Diggers under the Rump Parliament, see Chapter 3.

Fig. 5 *Hampton Court Palace*

Military opposition to Parliament, 1646–9

Initially the army sought redress of its grievances through the institution that commanded it, Parliament. As Parliament, dominated by the Political Presbyterians, failed to address the army's concerns, the statements of the New Model became progressively more radical. The war had taught the soldiers and officers of the New Model that parliamentary tyranny was just as dangerous as that of a monarch.

The New Model first petitioned Parliament for redress of their grievances in March 1647. Parliament condemned this petition. In May the Commons accepted Charles's third reply to *Newcastle Propositions*, by which he conceded Presbyterianism for three years and parliamentary control of the militia for 10 years. Charles wanted further negotiations. Both antagonised the army, as they felt that the terms were too lenient and Charles could not be trusted to honour them.

On 25 May the Commons voted to disband the New Model with only eight weeks' arrears, in response to which Fairfax ordered a general rendezvous at Newmarket. As the politicalisation of the army in reaction to Holles' parliamentary faction became more pronounced, the rendezvous at Newmarket (4–5 June 1647) saw the organisation of a more formal political structure, the General Council of the Army, to discuss strategy. It was to consist of two commissioned officers and two agitators from each regiment. It was to be through this body that the officers, in particular Commissary General Henry Ireton, sought to lead the army to settlement.

Fig. 6 *Charles I being led away by parliamentary troopers*

■ **Did you know?**

At the Restoration orders were given for Joyce to be arrested when the astrologer William Lilly claimed that he had been the masked executioner of Charles I. Joyce escaped with his family to the Netherlands.

■ **Key dates**

July 1647	*The Heads of the Proposals*
Dec 1647	Engagement between Charles I and Scots
Apr 1648	Windsor Prayer Meeting
Aug 1648	Battle of Preston
Nov 1648	*Remonstrance*
Dec 1648	Pride's Purge
Jan 1649	Execution of Charles I

Charles's seizure

The New Model Army's control of Charles I allowed them to directly negotiate with him their own plan for settlement, *The Heads of the Proposals*. Charles's failure to take these negotiations seriously further radicalised the army and made some contemplate removing the King.

What had really made the New Model the significant force in the politics of settlement was their physical control of Charles I. On 2 June 1647, Cornet (the lowest rank for an officer in the army) Joyce seized Charles from Parliamentary house arrest at Holmby House and took him to the army's headquarters at Newmarket. On 4 June Joyce wrote to Cromwell: 'We have secured the King. You must hasten an answer to us, and let us know what we shall do.' Waller, a leading Political Presbyterian, wrote of Joyce's seizure of Charles I: 'This egg was laid, in Cromwell's own chamber, and brooded between him, and Ireton.'

On 4 June the army produced a *Humble Remonstrance*, declaring that they would not disband until their grievances were met: indemnity and the removal of Holles' Presbyterian faction. The army decided to march towards London to put pressure on their enemies in Parliament. The first step in this process and statement of the Army's position was the *Solemn Engagement* of 5 June 1647. As with most of the significant documents that were to emerge from the army, the *Solemn Engagement* was principally the work of Ireton. The *Solemn Engagement* suggests real cooperation between the officers and the adjutators.

By June, with army headquarters at Cambridge, Fairfax, Cromwell and Ireton went to Childerley where Charles was now held. The meeting was the first of what became formal negotiations between the army leadership and Charles. In these Ireton was the army's chief spokesman. To reinforce the *Solemn Engagement*, impeachment charges were drawn up against 11 MPs, headed by Holles, who the army saw as leading Parliament against them. In another justification of their actions the army argued that 'It is not the desire of the Army to make themselves Masters of the Parliament, but to make the Parliament Masters of themselves'.

On 14 June, *A Representation of the Army*, drafted principally by Ireton and John Lambert, aided by Cromwell, appeared. The *Representation* declared that the New Model was 'not a mere mercenary army'. It outlined the fundamentals of the army's political position:

■ A purge of Parliament.

■ Future parliaments of fixed duration.

■ Guaranteed right of freedom of people to petition parliament.

■ Liberty of tender consciences.

The army declared itself dedicated to 'the defence of our own and the people's just rights and liberties'. Through its statements since March 1647, the army had made clear that settlement had to take their grievances into account. What made the political statements of the army carry weight was not just the military muscle of an army but that the army had secured physical control of the King.

The Heads of the Proposals

The most important immediate result of the army's politicisation and physical control of Charles was their own direct attempt to negotiate a settlement: *The Heads of the Proposals*, drafted by Ireton and Lambert.

At Reading, on 16 July 1647, the Army's General Council met. There appeared to be signs that the general unity of the army that had held to date was beginning to break down. The adjutators had become impatient with the slow progress in achieving their demands by following, for them, the too moderate path outlined by Ireton and Cromwell. The adjutators were pushing for a more immediate march on London to secure their demands. The alienation of the adjutators was only heightened by the fact that at Reading it became clear that the senior officers now had a more fundamental design for settlement and on the basis of it were negotiating directly with Charles. These negotiations opened Ireton and Cromwell up to charges of hypocrisy.

The main points of the *Heads*, published on 2 August 1647, were:

- regular biennial parliaments
- reform of parliamentary representation
- parliamentary control of army and navy
- parliamentary appointment of great offices of state for 10 years
- religious settlement that maintained national church with bishops, but no coercive power
- Act of Oblivion (pardon) that exempted only a few royalists from punishment.

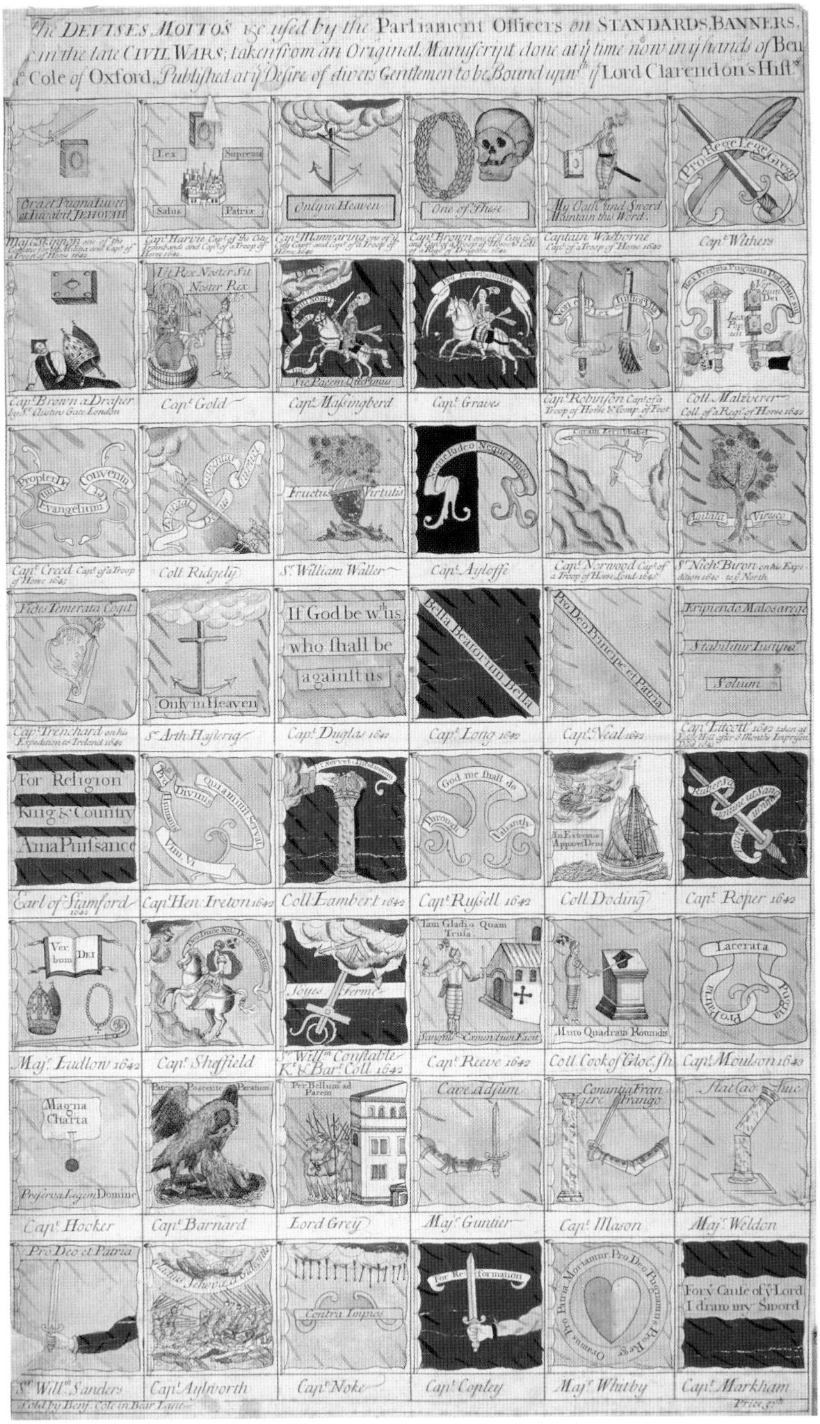

In negotiating with the King and Parliament on the basis of the *Heads*, Ireton and Cromwell illustrated their desire for an essentially moderate settlement. Their willingness to compromise with Charles brought division in the army to a head and would also be the basis of their own more hard-line attitude to Charles after the second civil war.

Fig. 7 *Examples of the banners carried by parliament's armies into battle*

One feature of the *Heads* was the limits on Parliament through biennial elections and redistribution of seats – a clear reflection of the experience of the army over the last two years, as was the issue of indemnity. Other crucial features were that while the King was limited by parliament and a selected council there was no check on his negative voice, episcopacy without disciplinary powers was to be allowed and there was an assurance of Charles's 'personal rights'. Tuck (1993), in *Philosophy and Government*, has argued that the *Heads* would have left Charles very similar to a Dutch *Statholder*. Indeed it is likely that Ireton had read or was aware of the work of the Dutch writer Grotius.

■ Key profile

Hugo Grotius (1583–1645)

A Dutch philosopher, imprisoned for life in 1618 as a result of his part in Dutch political divisions, Grotius escaped to Paris in 1621. There he completed his major philosophical works, notably *On the Law of War and Peace* (1625). Grotius was a key theorist of natural rights who sought to ground just war principles in natural law. Grotius's work influenced English philosophers such as Selden, Hobbes and Locke, as well as army theorist Henry Ireton.

It is very possible that these real concessions to Charles in the *Heads* came about as a result of Ireton's direct negotiations. On 3 July Ireton was noted to have stayed in conversation with the King from dinner until midnight. Berkeley, who was Charles's emissary with the army, had at the time of the *Heads* established a good working relationship with Ireton and believed that Ireton would be able to get the *Heads* through the Army Council. Berkeley also recorded Ireton modifying the *Heads* after negotiation with Charles. There is little doubt that Ireton and Cromwell went as far as they felt they could in trying to get Charles to accept the *Heads*.

Berkeley also commented on the political divisions that were opening up in the army as the result of the negotiations with the King over the *Heads*. If Charles did not accept the *Heads* 'ye temper of the Army' would turn against him. By the time of the Putney debates the army officers negotiating with Charles over the *Heads* realised that he was not negotiating candidly. Indeed Charles had the audacity to remark to Ireton that 'without me you will fall'.

The tension between the army and some in Parliament also increased. In response to the *Heads* and the army's increasing proximity to London, the Political Presbyterians organised demonstrations in favour of peace and on 26 July, with the connivance of Holles, a mob invaded the Commons and forced the passing of a resolution to invite the King to London. By 3 August the army was just outside London, where the Political Independents joined them after walking out of Parliament. On 6 August the army marched into Westminster and on 8 August the City of London.

Charles's duplicity was confirmed by his escape from Hampton Court on 11 November 1647. In response to the new military threat posed by Charles's escape and his negotiations with the Scots, the New Model officers and ranks reunited. An attempted Leveller inspired mutiny in the army at Ware was crushed.

The Engagement

At the end of December 1647, Charles rejected the Four Bills, an amalgamation of the *Newcastle Propositions* and the *Heads*, sent to him by Parliament just before his escape from confinement at Hampton Court.

Charles instead had signed the Engagement with the Scots, agreeing to Presbyterianism for three years in England, in return for a Scottish invasion to restore him to power.

The threat of a Scottish invasion and another civil war that Charles had brought about through the Engagement hardened views. Cromwell himself expressed such feelings.

> The former quarrel was that Englishmen might rule over one another: this is to vassalise us to a foreign Nation. And their fault who have appeared in this Summer's business is certainly double to theirs who were in the first, because it is the repetition of the same offence against all the witnesses that God has borne, by making and abetting a Second War.

4　　　　　　　　　　　　　　　　　　*Oliver Cromwell, 20 November 1648*

In January 1648, as a result of the Engagement, Parliament passed the Vote of No Addresses; in effect that there would be no further negotiation with Charles.

Windsor prayer meeting, April 1648

In April 1648, the New Model gathered at Windsor to pray before facing their enemies. They reflected on passages of the Bible and the preachers they heard appeared to declare that Charles I was that 'man of blood'. Major-General Thomas Harrison in particular reflected on *Numbers* 35:33: 'So ye shall not pollute the land wherein ye are; for blood it defileth the land: and the land cannot be cleansed of the blood that is shed therein, but by the blood of him that shed it'.

In 1650 the New Model, reflecting on the events of 1648, declared in Millenarian tone:

> We were then powerfully convinced that the Lord's purpose was to deal with the late King as a man of blood. And being persuaded in our consciences that he and his monarchy was one of the ten horns of the Beast and being witnesses to so much of the innocent blood of the Saints that he shed in supporting the Beast … we were extraordinarily carried forth to desire justice upon the King, that man of blood.

5　　　　　　　　　　　　　*Declaration of the Army from 1 August 1650*

At Windsor the army articulated regicide in public for the first time.

A closer look

The New Model Army as God's Instrument

The most detailed study of the New Model is Ian Gentles' *The New Model Army in England, Ireland and Scotland, 1645–1653* (1992). In a chapter on 'The Importance of Religion', Gentles outlined why religion was a significant element of the New Model's success:

- **Godly officers:** For Gentles the 'officers were the religious vanguard who set their stamp on the army'. A third of the New Model soldiers were conscripts but a core of the officers, particularly in the cavalry, were godly. They did much to give the whole army its religious drive.

Did you know?

Charles actually signed the Engagement while imprisoned on the Isle of Wight in Carisbrooke Castle. Having escaped from Hampton Court Charles, rather than heading for Scotland, went south hoping that Colonel Robert Hammond, the governor of Carisbrooke Castle, would act on his recent indication that he was unhappy with the army's political role. Hammond was, however, also Oliver Cromwell's cousin. When Charles arrived Hammond chose to obey Parliament's commands to secure Charles.

Activity

Revision exercise

Make a list of Charles's actions from 1642 to 1648 that might indicate that he could not be trusted.

- **Chaplains:** They were appointed for each regiment and were closely connected to the colonel of the regiment. They provided religious leadership through sermons, bible studies and steeling the army by accompanying them on their marches, campaigns and into battle. Preachers like Hugh Peter became key political figures in the English Revolution.
- **Visual iconography:** Each regiment had its own banner and the mottoes on them were usually religious.
- **Fasting and self-reflection:** These were used to prepare for the tests, whether military or political, that the army was to face.
- **Lay preaching:** The practice of soldiers undertaking preaching themselves.
- **Minority:** Alienation from rest of society reinforced their own self image of godliness, which led to high morale.
- **Equality:** The creation of the General Council of the Army in 1647 as well the Reading and Putney debates partly stemmed from a religious belief that even the humble were valued by God.

The Second Civil War

Parliament and the army not only faced an imminent Scottish invasion, but there were royalist/anti-Parliament risings starting in Canterbury at Christmas 1647; then in April–June 1648 across the country, notably in South Wales, Kent, Colchester, Norwich and Pontefract.

A pamphlet of the time outlined the bitterness felt at Parliament's intrusion on their lives.

> The common sort of people thought we should have had a golden age. They expected England to become a second Paradise. But the remedy of these pretenders to Reformation is worse than the disease: the two Houses have filled the Kingdom with Serpents, bloodthirstie Souldiers, extorting Committees, all the Rogues and scumme of the Kingdom have they set on work to torment and vex the people, to rob them, and to eat the bread out of their mouthes.

6	*The Declaration of many thousands of the City of Canterbury, or County of Kent, 5 January 1648*

In August 1648, the invading Scots army was routed by a force a third of their size led by Cromwell at Preston. This convinced many in the New Model that they were truly 'God's Instrument'. The Second Civil War was a turning point. Many, especially in the army, now regarded settlement with Charles as impossible. After ending royalist control of Colchester through a long and brutal siege in August 1648, the leaders of the rising were tried and executed by the army. Ireton, who took the leading role in prosecuting the royalist leaders at Colchester, told them: 'Know, your self as all others that engage a second time against the Parliament are traitors and rebels, and they doe employ us as soldiers by authority from them to suppresse and destroy'.

Political Independent MPs who had earlier supported the Army now moved for a reconciliation with the King in the summer and autumn of 1648. Scared by the increasing radicalism of the army and desperate to end war, Parliament repealed the Vote of No Addresses. Preparation was made to put proposals to the King, now held captive on the Isle of Wight. These negotiations became known as the Newport Treaty.

Fig. 8 *Newsbook image of Charles I as a prisoner in Carisbrooke Castle on the Isle of Wight in 1648*

The *Remonstrance of the Army*

The prospect of a treaty between Parliament and Charles, despite his defeat in another civil war, forced the army and, in particular, Henry Ireton to act.

> The work of breaking off the negotiations for a treaty fell to Henry Ireton. Fairfax was vocally committed to a settlement, and Cromwell, who had opposed a military coup in the past, was absent in the North. Ireton had always been the Army's strategist, the penman who could write the stirring propaganda of the Army's declaration and argue first principles with a schoolman's logic. He flourished in Cromwell's shadow, a cool head to contrast with his impetuous father-in-law. He was surely behind some of the subtle moves of the parliamentary radicals, though he left few tracks. Now he would have to guide the Army's course between cautious officers and rash soldiers, for there was no doubt of the sentiment within the regiments. Petition after petition arrived at headquarters demanding a purge or dissolution of Parliament and a trial of the King.

7　　　　　　　*M. Kishlansky, **A Monarchy Transformed: Britain 1603–1714** (1996)*

At the Windsor Prayer Meeting, the New Model had declared Charles 'that man of blood'. The Second Civil War forced officers who had still been rather circumspect, particularly Cromwell, about this in April to accept that justice should be enacted on Charles. The position of the army was more formally outlined by Ireton on 18 November 1648 in the *Remonstrance of the Army*. Ireton's *Remonstrance* demanded that Parliament put Charles on trial.

If Parliament refused to do this the *Remonstrance* called for a purge of parliament and then the King's trial. Ireton's *Remonstrance* outlined the consequences for a monarch who, once defeated, sought to overthrow this judgement, in effect the position of Charles.

> '[S]uch a person in so doing (wee may justly say is guilty of the highest Treason against the highest Law among men, but however) must needs be the authour of that unjust warre, and therein guilty of all the innocent blood spilt thereby, and of all the evills consequent or concomitant thereunto.

8   *The Remonstrance (1648)*

Pride's Purge

A vote in Parliament on 5 December – 129 for with 83 against – to continue the Newport Treaty with Charles made the army act on the threats of the *Remonstrance*. The next day Ireton organised the army and troops led by Colonel Thomas Pride purged Parliament of those regarded as most forward in negotiating with Charles. The removed MPs were taken by the army to a nearby pub called 'Hell'.

Cromwell arrived in London on the evening of 6 December 1648, after the purge had been completed, naturally much to the suspicion of some contemporaries. It is likely that Cromwell had concerns about the momentum being built up in the army by Ireton for a dissolution – not a purge – of parliament. However, although action against Parliament had been under discussion for some time, the exact timing of Pride's Purge was only forced by the vote in the Commons on 5 December by 129 to 83 that there was ground to proceed with the Newport Treaty.

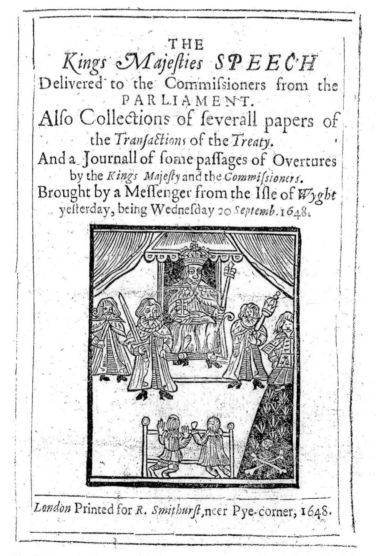

Fig. 9 *A newsbook report of the Newport Treaty negotiations that pushed the army into staging Pride's Purge*

Cromwell was on his way south before this vote. The timing of Pride's Purge had been dictated not by Ireton but by the MPs, and thus the timing of Cromwell's arrival was a coincidence.

■ A closer look

Historians: was Cromwell a 'reluctant regicide'?

John Morrill (2001) has referred to Cromwell as a 'reluctant regicide'. Cromwell's hesitancy has been noted by others. Coward has argued that after 'Cromwell reached London he rarely attended meetings of the Army Council, where Ireton pushed ahead with arrangements for the king's trial'. Instead, although Cromwell lived in Whitehall, it was only after the failure of the Denbigh Mission, a last attempt led by the Earl of Denbigh to get Charles to negotiate, that Cromwell 'at last joined Ireton's revolution'. Woolrych (2002) has stated that it is 'hard to escape the conclusion that he [Cromwell] still had doubts about Ireton's efforts'.

Much speculation has been concerned with determining when the regicides, and Cromwell in particular, decided that Charles should be executed. Cromwell and Ireton had already made the decision that Charles deserved to die by the time of the *Remonstrance*. There is unlikely to be a source that indicates clearly when the actual decision that regicide needed to be enacted was made, although for Ireton it can be argued that he had come to that conclusion as he drafted the *Remonstrance*. There was no moment; the determination to act developed and was confirmed by victory in the second civil war, the lack of other suitable alternatives and providence.

Cromwell's faith in providence is well known. Worden (1985) and Morrill, in particular, have highlighted the importance of providence throughout his life. Late 1648 and early 1649 was no exception. Once Cromwell reconciled himself to the necessity of regicide he was forceful in ensuring its enactment. However, in coming to that point Cromwell had, if anything, been looking to counter his belief that God had judged the King. His attempts at settlement derived more from his political concerns about the consequences of regicide rather than whether providence had made clear that killing Charles was just. Cromwell was searching for another form of justice. Cromwell's words after Preston indicate his confidence that God had owned the army as his instrument. In one of his letters of the time having recognised his membership of a despised minority, Cromwell displays the confidence of one that believed that God would sustain them 'despite of all enemies'. Cromwell certainly wanted action against Parliament and justice on Charles but, as Gaunt (1996) has commented, 'Neither in his letters nor in the army declarations do we find an unambiguous commitment to regicide'. If such a statement ever existed it is unlikely that it did for long.

■ **Did you know?**
Next to Parliament were three pubs named Heaven, Hell and Purgatory. That the removed MPs were taken to 'Hell' was doubtless a political judgement.

The purged parliament, the Rump, would bring Charles I to trial.

Fig. 10 *The execution of Charles I*

The trial and death of Charles I

Why Charles was executed

Religion:

■ Charles I seen as 'that man of blood'.

■ Charles trying to start another war through the use of Catholic troops in Ireland.

■ Charles's defeat in two civil wars was seen as a judgement of God.

Political:

■ Charles's failure to compromise with the army's *Heads of Proposals*.

■ Fear of Charles agreeing the Newport Treaty with Parliament.

■ Fear of Charles being able to start a third civil war.

> That the said Charles Stuart, being admitted King of England, and therein trusted with a limited power to govern by and according to the laws of this land and not otherwise; and by his trust, oath, and office, being obliged to use the power committed to him for the good and benefit of the people, and for the preservation their rights and liberties; yet nevertheless, out of a wicked design to erect and uphold in himself an unlimited and Tyrannical power to rule according to his will, and to overthrow the rights and liberties of the people.

9
The Charge against the King (1648)

A total of 135 commissioners were appointed to sit as the King's judges. Many of these refused to act. Fairfax attended only the first meeting. It is possible that some, including even Cromwell, saw the trial as a final means to make Charles realise that he now had to come to settlement.

Did you know?

John Bradshaw, the President of the Court, wore a bulletproof hat during the trial in case of assassination attempts. This hat still survives today.

Fig. 11 *The armoured hat worn by John Bradshaw to protect him from assassination when sitting as President of the Court that tried Charles I*

Charles, however, refused to even accept the court's legitimacy. Faced by Charles's continued intransigence, Cromwell was reinforced in his belief that it had become a 'necessity' to remove Charles to try to settle the nation, for if they didn't, he would continue to ferment further war.

The familiar picture of Charles during his trial as passive victim or noble martyr is romantic fiction. His conduct in Westminster Hall was consistent with his abiding preference for coercion over conciliation. In refusing to recognise the court's authority he was signalling his refusal to forswear the use of Scottish and Irish arms against his English enemies. In effect, he was playing out the hand he had acquired in signing the God's anointed. But his strategy contained a fundamental flaw. The various parties conjoined in Ormond's alliance were held together primarily by loyalty to the person of Charles I: remove him and the whole ramshackle structure would be undermined. In light of his intransigence, therefore, regicide became a matter of cold necessity.

10 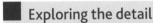 *D. Scott, **Politics and War in the Three Stuart Kingdoms, 1637–49** (2004)*

This political pragmatism was reinforced by 'providence'. God had led them to this decision.

Fig. 12 *Newsbook account of Richard Brandon's supposed confession to being the executioner of Charles I*

Activity

Class activity

Hold a class trial of Charles I. Have someone outline why Charles deserved to be executed and in turn have Charles defend himself. You could even call witnesses for both sides.

Exploring the detail

As was custom, Charles's executioner had his face covered. At the Restoration the soldier William Hulet was tried and found guilty of being Charles's executioner, yet the circumstantial evidence against him meant he was released. Hulet was, however, probably the assistant. A soldier was selected as assistant in case the executioner could not complete the deed. The assistant held Charles's severed head aloft. He did not call out 'behold the head of a traitor', but after waving the head around threw it to the scaffold's floor. The executioner is likely to have been Richard Brandon, London's common executioner.

Did you know?

The often repeated report that a 'groan' came from the crowd as Charles's head was severed is not actually in a contemporary account but added later by the editor of Philip Henry's Memoir. The manuscript actually reads: 'On the day of his execution, which was Tuesday, Jan. 30, I stood amongst the crowd in the street, before Whitehall gate, where the scaffold was erected, and saw what was done, but was not so near as to hear any thing. The blow I saw given, and, can truly say, with a sad heart.'

Charles was declared guilty and sentenced to die. Out of the 135 commissioners, many of whom never attended any sessions of the court, 59 became regicides by signing the death warrant of Charles I.

On 30 January 1649 Charles I was taken through the banqueting hall of Whitehall Palace with its Ruben's ceiling that he had commissioned to glorify the Divine Right of Kings to the scaffold for his execution. With one blow Charles's head was severed.

Fig. 13 *A print of the execution of Charles I*

Summary questions

1 Was settlement possible in 1646?

2 Explain why the army became politicised.

3 In what respects was religion a divisive issue in this period?

3   Republican Rule, 1649–53

In January 1649, England's only experiment with republicanism began with the public execution of Charles I and was confirmed by the abolition of monarchy, the Lords and a declaration that England was a Commonwealth. Alongside this, images of monarchy were destroyed. The most telling example of this was the literal beheading of one statue of Charles and its replacement with a statue depicting England's freedom from tyranny. The crown jewels were melted down to make coins and their stones sold. Some pubs even replaced their signs with ones that read 'Here was the King's head'.

Radical religious groupings: Fifth Monarchists and Ranters; Presbyterianism and Independency

Radical religion

Before 1640 Charles I, the Archbishop of Canterbury, William Laud and the bishops demanded conformity to a rigid Laudian Church of England. With the collapse of Charles's authority after 1640, the Church of England was also undermined and there developed greater religious expression. Civil war and revolution accelerated that process to the point that those who had been regarded as radicals in 1640 – Presbyterians and Independents – were conservative in comparison to new groups like the Fifth Monarchists or the Ranters.

Fifth Monarchists

The Fifth Monarchists' belief in the imminent establishment of the kingdom of heaven on earth was driven by the reading of the Bible, specifically the *Book of Revelation*.

Fifth Monarchism was not solely Bible-led, however. Astrology, which was widely accepted at the time, also provided material for those who believed the Fifth Monarchy was imminent.

The Fifth Monarchists wanted a regime run exclusively by the 'saints' based on their interpretation of *Daniel* and *Revelation*. These books suggested to them the thousand-year kingdom of saints was close. This belief was not unusual and derived from millenarianism, which was a widely held belief of the time that God would establish Christ's rule on earth. The Fifth Monarchists believed, however, that action could hasten Christ's kingdom. The Fifth Monarchists had support in the army and the revolutionary context of civil war and revolution merely strengthened the belief that these were truly the end of days.

In April 1648, as the army prepared to face a Second Civil War and Scottish invasion that Charles had brought through his Engagement with the Scots, the army met in prayer at Windsor Castle. Here a leading Fifth Monarchist, Major-General Thomas Harrison, reflecting on *Numbers 35:33*, declared Charles I 'that man of blood'.

The Rump set up commissions for the Propagation of the Gospel in the north and Wales. The Welsh commission was taken over by Welsh Fifth Monarchists, Vavasor Powell and Morgan Llwyd, who were linked to Harrison. The Fifth Monarchists, like many in the army, increasingly

Did you know?

The actual term Fifth Monarchy derived from the *Book of Daniel*. In *Daniel 7–12* Daniel had a vision of a kingdom that would last forever that would follow the four great earthly monarchies. For Daniel these were the Babylonian, the Medo-Persian and the Greek. The fourth was to be led by a 'master of intrigue', who would take a stand against God. In the 17th century these monarchies were regularly identified as:

- Assyrian
- Persian
- Greek
- Roman
- Christ's.

regarded the Rump as preventing the establishment of godly rule. In this context the Fifth Monarchists became, according to Capp (1972), a pressure group that aimed at removing the Rump and establishing godly rule. At the forefront of this pressure was Harrison.

■ **Key profile**

Thomas Harrison, 1606–60

The son of a butcher who entered Essex's Parliamentary army, transferring to the Eastern Association in 1644 as Major to Fleetwood's regiment. Part of the New Model and a **Recruiter MP** in 1646. One of the most radical in the army, he was clear in his judgement of Charles Stuart as 'that man of blood'. Harrison commanded the troops that brought the King from Windsor to his trial in London. Attending nearly all the sessions of the trial, Harrison was a prominent regicide. In 1650 Harrison was made President of the Commission for the Propagation of the Gospel in Wales, giving him enormous influence in Wales. In 1651 he became a member of the Council of State and a major-general. The most prominent Fifth Monarchist, Harrison was at the forefront of calls to remove the Rump, wanting it replaced by a body of the 'Saints' modelled on a Jewish Sanhedrin. With the removal of the Nominated Assembly and his refusal to accept the Protectorate, Harrison had his army commission removed. During Cromwell's Protectorate Harrison was imprisoned four times. During 1658–60 Harrison remained passive. At the Restoration he was the most prominent surviving regicide and the first executed.

With Cromwell's dissolution of the Rump (1653), Harrison argued for an assembly based on a Jewish Sanhedrin, a parliament of 70 men. He was opposed by Lambert who, in the short term, sought rule by a council of about 12 men. The focus for many Fifth Monarchists was the method of selection for the next parliament. Selection by the saints would ensure an assembly of saints. Other Fifth Monarchists, such as John Rogers, actually argued, however, that Cromwell should rule on his own or that he should select the members of the next assembly. They equated him with Moses who was chosen by God to lead his people out of bondage.

The choosing of Nominated Assembly was not, however, as the Fifth Monarchists would have wanted and Harrison in particular seems to have quickly lost interest in the body. The Nominated Assembly may have been the height of the influence of the Fifth Monarchists on central government, but that influence proved limited.

> The widespread notion that Fifth Monarchy men made most of the running in Barebone's Parliament is largely mistaken. It is entirely understandable, however, for it was sedulously fostered after the assembly's demise by hostile pamphleteers, and so far as the original intentions of Harrison, Carew, and their preacher friends went they were not far wrong. But there were in fact only twelve or thirteen Fifth Monarchists in the House.

 *A. Woolrych, **Commonwealth to Protectorate** (1986)*

■ Key terms

Recruiter MPs: a term used by royalists in referring to the recruitment of MPs to replace those that were with the King to maintain numbers in the Commons.

■ Cross-reference

For more on the Nominated Assembly, see page 50.

■ Activity

Thinking point

In what ways were the Fifth Monarchists an influential group in this period?

The establishment of the Protectorate saw the Fifth Monarchists forced into opposition.

Ranters

The Ranters emerged in the late 1640s, like other radicals, from the experience of civil war and revolution. Ranters took **predestination** to what they saw as a logical conclusion that as they were saved they could lead life as they wanted.

Some who were seen as Ranters denied the concept of sin. They denied that God existed independently, instead arguing that God could be found in man or nature, the pantheistic belief that God was in everything. The Ranters became the epitome of the religious radical feared by the conservative gentry. Ranters argued that those who had discovered the 'godhead' within them did not need to conform to conventional morality. As with other religious radicals Millenarianism was part of what can be seen as Ranter writings.

Key terms

Predestination: a belief in salvation being preordained by God and reflected in the Puritans referring to themselves as the 'elect' or 'godly'.

Fig. 1 *A pamphlet 'reporting' apparent Ranter activity. Some historians have seen the Ranters more as a product of such sensational newsbooks than an actual movement*

Key terms

Presbyterianism: Presbyterians were those who supported a church with a government of equal presbyters, or elders, often appointed by the congregation, rather than others systems such as episcopacy (bishops).

Independency: a broad term that embraced the Independent sects who had rejected the concept of a state church for gathered churches of fellow believers.

Rump Parliament: a name derived from the nature of the body as a result of Pride's Purge of 6 December 1648, which removed MPs to enable the trial of Charles I.

In *A Fiery Flying Roll* of 1650 Abiezer Coppe wrote:

> Wherefore be it known to all tongues, kindreds, nations, and languages upon earth, that my most excellent majesty, the King of Glory, the eternal God, who dwelleth in the form of the writer of this roll hath in the open streets proclaimed the notable day of the Lord.

There was no Ranter work printed after 1650. There is little evidence of organisation or a group apart from those who followed Laurence Clarkson or Thomas Webb. Such was the lack of any defined Ranter 'movement' that doubts have been expressed as to whether the Ranters existed at all. The term Ranter came to be applied generally to those whose behaviour was seen as abnormal as well as those who questioned the nature of sin. The accounts of Ranters, coming from hostile sources, invariably focus on their blasphemy and excesses, whether alcoholic or sexual. The Ranters should be seen in the context of fear of a breakdown of authority.

Presbyterianism and Independency

Presbyterians desired to establish a national structure in the Church that would enforce a uniformity of practice. After the Solemn League and Covenant, Scottish Presbyters hoped for the enforcement of **Presbyterianism** in England. Supported by some Political Presbyterians, like Holles, their hopes of establishing this were seriously weakened with the emergence of the army as a political force and its support for **Independency**.

In Independency, each congregation was independent to decide practice for itself. Many were influenced by experience of worship in the Netherlands or New England, where such a looser framework prevailed. For Independents there could be a local or national structure, but this would only act in a supporting role to each congregation which, ultimately, held authority over its own members and practice.

During the civil war each term became associated with political positions. The Presbyterians, in line with their ideas about church structure, were more conservative, opposing religious toleration and more keen to negotiate with Charles. They also became allied with the Scots as a counter-weight to the Independents' links with the New Model.

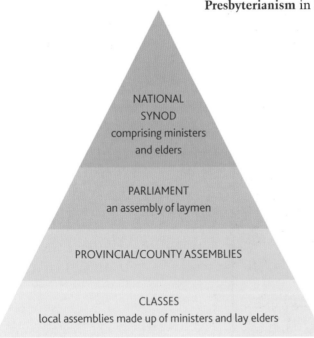

Fig. 2 *Presbyterian church structure*

NATIONAL SYNOD
comprising ministers and elders

PARLIAMENT
an assembly of laymen

PROVINCIAL/COUNTY ASSEMBLIES

CLASSES
local assemblies made up of ministers and lay elders

The establishment of the Rump Parliament and the Commonwealth

The establishment of the **Rump Parliament** and the Commonwealth were to a degree determined by the nature of the Revolution, of which there have been different views.

Historians and the English Revolution

Manning saw the Revolution in the Marxist context of class struggle:

> The events of 1649 were the climax of the English Revolution, not only because a king was publicly tried and executed and a republic established, but also because people from outside the governing class – soldiers, women and the middle ranks of society – intervened in the great affairs of politics and religion. Their radicalism was not simply a reaction to the breakdown of the old constitution and ecclesiastical order in the first civil war, or merely forced on them by the actions of Charles I in causing the second civil war. It arose from long held and deeply felt hopes and expectations of profound changes for the better in their world: in other words, they were revolutionaries.

3   *B. Manning, **1649: The Crisis of the English Revolution** (1992)*

Coward has pointed out the lack of popular support for the regicide:

> Unlike the French or Russian Revolution there was no hint of any mass popular enthusiasm for the English Revolution. There was no popular rejoicing on 30 January 1649. Ironically Charles I was more popular at his death than at any time in the 1640s. The English Revolution was carried out by a minority, whose decisions to become regicides were taken at a very late stage. The two men who took the lead in bringing the King to trial, Ireton and his father-in-law, Cromwell, had been fully committed only a year before to securing a monarchical settlement. They were driven to become regicides by a combination of 'functional' (political) and 'ideological' (religious) pressures. This is what Cromwell meant by 'necessity' and 'providence'.

4   *B. Coward, **Stuart England 1603–1714** (1997)*

> ### Activity
> **Source analysis**
>
> How does Source 3 differ from Source 4?

Morrill has stressed that 1649, while enacted by a minority, was still a revolution:

> The events of January 1649 constitute a truly revolutionary moment. The abolition of monarchy, the abolition of the House of Lords, the closely linked abolition of the Church of England and of the principle that all men and women ought to be members of a single national Church, represent the destruction of those very institutions around which men and women organized their view of the natural order in the world.

5   *J. Morrill, (ed.), **Revolution and Restoration: England in the 1650s** (1992)*

The limits of the support for the revolution and its enactment by a minority based in the New Model shaped the Interregnum regimes. The Rump, established by Pride's Purge, was always equated with the regicide as well as a revolutionary army. This was despite the fact that key figures in the Rump, notably Haselrig, were deeply antagonistic to the New Model. The link to the regicide and the army was an issue for all Interregnum regimes who faced two key problems:

- Conservative demands for a return to political normality set against a radical minority, especially in the army and the sects who wanted to follow up what they saw as the limited political revolution of 1649.

Fig. 3 *Thomas Hobbes: philosopher who saw the Commonwealth and Protectorate as legitimate forms of government through their hold on power*

Fig. 4 *Thomas Hobbes'* Leviathan, *1651*

Did you know?

The Levellers regarded the use of 'Norman French', Latin and illegible 'court hand' in law as a deliberate means of exerting control by the elite and continuing the 'Norman Yoke' of feudalism imposed on the 'freeborn English' from 1066. Cromwell commented that the 'law as it is now constituted serves only to maintain the lawyers and to encourage the rich to oppress the poor'.

The relationship between Parliament/State and the New Model was fragile. While, nominally, the authority in the land was parliament it was obvious that parliament could only function under the protection of the army which held real power.

These were the contradictions at the heart of the Rump.

The Rump Parliament and the Commonwealth

The Rump voted on 6 February 1649 to abolish the House of Lords and on 7 February to abolish monarchy and the apparatus of monarchical government. The legislation to enforce these measures was, however, slow. It was not until 19 May 1649 that the act establishing the Commonwealth of England was passed. On 2 January 1650, the Rump passed an Engagement Act by which all adult males had to declare loyalty to the Commonwealth. This was reinforced in July 1650 by a Treason Act by which it was illegal to deny the authority of the regime as vested in the Commons. In practice it proved impossible to enforce the Engagement; even Fairfax objected to it.

Key profile

Thomas Hobbes 1588–1679

From 1640–1652, philosopher Thomas Hobbes was based in Paris where he wrote *Leviathan* (1651). The final section of this work was a justification of submission to England's new republican regime. Hobbes argued that as Charles Stuart could not protect the English people they were compelled to obey the new state. Furthermore, the new republican state had as much authority as monarchy. For Hobbes all religious authority should come under the authority of the state. In 1652 Hobbes returned to England. The Restoration also brought the 1662 Printing Act by which all books were required to have a licence by Episcopal authority. Hobbes subsequently produced nothing of note that was controversial.

Hobbes put forward the idea of absolute sovereignty whereby a state was legitimised if it could protect the people under its power. The Rump sought to secure stability and its own power and thereby gain *de facto* legitimacy.

It was the Rump's attempt to appeal to consolidate its base after the revolution that made some regard the regime as too conservative; not only groups like the Levellers but, more notably, the army. None of the recommendations of the Hale Commission on law were put into action, the Presbyterian system, set up between 1644 to 1648, remained in place and moves to abolish tithes (financial support for the clergy through a tax) received little support. Furthermore in 1650 measures against religious nonconformity, particularly the Blasphemy Act of August, marked the Rump as more religiously conservative than the army.

Despite these impulses to conservatism the Rump did introduce some reform. In September 1650 the Rump brought an end to compulsory attendance of national church. Also in 1650 it was decided that all legal proceedings would henceforth be in English rather than Latin.

The Rump established Acts for the Propagation of the Gospel in Wales, Ireland and the North.

A closer look

The Adultery Act and Mosaic Law

Under the Rump moves were taken, influenced by Millenarianism, to prevent what was seen as moral, and therefore religious, delinquency. Parliament passed a Blasphemy Act and an Adultery Act in May 1650 by which the death penalty was introduced for adultery, fornication and incest.

> For suppressing of the abominable and crying sins of incest, adultery and fornication, wherewith the land is much defiled and Almighty God highly displeased, be it enacted by the authority of this present Parliament … that in case any married woman shall from and after the four and twentieth day of June 1650 be carnally known by any man (other than her husband). Every person offending shall suffer death.
>
> **Adultery Act 1650**

Some wished to go even further and establish Mosaic Law, the Law of Moses. This was in effect the Ten Commandments, moral law as an expression of God's will. Throughout *Exodus*, *Leviticus* and *Deuteronomy* in the Bible there are approximately 150 paragraphs that can be seen as focused on law or prescriptions. John Milton was one who opposed Mosaic Law, believing that Christ's sacrifice and the Gospel had abolished Mosaic Law. Milton outlined his position in *De Doctrina Christiana*.

Exploring the detail

The stoning of James Nayler

In the parliamentary debates of 1657 on what to do to the leading Quaker James Nayler, one MP, the Major-General William Boteler, commented that 'by the Mosaic Law, blasphemers were to be stoned to death'. Stoning was a traditional Hebrew form of execution, outlined in *Deuteronomy 13:9–10*. It required at least two prosecution witnesses who would then have to cast the first stone. If the victim survived spectators would complete the sentence.

Cross-reference

For more on James Nayler, see Chapter 5.

Activity

Revision exercise

In what ways might the Rump Parliament be considered a conservative, non-radical regime?

The real issue for the army was the Rump's failure to introduce constitutional reform. Their disappointment with the Rump was voiced and grew as their victories against the external enemies of the regime made them more convinced that this moment needed to be seized to establish godly rule. Vanquishing the enemies of the new state prevented them, however, from acting on their frustration at the limits of reform.

The Rump at war: Ireland, Scotland, Charles Stuart and the Dutch War

After the execution of the King, the Rump faced external threats from Ireland, Scotland and Charles I's eldest son, Charles Stuart. It was the New Model that had to deal with these threats.

Ireland

England became Protestant after the Reformation of the 1530s. Ireland remained largely a Catholic country, despite the settlement of Protestants in Ulster and English control of Dublin and the surrounding region. Ireland had been a real problem for England ever since 1641 when Catholic inhabitants killed English Protestant settlers. After the regicide some Irish supported Charles Stuart. Cromwell landed with 10,000 Parliamentary troops in Ireland in August 1649 to put down rebellion and, in his eyes, as with most other Protestant English, punish the Catholics for their 1641 rebellion. Not only would Ireland be made to pay for the bloodshed of 1641 but it would also be exploited financially by the new regime. Cromwell's stance is clear in his Declaration to the Irish Catholic clergy of January 1650.

You Irish, unprovoked, put the English to the most unheard of and most barbarous massacre in 1641 (without respect of sex or age) that ever the sun beheld. This came at a time when Ireland was in perfect peace. You are part of Antichrist, whose Kingdom the Scriptures so expressly speaks should be laid in blood. Before long, you must all of you have blood to drink; even the dregs of the cup of the fury and wrath of God, which will be poured out unto you.

---

6   *Cromwell's Declaration to the Irish Catholic clergy*
(January 1650)

Cromwell's Irish campaign of 1649–50 involved a series of bloody sieges of Irish Catholic strongholds. The most infamous took place at Drogheda and Wexford. Ireland was subjected to more English control than ever before.

Fig. 5 *Caricature of Charles Stuart being forced to take the Covenant to get Scottish support to launch an invasion of England*

Scotland

The arrival of Charles Stuart in Scotland made another Scottish invasion imminent. Cromwell returned from Ireland as part of the preparations to meet this threat. When Argyll succeeded in persuading Charles Stuart to accept the Covenant, the Rump decided to strike first. Despite the attempts of Cromwell and Lambert to persuade him, Fairfax would not lead the invasion. In Fairfax's place Cromwell became Commander-in-Chief.

At Dunbar on 3 September 1650, Cromwell defeated a larger Scottish army. Some 3,000 Scots were killed and 10,000 captured.

No more than 20 of the New Model were killed. Lambert's victory at Inverkeithing in July 1651 forced Charles Stuart to invade England with what Scottish forces he could muster.

In England few rallied to support Charles Stuart. His Scottish army were allowed as far south as Worcester as the New Model coordinated its forces. Here, exactly one year after their victory at Dunbar, Cromwell routed Charles's army.

By their victories in Ireland and Scotland, the New Model had made the republic secure at home. The politicians and merchants of the Rump had, however, started their own war.

The Dutch War

The Protestant Dutch Republic appeared a natural ally. During the years of Laudian persecution, the Dutch, with their greater degree of religious toleration, were a haven for many English religious radicals. Such were the apparent bonds between the two countries that an international Union was seriously considered in 1649.

Holland, the wealthiest of the Dutch United Provinces, had a merchant class that was strongly republican but they were opposed by the Orangist party led by William II of Orange as a quasi-monarch. The Orangists made royalist exiles welcome. The Dutch, while wanting some form of agreement, did not want to lose their sovereignty or give away their economic advantages. The Rump's Navigation Act of 1651 specified that only English ships or those of the place of manufacture should bring goods into England and its colonies. Furthermore only English ships should land fish into England.

There were escalating clashes at sea until a full naval engagement between the pro-royalist Orangist Dutch admiral van Tromp and England's republican admiral Robert Blake in May 1652 pushed the two countries to war. The momentum for war had been underpinned by economic competition that saw the merchant class also keen for a conflict. The Dutch carrying trade was five times greater than the English, dominating the Baltic, other northern European waters, the Mediterranean and the Caribbean as well as along the coasts of Africa and America. Some Rumpers saw the war as a means to build up the navy as a counter-weight to the army.

The Dutch War created not only practical problems but army resentment at:

- the money spent on the navy
- the navy being used as a political counter-weight to the army
- fighting another Protestant republic.

The Repression of the Levellers

The Levellers denounced the Rump, especially its extremely narrow representative nature. In 1649 Lilburne produced *England's New Chains Discovered*. In this he attacked the grandees for betraying what people had fought for. He appealed to the army, Londoners and others to reject the rule of what he regarded as a military junta, a self-seeking Council of State and their 'puppet' Parliament.

The Rump sought to counter such criticism by a September 1649 Act limiting the freedom of the press and employed the republican poet John Milton as a kind of propaganda and censorship minister.

Did you know?

The escape of Charles Stuart

After his defeat at Worcester, Charles Stuart spent six weeks travelling to avoid capture and reach the safety of the continent. He only avoided capture due to luck and the support of Catholics and royalists who supported him in his escape. The initial stages of Charles's escape gave rise to the use of the term 'Royal Oak' for public houses as Charles hid in the branches of an oak tree.

Activity

Talking point

Discuss the political impact on the New Model Army and its relationship with the Rump as a result of the army's victories in Ireland and Scotland.

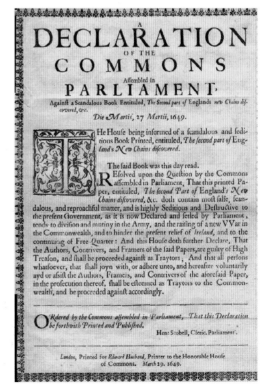

Fig. 6 *A negative response to John Lilburne's pamphlet* England's New Chains Discovered *(1649)*

Fig. 7 *John Milton (1608–74): Puritan, republican and poet*

■ **A closer look**

John Milton (1608–74), poet and polemicist

England's greatest poet, Milton, produced numerous political works during the English Revolution. During the siege of Colchester (1648), Milton wrote a sonnet to Fairfax. More notably Milton produced a defence of proceedings against Charles I, published in February 1649. On the title page Milton proclaimed that 'it is lawful for any who have the power, to call to account a tyrant or wicked King and after due conviction, to depose, and put him to death'. In March the Rump employed him to be Secretary for Foreign Tongues, effectively translating material mainly from Latin. In October 1649 Milton produced *Eikonoklastes*, 'image breaker', defending the regicide, the title also being a reference to the surname taken by Greek emperors who destroyed superstitious images. Milton followed this by further support for the regicide in the *First Defence* (1651) and *Second Defence* (1654).

In 1652 Milton produced sonnet 16, 'To the Lord General Cromwell' and in 1655 sonnet 18, 'On the late massacres in Piedmont'. Faced with the increasing prospect of the Restoration Milton sought to outline how the republican forces should respond. Expressing his dismay at Lambert's removal of the Rump in October 1659 in *A Letter to a Friend, Concerning the Ruptures of the Commonwealth* Milton followed this by proposing the idea of a ruling Council in *The ready and easy way* (February 1660). At the Restoration Milton went into hiding as his books were burned. Briefly incarcerated in the Tower, Milton secured a pardon. In 1658 he had started *Paradise Lost*, eventually published in 1667. These later years were marked by other major works, *Paradise Regained* (1671) and *Samson Agonistes*.

A government newspaper, *Mercurius Politicus*, launched in June 1650, was designed to defend the Rump. It was edited by one of Milton's friends and the most talented journalist of the age, Marchamont Nedham.

■ **Key profile**

Marchamont Nedham, 1620–98

Journalist and pamphleteer. A legal clerk in 1643, Nedham became editor of the pro-parliamentary but anti-Presbyterian newsbook, *Mercurius Britanicus*. In 1646 Nedham was imprisoned for referring to Charles as a tyrant. By 1647 Nedham emerged as editor of the pro-royalist newsbook, *Mercurius Pragmaticus*, before again supporting republicanism with his 1650 *The Case of the Commonwealth of England Stated*. During the next decade Nedham was editor of *Mercurius Politicus*. At the Restoration he only returned to pamphleteering in 1676 with three pamphlets that linked the Earl of Shaftesbury's politics with the crisis of 1641.

The Levellers were also regarded as a threat by the grandees. The alliance of army leaders and Levellers had collapsed before the King's execution. Furthermore the Levellers' Second Agreement (December 1648) differed significantly from the Officers' Agreement (20 January 1649), especially on the extent of religious freedom that should be allowed.

In March 1649, the leading Levellers, including Lilburne, were arrested. They continued their propaganda war, however, against the Rump and army. In *The Hunting of the Foxes* Cromwell was particularly attacked as a hypocrite. The Levellers' Third Agreement of 1649 was an attempt to inspire army mutiny. The response was limited and quickly crushed by Cromwell and Fairfax at Burford in May 1649.

It was not only the determination of the Rump and the army leadership to quell the Levellers that limited the movement, but also the fact that the Rump had money to pay the army. This prevented much unrest among the troops. Although Lilburne was acquitted at his trial in September 1649, the Leveller influence in the army was effectively over and thus any real threat the Levellers may have posed to the state.

The Repression of the Diggers

In March 1649 a group led by a William Everard, but including Winstanley, occupied waste ground at St George's Hill, thereby taking direct action to achieve their central goal: equality, especially economic, but also social. Winstanley claimed that the Diggers' idea of equality through communal living had been confirmed by a vision from God. Certainly compared to the Levellers there was a much greater religious element to the Diggers. The Diggers' ultimate failure was due to the hostility of those who owned the land. After a year of continued hostility the Digger community at St George's collapsed. Hill (1972) has outlined how other Digger communities were established in Northamptonshire, Kent, Buckinghamshire, Hertfordshire, Middlesex, Bedfordshire, Leicestershire, Gloucestershire and Nottinghamshire.

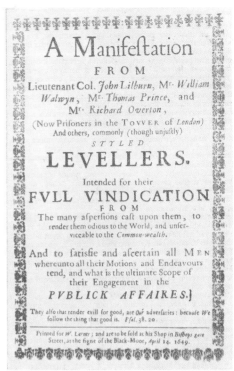

Fig. 8 *A Leveller pamphlet. Lilburne, William Walwyn and Richard Overton were regarded as the leading Levellers*

Despite their immediate failure the Diggers' significance lies in the path they laid for future radicals from the following central ideas:

- **Direct action:** Although not the first, Winstanley and the Diggers represent one of the most obvious examples of direct action politics. Winstanley stated 'action is the life of all, and if thou dost not act, thou dost nothing'.

- **Communism:** In the establishment of their communes the Diggers provide an example of Communism in action 200 years before Marx and Engels produced their Communist Manifesto (1848).

- **Liberation theology:** The ideas of the Diggers predate a radical Christian movement which aimed to eliminate poverty and injustice.

- **Environmentalism:** In their establishment of communes and living off and in harmony with nature the Diggers can be seen as forerunners of the environmental movement.

The failures of the Rump Parliament and Cromwell's reasons for its dissolution

It was not only the army who grew increasingly frustrated with the Rump's limited reform. There were various radical groups who also posed a threat to the Rump. Radicals, like many in the army, became frustrated with the Rump's lack of reform. There were a number of reasons for the Rump's conservatism:

- **The Conservatism of the MPs:** Of the 41 MPs on the Council of State, 22 refused to swear an oath approving of the regicide, the abolition of the Lords and the monarchy. Furthermore by seeking to broaden support for the regime, to counter the impact of Pride's Purge,

> **Activity**
>
> **Talking point**
>
> Was there any chance of the ideas of the Digger movement being successful?

MPs made it more conservative. The MPs were part of a social order, the majority being lawyers and merchants, that was resistant to reform.

■ **Economic factors:** The Rump came to power at the time of the worst economic crisis of the 17th century which necessitated a more conservative approach. There were simply not the funds to initiate extensive reform.

■ **Security situation:** The threat from Ireland and Scotland as well as the animosity of other European states meant that establishing the regime was more of a priority than reform.

■ **Bulwark against radicals:** Some supported the Rump as a conservative force to counter the army's radicalism.

■ **Fear of radical religious groups:** The Ranters, for example, made the MPs fearful of religious reform.

■ **The Dutch War:** The Rump's war against the Dutch became the focus of their attention and resources.

In the face of the apparent collapse of order the Rump sought to bring stability. Figures compiled by Morrill in *Revolution and Restoration* (1993) indicate the decline in the measures taken by the Rump, the key role of a core of MPs and where their focus lay. There were 210 MPs between January 1649 and April 1653, but only 60 to 70 were regularly active with an average attendance of 50 to 60 MPs at sittings. Acts passed by the Rump declined over the period.

Cross-reference

For religious radicalism see Chapter 5.

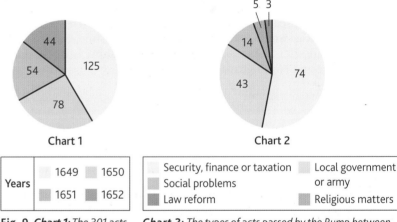

Years	1649	1650
	1651	1652

Security, finance or taxation	Local government or army
Social problems	
Law reform	Religious matters

Fig. 9 *Chart 1:* The 301 acts passed by the Rump between January to May 1649, January to May 1651 and January to April 1653

Chart 2: The types of acts passed by the Rump between January to May 1649, January to May 1651 and January to April 1653

These figures should be balanced, however, by historical judgements setting the Rump's achievements in a broader context.

> The Rump did not idle away all its time. The laws relating to debtors had been eased. The poor need no longer languish in jail, their families beggared, while rich men evaded their debts. Legal proceedings would be written in a normal hand rather than in a script which only the trained could decipher. The Elizabethan statute requiring weekly attendance at the parish church was repealed. The special needs of the north, Wales and Ireland were catered for by Acts to assist the propagation of the gospel in those regions. The Rump's achievements were not derisory, especially when it was simultaneously struggling to survive and to raise money.

7 — *T. Barnard, **The English Republic** (1997)*

If the Rump's policy accomplishments were to a significant extent restricted by its narrow sociopolitical base, there remained one field in which it was able to achieve really striking successes, and that is the realm of commerce and diplomacy. England's dramatic rise as a military-commercial power in this era was perhaps the achievement most characteristic of the Rump's overall political orientation. Contemporaries saw a clear connection between republican politics and overseas commercial and military power.

8   *R. Brenner,* **Merchants and Revolution** *(1993)*

Activity

Source analysis

How far does Source 8 differ from Source 7 in relation to the achievements of the Rump?

Cromwell and the Dissolution of the Rump

In the aftermath of victory at Dunbar, Cromwell wrote to urge the Rump to reform: 'Relieve the oppressed, hear the groans of poor prisoners in England; be pleased to reform the abuses of all professions; and if there is anyone that makes many poor to make a few rich that suits not a commonwealth.' Cromwell and the army ultimately made the decision to remove the Rump, justifying it by a desire for reform. Yet, Cromwell himself was, in some ways, one of the other reasons for the Rump's conservatism. Cromwell, although a religious radical, was a political conservative. He did not want to overturn society's norms.

The rift between the Rump and the army was now so wide that Cromwell had to take an unequivocal stand on the side of the army and reform. Cromwell retreated from his policy of cultivating moderate opinion. Cromwell and the army leadership did not wish to take a direct political role; they believed that Parliament should rule. Yet the crucial issue for Cromwell, and the army, was the Rump's perceived conservatism. Campaigns in Ireland and Scotland had prevented the army taking any action against the Rump. What the campaigns also did was radicalise the army's demand for reform.

Cromwell shared these concerns about the Rump's lack of progress. Although he was a constitutional conservative, his millenarianism meant he was impatient with the Rump's ending of the Propagation of

Fig. 10 *A depiction of Oliver Cromwell dissolving the Rump Parliament. In the top right corner are the words 'This House is to Let' which, apparently, someone had posted at the time as a comment on the removal of Parliament*

Did you know?

The continuing doubt over Cromwell's exact motivation and the nature of the Rump's bill is due to Cromwell's actions on the day of the dissolution. As he harangued the MPs in dissolving the Rump Cromwell stuffed the bill under his cloak. It was never seen again.

the Gospel and valued army unity over parliamentary authority. The exact cause of his expulsion of the Rump cannot, however, be known. He destroyed the evidence.

In the winter of 1652–3 Cromwell still sought to avoid the use of force, acting as a moderator between the army and the Rump and securing a date for the Parliament to dissolve itself in November 1653. He probably then planned for some form of interim council until it was safe to hold elections but when he discovered in April 1653 that the Rump intended to dissolve and have its own committee to judge those who would be elected he felt this would, in effect, maintain their power and would still prevent reform. Thus he acted.

A closer look

The major studies of this episode, Worden's *Rump Parliament* (1974) and Woolrych's *Commonwealth to Protectorate* (1982), differ over Cromwell's reasons for the dissolution of the Rump. For Worden the Rump's bill provided for completely new elections. The Rump was therefore not 'determined to perpetuate its power'. For Worden, the crisis of April 1653 'was not between a parliament determined to perpetuate its power and an army resolved to hold elections, but between a parliament which had resolved to hold elections and an army determined to prevent it from doing so'. At some point before the dissolution, the roles of Parliament and the army were reversed. Cromwell and the army were concerned about the Rump's plans to hold fresh elections that would see the return of more of the kind of men whom the army had removed through Pride's Purge and thus even less chance that their interests would be protected. For Worden, what 'the Rump was planning on 20 April was not the perpetuation of its authority; it was revenge for Pride's Purge'.

Woolrych has generally agreed with Worden's interpretation, but has also pointed out that while the final bill did not provide Parliament with the means to perpetuate itself, the fact that the army believed that there was a clause in it that allowed for recruitment of MPs was what made them act. Woolrych has suggested that the bill originally provided for recruitment, but that this was removed at the last moment. Woolrych has also pointed out that Cromwell and the army also had other concerns. One was the lack of clarity over who was to judge whether prospective future MPs were 'persons of known integrity, fearing God, and not scandalous in their conversation'. Furthermore on 20 April some reports suggest that the bill would have removed Cromwell as commander and given the Rump power over army commands through a committee. Officers were also to be prohibited from serving as MPs. Alongside this the Rump planned to reduce the army's budget to only £31,000 a month which would only have paid for 14,000 soldiers.

In short Cromwell removed the Rump for the following reasons:

- Fear over what the Rump's bill for a new representative included.
- The cutting of the army budget.
- Parliamentary control of army commands.
- Preventing the ungodly returning to political power.
- Cromwell's own vision of a godly nation and political settlement.

Activity

Thinking point

Write a speech that Cromwell might have presented to the nation in order to justify the removal of the Rump.

The Parliament of the Saints: reasons for its creation, its failures and the decision to abandon it

Reasons for its creation

The Rump's dissolution left power in Cromwell's hands. Cromwell was not, however, interested in being a military dictator. As a political conservative he sought another Parliament as a means of settlement. The question was what kind of Parliament and more specifically the means of selecting MPs. Cromwell decided to turn to those he felt he could trust, the godly. The Fifth Monarchist Harrison in particular seems to have helped persuade Cromwell that this was the way forward. In contrast Lambert was counselling Cromwell to turn to a small body of about 12 men in the short term. Cromwell went for the more godly option, but rather than Harrison's desire for an assembly modelled on a Jewish Sanhedrin the army officers selected 139 MPs nominated by separatist congregations across the country. Cromwell's summons for the Assembly referred to 'divers persons fearing God and of approved integrity and honesty are, by myself, with the advice of my Council of Officers, nominated; to whom the great charge and trust of so weighty affairs is to be committed'.

Names given to the Assembly of July–December 1653	Reason for name
Nominated Assembly	Members were nominated rather than elected. Cromwell referred to it as an Assembly rather than a Parliament.
Little Parliament	There were only 140 members. In the 1640 Parliament there had been 507 MPs.
Barebone's Parliament	A term of abuse derived from the name of one of its members, Praise-God Barbon.
The Parliament of Saints	A positive term from those who saw the members as the godly.

Its failures

Derided as the 'Barebone's Parliament', and particularly attacked after the Restoration, there was actually much that was positive about the Nominated Assembly. Aylmer in his *State's Servants* (1973) commented on the development of public administration under the body into a much more professional civil service than had existed under Charles I.

The Assembly also looked at many proposals that were ahead of their time:

- The reform of the law on debt.
- More humane treatment of the insane.
- The civil registration of births, deaths and marriages.
- Tougher measures against thieves and highwaymen.

None of these measures were too radical to frighten moderates. There were some, however, in the Parliament who wanted to go much further.

Religious radicals, including Fifth Monarchists, might actually have been relatively small in numbers. Capp, in his study of the *Fifth Monarchy Men* (1972) could only find 12 definite Fifth Monarchists, but they were

Did you know?

Barebone's Parliament derived its name from the religious radical Praise-God Barbon MP. Some religious radicals used Christian names as a symbol of their godliness. Praise-God baptized his own son 'If-Jesus-Had-Not-Died-For-Thee-Thou-Wouldst-Be-Damned Barbon'. This son went by the name Nicholas and became a leading London property developer after the Restoration, making himself a fortune. The apparent arrogance of Puritans convinced of their own godliness had been satirised earlier by writers like Ben Johnson with characters like the hypocritical Puritan Zeal-of-the-Land-Busy in his Bartholomew Fair. After the Restoration, John Bunyan in *Pilgrim's Progress* took this a stage further with all his characters named in an exaggerated form to reflect their nature.

■ Exploring the detail

Justices of the Peace (JPs) had been appointed by the Crown to enforce the law in the localities. JPs conducted their formal business four times a year, quarter sessions, in the main county towns and at commissions of the peace. The men who were appointed JPs were from the traditional governing gentry of the nation.

■ Exploring the detail

Reform of Chancery: radicals saw the law and lawyers as a bastion of privilege. The legal process was kept deliberately complex to raise costs and thereby the incomes of the legal profession. The court of Chancery was particularly attacked for its costly procedures partly as a result of which cases could drag on for years. The failure to reform saw Chancery become even more archaic to the point that Charles Dickens still felt it necessary to attack it in his novel *Bleak House* in 1853.

■ Activity

Revision exercise

1. Explain why the Levellers and Diggers failed to achieve their aims.

2. In what ways can the Rump Parliament be regarded as a success?

3. Explain why and how the New Model Army was important in this period.

very well organised. They were able to get through the Assembly contentious votes to abolish Chancery, to abolish lay patronage of church livings as well as signalling their desire to get rid of tithes. From July to October 1653 many JPs who had supported the Rump were ejected from commissions of the peace, leaving fewer greater gentry on them than ever before.

Such measures alienated the moderates in and outside the Assembly, including Cromwell. He told his Parliament of 1657 that if he had allowed the Assembly to continue it would have resulted in 'the subversion of your laws and of all the liberties of this nation, the destruction of the ministers of this nation: in a word, the confusion of all things'. The suggestion by radicals to cut army pay, including not paying senior officers for a year, was provocative to a group that they were dependent on. The leading army officer after Cromwell, Lambert, was in contact with moderates in the Assembly.

The removal of the Nominated Assembly

The reasons for the calling of the Nominated Assembly as well as its failures were why moderates wanted to abandon it. They had never really supported it and its failures confirmed to them the need for a different form of settlement. On 12 December moderates from the Nominated Assembly met very early and outvoted the radicals to hand power back to Cromwell. The key figure behind what was in part a military coup was Lambert, working in alliance with moderate MPs. On 12 December soldiers dispersed the Nominated Assembly. With regard to the responsibility for the removal of the Nominated Assembly, Woolrych (1982) in his *Commonwealth to Protectorate* has argued that the 'finger points not at Cromwell but irresistibly at Lambert. His dominant role in framing the *Instrument* and afterwards in persuading Cromwell to accept it makes Lambert the obvious man to have organised the military side of the coup'. This coup was to establish Cromwell as Lord Protector.

Fig. 11 *Coins of the Commonwealth of England, 1649–53*

Learning outcomes

From this section you will have gained an understanding of the reasons for the defeat of the royalist cause in the first civil war and why settlement was not achieved with Charles I in the years 1646 to 1649. You will also have gained an understanding of the different radical groups of the period and the achievements and failures of early Republican government, notably in relation to the demands of the New Model Army. You have considered how the position of the New Model Army from 1647 made it a central feature of the period. It was to remain so until 1660.

AQA Examination-style questions

To what extent was the abolition of monarchy in 1649 the result of political and religious radicalism rather than the intransigence of the King?

Essays require a clear structure on which a thorough argument needs to be constructed. In helping you to structure your essay, a chart like the following may help:

Paragraph headings and key content	Evidence/details to include in paragraph	Analysis/comment on details in relation to question	Historiography/sources that can be used as support of argument
1. Introduction			
2. Newcastle Propositions			
3. Politicisation of NMA			
4. Heads of Proposals			
5. Engagement/Second Civil War			
6. VNA/Windsor			
7. Repeal of VNA and Newport Treaty			
8. Remonstrance			
9. Pride's Purge			
10. Trial and Regicide			
11. Conclusion			

Always remember the basic structure of a paragraph:

- A sentence introducing the theme of the paragraph.
- The evidence to illustrate the theme of the paragraph.
- Comment on the evidence and theme of the paragraph in relation to the specific wording of the question.

In this chapter you will learn about:

- Cromwell's establishment as Lord Protector
- the *Instrument of Government*
- other theories of government
- Cromwell as Lord Protector
- the republican, royalist and military opposition to the Protectorate.

Fig. 1 *Oliver Cromwell, Lord Protector (1653–8)*

On 16 December 1653, Cromwell was taken by coach from Whitehall to Westminster Hall, the scene of the trial of Charles I, to be invested as Lord Protector. He was accompanied by a mounted guard with soldiers lining the route. In front of Cromwell were coaches taking other leading figures of the new regime. In the carriage with Cromwell was Lambert. He preceded Cromwell as they entered the Hall carrying the sword of state. The articles of the *Instrument of Government*, Britain's first written constitution drafted by Lambert, were read out before Cromwell took an oath to uphold them. The ceremony was a symbol of not only the military nature of the Protectorate, but also a desire for it to be seen as a more traditional form of government.

Cromwell as Lord Protector and theories of government

The establishment of Cromwell as Lord Protector

Woolrych (1982) has highlighted Lambert as the prime mover in the removal of Nominated Assembly and the establishment of the Protectorate. The officers of Scotland addressed their support of these events to Lambert. One contemporary simply commented, 'what Lambert hath aimed at he has affected.' Lambert organised and carried off a very successful and remarkably smooth military coup. This was the context for Cromwell's establishment as Protector which was inaugurated through Lambert's *Instrument of Government*.

The *Instrument of Government*

Lambert's *Instrument* comprised 42 clauses with just over 4,500 words. The *Instrument's* key features were:

- **Protector:** head of state
- **Parliament:** elected every three years, to sit for a minimum of five months
- **Council of State:** central role especially in finance, appointments, control of armed forces
- **Militia:** controlled by Protector and Parliament.

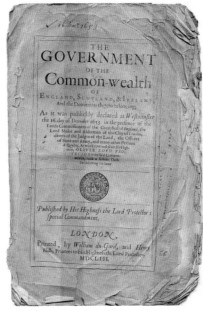

Fig. 2 *A printed copy of Britain's first written constitution, the* Instrument of Government, *1653*

Cross-reference

For more on the establishment of the Protectorate and the removal of the Nominated Assembly see Chapter 3.

Activity

Class debate

Divide into two groups in order to debate the advantages and disadvantages of a written constitution. One group should prepare a speech on the advantages while the other prepares a speech on the disadvantages. After the speeches have been delivered take a vote on whether the advantages outweigh the disadvantages.

Exploring the detail

The *Instrument of Government* was Britain's first written constitution. With the Restoration there was a reversion to monarchy and the ambiguity of an unwritten constitution. Britain still has no written constitution.

A key facet of Lambert's political thinking was the belief that Parliament had to be subject to some check if it was not to simply take over the royal prerogative. Parliament and Protector were to be balanced by a powerful council. Lambert, through the *Instrument*, dealt with the political reality that there would have to be minority rule and that the army had to become, in effect, part of government and legislature through the Council. The military men who had secured the victory needed protection. Lambert argued that:

> If a Parliament should be chosen according to the general spirit and temper of the nation, and if there should not be a check upon such election those may creep into this House, who may come to sit as our judges for all we have done in this Parliament, or at any other time or place … We cannot tell what kind of Parliaments other ages may produce. We ought to take care to leave things certain, and not expose the people's liberties to an arbitrary power.

1

Key terms

Recognition: at the start of the Protectorate some republican MPs questioned the legitimacy of the *Instrument of Government*. In response Cromwell declared 'four fundamentals':

- government was by a single person and parliament

- there was to be no perpetuation of parliaments

- there was to be liberty of conscience

- the militia was to be controlled by the Protector, Council and parliament.

The Recognition required that MPs give an oath recognising the first of these fundamentals. This forced the withdrawal of about 100 republican MPs.

Ordinances: by the terms of the *Instrument of Government* Cromwell and the Council of State could legislate by Ordinance between the sittings of Parliaments. Between 24 December 1653 and 2 September 1654 Cromwell and the Council brought in 83 Ordinances. The majority of Ordinances dealt with finance, making the tax collecting system more efficient.

'Civilian Cromwellians' and 'military Cromwellians': the terms were not strictly accurate in that some members of the army can be classed as 'civilian Cromwellians' and some civilians can be classed as 'military Cromwellians'. These terms are used for supporters of Cromwell during the Protectorate who had different ideas about the direction of settlement. What they most closely denoted was those who sought a more conservative traditional form of settlement, the 'civilians', and those more radical, including more religiously radical, 'military'.

A problem for some was the means by which a check had been imposed on Parliament. The **Recognition** of 1654 implied that there was a power equal to Parliament.

Activity

Thinking point

Explain briefly why (i) the manner of the establishment of the Protectorate and (ii) the role of Lambert were significant in the way the regime was viewed by contemporaries.

The Council of State

The *Instrument*'s essential check on Parliament was the power given to the Council. It would select Cromwell's successor and guide the Protector on policy. The Council was not controlled by Parliament, and recruited its own members, who held their position for life.

In the months up to the first Protectorate Parliament, Cromwell, Lambert and a small group of councillors ran the state. They were most active in producing the Protectorate **Ordinances**.

Despite the Council's role, it would be unwise to underplay Cromwell's influence. There was a difference between the theory and practice of power. While formally the Protector, like Parliament, had limits on his power, and while Cromwell himself was later keen to emphasise the role of the Council, constitutionally Cromwell was still very much the dominant force in the Protectorate.

While the army secured some institutionalisation of its power through the positions of the leading officers in the Council they, or their allies, were not a dominant force in it, or united on all matters. Terms such as **'civilian'** and **'military'**

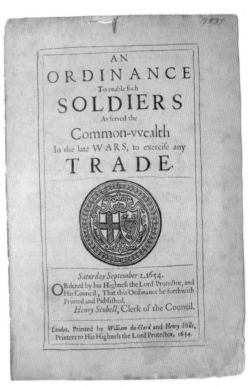

Fig. 3 *A printed copy of an Ordinance issued by the Protectorate Council of State in 1654*

to describe faction within the Council can be artificial. Fundamentally the term 'military' denotes men whose experience of battle was the root of their political goals. Yet most, whether 'military' or 'civilian', were bound to Cromwell.

The positions of the military and civilian Cromwellians

Military:

- Key example: John Lambert.
- Religious radicalism.
- Influence of the Army.
- The continuation of the Protectorate.

Civilian:

- Key example: Lord Broghill.
- Religious conservatism.
- Influence of Parliament.
- Kingship.

Electoral Qualifications

The way MPs were to be elected also should have provided some check on Parliament. MPs were supposed to agree to an indenture, a political contract that should have limited them and electors alike by making them recognise the new regime. Unfortunately, some MPs felt no qualms about agreeing to the indenture and Recognition, and then proceeding to act against the Protectorate.

The Council did interfere in the 1654 elections. Some MPs were excluded. In the elections for the second Protectorate Parliament, even more influence was used to shape who was elected. This was part of the reason for the Major-General's resort to a Parliament, the belief that to a large degree they could influence its composition, reinforced by a willingness to use their exclusion powers much more readily than in 1654 when they, but particularly Cromwell, were more optimistic of achieving a working Parliament.

Other theories of government – Harrington and Vane

Fifth Monarchists like Harrison disapproved of the Protectorate. For them it marked the defeat of the Nominated Assembly, as well as a retreat from placing power in the hands of the saints. Others had more secular reasons for proposing different theories of government. Republicans objected to the *Instrument* and opposed it in parliament. For republicans authority should be in a single chamber parliament like the Rump.

Classical Republicanism

With no English republican tradition, some republicans turned to a long-established European republican language originating in classical Greece and Rome, called Classical Republicanism. These ideas became established in the political culture of the Renaissance period, particularly the work of the classical writers Aristotle, Livy, Tacitus and the Renaissance writer Machiavelli. Immediately after the regicide English republican writing was defensive, such as John Goodwin's *Right and Might Well Met* (1649) or, less so, Milton's *The Tenure of Kings and Magistrates* (1649).

By 1651 English republicanism was positively declared to Europe in Milton's *Pro Populo Anglicano Defensio* (In Defence of the English People) using classical writers Plato, Aristotle, Cicero and Livy. This stance was to be reinforced by Nedham in the Commonwealth's weekly newspaper, *Mercurius Politicus*. A central argument for Nedham was the link between liberty and military power, a soldier citizen, which could

Fig. 4 *A Roundhead and a civilian MP*

Activity

Revision exercise

Construct a chart from the information in this chapter showing Cromwell's influence on one side and how his influence was limited on the other.

Cross-reference

For the Fifth Monarchists see Chapter 3.

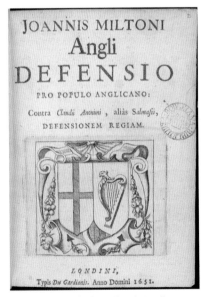

Fig. 5 *Cover of John Milton's* Anglicano Defensio *of 1651 that defended the regicide*

be found in the work of Aristotle, Livy and Machiavelli. For Classical Republicans the Rump was a legitimate form of government.

James Harrington's *Oceana*

Harrington's *The Commonwealth of Oceana* (1656) was a key work of republican political thought. It was better received and more widely read than the other major work of political philosophy of the time, Hobbes' *Leviathan*.

■ Cross-reference

For more on Marchamont Nedham, see page 44.

■ Cross-reference

For Thomas Hobbes' *Leviathan*, see page 40.

Harrington was critical of the Protectorate rather than calling for resistance. He argued that for stable government the form must match the distribution of property, especially land. Thus, according to Harrington, as property distribution had become more 'popular' only a republic could provide stable government. Society was to be divided into three parts which was linked to military duty. Similarly a two chamber (Senate and Assembly) elected Parliament was to be divided in relation to property and military duty.

Elections were to be by secret ballot and Parliament would sit continually with a system of rotation; a third of each chamber would retire each year. The Senate had sole right to propose and debate measures whereas the Assembly would vote for or against them in silence. Officers of state were to be elected by and from the Senate.

Although a theoretical model was never adopted, a clear example of the real impact of Harrington's work can be seen by the articulation of his theory in the Second Protectorate Parliament by the MP and client of Lambert, Captain Adam Baynes.

■ A closer look

The 'new men' made by war and revolution – Captain Adam Baynes 1622–71

Baynes' family were of relatively humble origins from the Leeds area, Baynes' father being a yeoman and Baynes himself may have been apprenticed to a cloth merchant. In 1642 he joined Parliament's northern army and by 1646 was an officer in Lambert's regiment. In the winter of 1648-9 Lambert appointed him as his and his brigade's financial agent in London. Here he acted as their attorney in purchasing crown and church lands. Baynes was a republican who favoured the trial and execution of Charles I. Evidence suggests that he was well disposed to the Leveller leader Lilburne. He regarded the Rump as contrary to the interests of the army and godly. Through Lambert's patronage, Baynes was appointed to the Protectorate's army committee and after the enfranchisement of Leeds in 1654, again probably through Lambert's influence, Baynes became an MP. Baynes' influence waned with Lambert's in 1657 but he was returned to influence as an MP in 1659 and worked with Lambert to oppose Richard Cromwell being made Protector, being outspoken in his criticism of the Other House. At the Restoration Baynes suffered imprisonment and persecution.

A practical problem for Harrington became clear when he produced five pamphlets promoting his ideas between May and August of 1659. Republican politicians were not impressed with the idea of rotation of office holders as this would destroy their hold over power. Others took Harrington's ideas more seriously and in October 1659 the Rota Club was set up to discuss them.

Henry Vane's *A Healing Question*

In *A Healing Question* (1656) Vane argued that Cromwell, through his authority as commander of the army, should call a new assembly chosen by the 'well-affected'. Vane wanted a broad coalition of the 'good Party', those who stood for civil and religious liberty. The basis of government would be a Senate. Vane's pamphlet was the source for the phrase the 'Good Old Cause'.

Fig. 6 *A later edition of James Harrington's republican model,* Oceana

Key profile

Henry Vane 1613–62

Vane was at the heart of parliamentary government until Pride's Purge. Vane returned to Parliament after the regicide and was a member of the February 1649 Council of State. After the removal of the Rump, Vane retired again, producing *A Healing Question*. An MP again in 1659, Vane sought to bring together men such as Ludlow and Lambert, with whom he had developed an alliance. His *A Needful Corrective or Balance in Popular Government* was a response to Harrington. Imprisoned in the Tower and then on the Scilly Isles at the Restoration, the Cavalier Parliament demanded his trial. In 1662, refusing to beg for mercy, Vane was beheaded.

In Vane's letter to Harrington, *A Needful Corrective or Balance in Popular Government*, the idea of a Senate was again propounded to guide people to support the 'public interest' rather than their own. Vane had become increasingly close to Lambert and this may be reflected in Vane's thinking with regard to the 'Saints'. Selection of the Saints was left to the army, the 'well affected'. Commonwealthsmen and Fifth Monarchists met to discuss the practicalities of Vane's scheme, but decided that it would not be godly enough.

Cromwell and Parliament

Cromwell wanted settlement through a Parliament. The problem was that any traditional Parliament would not support Cromwell's other main aim, a godly reformation. These two aims have thus been seen as contradictory. The goal of a godly reformation marked Cromwell off from the traditional conservative political elite who were normally represented by Parliament. This reinforced his reliance on the army which in turn hampered his search for settlement through Parliament.

Activity

Revision exercise

Write a paragraph explaining which of Harrington or Vane's ideas had more chance of bringing political settlement in these years.

Cromwell's contradictory impulses and the problems it caused in his Parliaments was seen clearly in the Nayler Crisis during the Second Protectorate Parliament but the tension created by the question of the extent of religious toleration also came to a head during the First Protectorate Parliament with the case of John Biddle.

Biddle was a Socinian, someone who denied not only the Trinity (the Father, Son and Holy Spirit) but the divinity of Christ. (The term derived from a 16th century theologian, Faustus Socinus.) Accused of Blasphemy, his case became illustrative of the tensions between army and Parliament as well as Cromwell's own aims at the end of the First Protectorate Parliament because it highlighted the conservatism of MPs generally in religious questions. Cromwell was already frustrated with MPs because rather than relieve the godly they had focused their attention on attacking the *Instrument*.

On 7 December 1654, Parliament effectively resolved that it was the body that would control religion. It should be noted that some leading figures in the 1654 Parliament had been purged by the army in 1648 partly due to their political Presbyterianism. Alongside these men it is likely that the representatives of Scotland and Ireland, allowed to sit in this first British Parliament under the terms of the *Instrument*, were also religious conservatives. For example, Broghill, a representative of Ireland, became a pre-eminent 'civilian Cromwellian'.

For Cromwell the Parliament was putting discipline over liberty. More importantly in their resolutions of 7 and 15 December, Parliament declared their intention to assert legislative supremacy over the Protector and his Council by declaring that what they had decided with regard to ministers and as action against heresy and blasphemy would 'pass into, and become laws, within twenty days after their presentation to the Protector, although he shall not give his consent thereunto'. It was therefore not only the issue of Parliament's more conservative approach to religion that concerned Cromwell and his councillors but their attack on the constitutional position of the Protector which Lambert had constructed deliberately because of fears of the potential arbitrary nature of parliamentary power.

For London Presbyterians and their parliamentary allies, Biddle's case became the test case for assessing blasphemy and heresy but, more importantly, the authority of Parliament or Protector to decide the limits of toleration and who should deal with those seen as having transgressed. Biddle was interrogated by a parliamentary committee and the Commons declared that he should be imprisoned and his written work burned. The prosecution of Biddle was followed by the preparation of a bill focusing on the threat of the Quakers.

Under the *Instrument*, it was debatable how far Cromwell could intervene directly in parliamentary proceedings. Cromwell's political conservatism also meant that he was fundamentally unwilling to intervene directly with Parliament to protect Biddle. Instead Cromwell imprisoned Biddle on the Scilly Isles, outside the reach of Parliament, and granted Biddle a generous weekly allowance.

The Biddle episode and MPs' further attacks on the *Instrument* forced Cromwell into a dissolution of parliament after the minimum constitutional period of 5 lunar months.

Cromwell and Kingship

The 'civilian' Cromwellians, centred on Broghill, reacted to the imposition of the major-generals by attempting to push the Protectorate in a more conservative direction. The centrepiece of their proposed constitutional changes was the offer of the Crown to Cromwell. Cromwell was certainly drawn to the idea. He recognised the advantages it would bring in aiding settlement with the traditional political nation.

Advantages of Kingship	Disadvantages of Kingship
More recognised form of government for gentry	Cromwell seen as a usurper
Establish a line of succession	Provoke more vigorous opposition from royalists
Achieve settlement with a Parliament	Opposition from some of the New Model
	Opposition of the leading 'military Cromwellians'
	Opposition from republicans

There was bitter opposition to Cromwell taking the Crown from republicans and most notably army officers. Some historians like Hutton have stressed the importance of this army opposition in Cromwell's refusal of the Crown. Others, like Barnard, have stressed Cromwell's pragmatic reasons for rejecting kingship.

> What happened is too often explained in terms of Cromwell's instinctive reaction against Kingship because it was precisely the sort of vanity to which God had often seemed hostile. Yet more practical considerations had some importance. On 6 May 1657 Cromwell informally expressed his willingness to accept the Crown. This aroused the army to a last effort. Lambert, Fleetwood and Desborough said they would resign. Then Cromwell heard that Colonel Pride had raised a petition, drafted by John Owen, against monarchy from most of the regiments in London, and was taking it to the Parliament. This impending confrontation compelled Cromwell's decision. On 8 May 1657, as the petition reached Parliament, Cromwell removed the need to deal with it by refusing the Crown.

2 *R. Hutton, **The British Republic 1649–1660** (1990)*

> A rational explanation of Cromwell's refusal of the crown would assume that he feared the spread of disaffection through the army and the sects. Yet events showed that unrest in the army was slight. Cromwell may have rejected the title for less rational reasons. It was distressed by allegations that he had worked for his own family's aggrandizement, and that in restoring monarchy he would be disobeying God's commands. Cromwell tended to dismiss the authority of King as inconsequential, 'a gaudy feather in the hat of authority', and to believe he could have all the benefits of the new settlement – the right to choose his successor, a second House and a solid body of provincial supporters – without it.

3 *T. Barnard, **The English Republic 1649–60** (1982)*

Cross-reference

For the Quakers, see Chapter 5.

Activity

Thinking point

Explain why religion was such a divisive political issue in the first Protectorate Parliament.

Activity

Challenge your thinking

In 2007 Smith and Little published their book *Parliaments and Politics during the Cromwellian Protectorate*. They argued that Cromwell's problems with Parliament could be equated with Conrad Russell's (1979) argument that the early Stuarts' problems were 'not difficulties with their Parliaments; they were difficulties which were reflected in their Parliaments'. Consider ways in which Cromwell's relationship with Parliament under the Protectorate fits Russell's argument.

Activity

Source analysis

How far does Source 3 differ from Source 2 in explaining why Cromwell refused the Crown in 1657?

A key part of Cromwell's refusal was religious. The army's opposition was linked to Cromwell's religious motivation. For Cromwell the army was God's Instrument populated by the Saints. Army opposition would have been telling for Cromwell in his conclusion that God had judged against kingship. Cromwell expressed his reasons to a parliamentary committee in April 1657:

> I wait as a person under the dispensation of the providence of God. As far as I can I am ready to serve not as a King, but as a constable to keep the peace of the parish. I am not a man scrupulous about words or names or such thing. Truly the Providence of God has laid this title [of King] aside providentially. God has seen providentially not only to strike at the title but the name. It is a thing cast out by Act of Parliament. I would not seek to set up that Providence hath destroyed and laid in the dust.

4

Republican, royalist and military opposition to the Protectorate and Cromwell

Republican opposition – Protectorate Parliaments

Republicans proved to be the most problematic opposition grouping for Cromwell, as their opposition was centred in the Protectorate Parliaments. Republicans were also known as 'Commonwealthsmen' because of their support for the Rump. For Republicans, Cromwell's removal of the Rump had removed the legitimate authority of Parliament, which should be the nation's ultimate authority. The leading Commonwealthsman was Haselrig. Their opposition was based on the fact that they saw the Protectorate as a drift towards kingship. The offer of the Crown to Cromwell appeared to confirm this.

1654 Parliament

Cromwell's position as Protector immediately came under attack from Republicans. Their opposition was more problematic because of Cromwell's unwillingness to manage parliament, due to his wish that Parliament lead the nation to settlement. Furthermore, managing Parliament was actually harder under the redistribution of seats that took place as part of the *Instrument*. Two thirds of the 400 MPs for England and Wales would now be 'county' rather than 'borough' MPs and as a result less open to influence.

Republicans focused on the *Instrument's* powers. In particular they were concerned with:

- the authority to enact Ordinances when Parliament was not in session
- control of the army
- reduction of the armed forces.

Cromwell's response was to make clear what he regarded as the 'fundamentals' of government:

- Government by a single person and parliament.
- No perpetuation of parliaments.
- Liberty of conscience.
- Militia controlled by Protector, Council and Parliament.

Exploring the detail

The idea of a Commonwealth as distinct from the interests of the Crown became established in Elizabethan England among some of the elite. This perception of the interests of the Commonwealth focused on the threat from France and Spain as well as the humanist idea of a community charged with civic duties. Thus some had a clear idea of what they felt were the responsibilities of the Crown and political nation which could be distinct from loyalty to the Crown. In this sense there was a republican tradition in England within the context of European humanism and republicanism.

Did you know?

The Protectorate Parliaments were the first fully British and Irish Parliaments to assemble until 1801. The reform of how seats were reapportioned was the most radical until the Great Reform Act of 1832. The redistribution of the constituencies under the *Instrument* gave representation to the growing towns of Manchester and Leeds for the first time.

Key profile

Arthur Haselrig 1601–61

Haselrig was one of the Five Members Charles I tried to arrest in 1642. Although a republican he refused to sit at the King's trial but was subsequently a leading figure in the Rump. Haselrig opposed the Protectorate being removed as an MP for his refusal of the 1654 Recognition and excluded from the first session of the Second Protectorate Parliament. Haselrig was a key figure in alienating the army leaders, particularly Lambert following Cromwell's death. Following the army's coup of 1659 Haselrig was one of those who appealed for the intervention of Monck. Leader of the restored Commonwealth, Haselrig was imprisoned in the Tower and died awaiting trial for treason in 1661.

The opposition of hardened civilian republicans led Cromwell and the Council to introduce the Recognition. About 100 MPs rejected it on principle.

It was not just the Republicans, however, who sought to attack the *Instrument*. Having seen the problems in Parliament and disliking the influence of the military figures, 'Cromwellian Civilians' like Broghill sought to adapt the *Instrument* and shift the emphasis of settlement to more traditional conservative forms.

Second Protectorate Parliament, September 1656

After the major-generals experiment, Cromwell, under financial pressure, persuasion from 'civilian Cromwellians' and his own conservative political impulses, called his Second Protectorate Parliament.

Cromwell, the Council and the major-generals used the powers of Exclusion. By the *Instrument* the Council could exclude those who were not 'persons of known integrity, fearing God, and of good conversation'. A hundred were excluded and 60 chose to decline their seats in the Parliament in protest.

The exclusions initially helped the conservatives and Cromwell to cooperate. This was centred on the shift symbolised by the beginnings of work on the *Humble Petition*. As a result the initial weeks of the Parliament witnessed work on the war against Spain, progress with legislation to regulate alehouses and the setting of the poor to work. This positive start was, however, brought to a halt by the debates surrounding kingship which symbolised the growing tensions between the 'military' and 'civilian' Cromwellians.

The Republicans, Kingship and the *Humble Petition and Advice*

Republicans naturally opposed the plan to make Cromwell king which was central to the new 'civilian Cromwellian' proposed constitution, the *Humble Petition and Advice*. Some referred to Harrington's *Oceana* and the idea of property distribution supporting the non-monarchical forms of government.

Even though Cromwell refused the Crown, there is little doubt that for Republicans the acceptance of the rest of the *Humble Petition* increased the emphasis on Cromwell as 'King in all but name' that had started with the inauguration of the Protectorate.

Cross-reference

For the Recognition, see page 54.

Cross-reference

For the major-generals, see Chapter 5.

Fig. 7 *A 19th century engraving of Oliver Cromwell, English soldier and statesman, with his wife, standing in front of a portrait of Charles I*

■ **Did you know?**

The Coronation Chair

For Cromwell's 1657 investiture as Lord Protector, the Coronation Chair, sometimes known as St Edward's Chair, after Edward the Confessor, was moved from Westminster Abbey for the only time in its history. Used at the enthronement of monarchs since Edward II in 1308 the chair had been made for Edward I so that he could place the Stone of Scone under it after he had removed it from Scotland in 1296 following his war of conquest. Only in 1996 was the Stone returned to Scotland.

■ Activity

Talking point

Should the Republicans have compromised with the Protectorate to strengthen non-monarchical rule?

This was clear in the different ceremony used to invest Cromwell as Protector in 1657 under the *Humble Petition* from the one in 1653 under the *Instrument* where Lambert, symbolising the military, had taken a prominent role. Sherwood (1997) has argued that 1657 was 'to all intents and purposes a king-making ceremony, transforming Cromwell from a de facto into a de jure King while retaining the title Lord Protector'.

It was not only the offer of the Crown that concerned Republicans. When Parliament met after Cromwell's acceptance of the *Humble Petition*, without kingship, Republicans were vocal in their opposition to the new constitution. Part of the *Humble Petition*, and partly as a result of the problems Republicans had created during the First Protectorate Parliament, was the addition of an Upper House, a second chamber that looked like the House of Lords, and was to act as a balance against the Lower House. Despite being nominated to this Upper House, Haselrig led republican opposition to the *Humble Petition*. Republicans argued that the people, as represented in a Commons, could not be subjected to the authority of another chamber. They regarded the Rump as the ideal form of government.

Republicans also organised a petition to get army support. During the debates on the *Humble Petition*, they circulated the petition through London and the army for signatures. The appeal to the army is clear in the petition not claiming that Parliament had power over the army and by avoiding clear religious proposals. Generally the petition was constructed deliberately broad to appeal to all but royalists and Fifth Monarchists. As a result of the petition, Cromwell dissolved Parliament on the day it was due to be presented, 4 February 1658. By depriving Republicans of a platform Cromwell weakened their opposition. Cromwell was most concerned about the impact of their opposition on the army and the more real threat it posed.

Royalist opposition – The Sealed Knot and Penruddock's Rising

On 3 September 1651, Charles Stuart and the invading Scottish army were crushed by Cromwell at Worcester. Charles Stuart escaped and fled to the continent, not to return until 1660. There was, therefore, no figurehead for rebellion in England. Furthermore, Charles Stuart provided no clear guidance to those royalists in England prepared to take action against the Rump or Protectorate. There was very little chance of a royalist rising being successful but Cromwell was most worried by royalists and exaggerated their threat. The majority of the royalists were not interested in plotting, but more concerned with securing their estates.

Charles Stuart was not really known in England. What people knew of him was not encouraging. Although it is now clear that Charles did not wallow in vice, he was a womaniser and heavily in debt. He certainly did not appear a model king. Furthermore there was division in the exiled royalist court where Henrietta Maria's position at the French court gave her and her 'Louvre Circle' influence over Charles. The differing outlooks of the moderate Hyde and 'swordsman' Rupert also hampered a concerted royalist opposition.

The Sealed Knot, founded in 1653 to coordinate royalist opposition in England, was a conservative cautious organisation centred on men of substance who were thereby discouraged by the threat of losing

■ **Did you know?**

The Sealed Knot today is an organisation founded in 1968 to 'promote research into and the study of and public interest in the history of the Civil Wars'. They do this through re-enactments, education and the erection of memorials.

their estates. They also exacerbated the divisions in the exiled royalist court by insisting that only Charles Stuart and the Hyde-Ormond faction were aware of their plans. What also made the Sealed Knot so cautious were the disastrous attempts to assassinate Cromwell in May 1654. A plan to ambush Cromwell's coach was foiled by Thurloe's intelligence and he also prevented the attempt to kidnap Cromwell a week later.

Royalist leadership in England was taken on by the younger sons and less well off who had less to lose and therefore could be more radical, attempting to win over Political Presbyterians and Levellers.

Charles broke his agreement with the Sealed Knot and commissioned the Earl of Rochester to command any forces raised in England. The planned rising was delayed until eventually by March 1655 Thurloe was well aware of the plans. The plotting was localised and poorly coordinated. Across the country the pre-emptive actions of the state meant there was no real significant royalist threat anywhere, apart from Penruddock's Rising in Devon, itself quickly crushed by Major-General Desborough.

Key profile

John Desborough (1608–80)

Desborough was from Cambridgeshire. In 1636 he married the sister of Oliver Cromwell. Joined Cromwell's troop of horse in the Eastern Association and was a Major-General in the New Model. Desborough was not a regicide, being the governor of Yarmouth at the time of the execution. In 1649 he was assigned to guard the west. His role during Penruddock's Rising of 1655 partly shaped the development of the major-generals scheme. During his role as Major-General and in the west generally Desborough tried to work with the local gentry.

He was part of the Wallingford House group that failed to prevent the restoration. He was disqualified from public office for life at the Restoration and after being imprisoned in the Tower for allegedly plotting to kill Charles II and Henrietta Maria. Desborough escaped to Holland but on his returned to England in 1665 he was imprisoned in the Tower again, this time for two years. Following his release Desborough lived out his life in Hackney, being a member alongside his old comrade Fleetwood, of John Owen's Independent congregation.

The most significant reaction by the state to the rising was the imposition of the major-generals.

Charles Stuart sent John Mordaunt from the continent to promote further royalist rebellion. Mordaunt's plans for a 1658 rising were exposed and his own attempt at the time of Booth's Rising of 1659 only drew 30 supporters. As with all other forms of opposition, the royalists' impact was limited by the work of Thurloe's intelligence network. Thurloe had letters seized and had agents who could recognise the writing of leading royalists. Thurloe had his network carry out preventive arrests when there were rumours of risings.

Did you know?

There have been two recent novels with Thurloe as a character – Iain Pear's *An Instance of the Fingerpost* (1997) and Susanna Gregory's *A Conspiracy of Violence* (2006). Other examples of historical fiction centred in the early modern period are Peter Ackroyd's *Milton in America* (1996) and Nigel Williams' *Witchcraft* (1988).

Activity

Talking point

Historical novels are usually regarded as a source for the period in which they are written rather than an historical source for the time about which they are writing. Does this mean that such historical fiction is of little value to the historian or that such fiction can add nothing to our historical understanding?

Key profile

John Thurloe, 1616–68

A lawyer who worked for Cromwell as early as 1647. In 1652 he became secretary to the Council of State and in July 1653 he succeeded Thomas Scot as director of intelligence and carried on in this role under the Protectorate. He also became an MP and Secretary to the Protectorate Council of State. He acted as a government spokesman in Parliament for the 'civilian Cromwellians' and Cromwell. Dismissed with the return of the Commonwealth, Thurloe was reappointed by Monck. Arrested at the Restoration he was released on condition that he gave information when requested by the Restoration regime. He was approached occasionally by Clarendon. Thurloe's papers were found hidden in a false ceiling in his Lincoln's Inn chambers during the reign of William III.

Miles Sindercombe's assassination plot

One plan to assassinate Cromwell was the work of the ex-Leveller and ex-army officer Edward Sexby who in the 1650s developed links with royalists.

A closer look

Edward Sexby and Silus Titus, Killing Noe Murder (1657)

Sexby had been in the New Model and emerged as a Leveller sympathiser in 1647 but left the army after the failure of the Ware mutiny. He worked for the Rump and in 1651 was working in France with the aim of annexing La Rochelle and Bordeaux for England. In 1655 he was discovered plotting with Wildman against the Protectorate and fled to Holland. From here with Silus Titus he authored a justification of attempting to assassinate Cromwell. The argument of the pamphlet was that it was a patriotic duty to assassinate the Protector and in doing so one would be acting for the people as Cromwell could be regarded as a tyrant who had usurped power and wielded it absolutely.

Titus had fought for parliament but converted to royalism when attending Charles I during the King's imprisonment. The pamphlet was produced at the time of the offer of the Crown to Cromwell and was designed to stoke up opposition. To further this it was printed under the name of William Allen. Allen had been one of the agitators alongside Sexby and the idea seems to have been to tap into army unrest at the prospect of Cromwell becoming king. Sexby failed however to get copies of the pamphlet into England until after Cromwell had refused the Crown. When trying to return to Holland he was seized and died in the Tower in 1658.

Sexby selected one Miles Sindercombe to assassinate Cromwell. Sindercombe had also been in the army and a Leveller, taking a leading role in their failed mutiny of 1649. Sindercombe with two associates planned to shoot Cromwell as he rode in his carriage to the opening of the 1656 Parliament. Cromwell's protection forced them to plan to attempt to blow him up in Whitehall Palace. As the matches were actually lit on the fire-bomb they had constructed, one of Sindercombe's associates informed on Sindercombe. His other accomplice then gave all the information he had to Thurloe. With the three under arrest, Thurloe revealed the details to Parliament in January 1657.

Military opposition – *Three Colonels' Petition*

Three Colonels' Petition

It was reported that Lambert told those who did not agree with his *Instrument* that they 'might leave their commands then: Do you think that we are such children, having begun a business, not to go through with it?' When Major-General Overton came out in opposition, he was arrested and his supporters purged. The most visible army opposition came in the *Three Colonels Petition*, of Colonels Alured, Saunders and Okey, published in October 1654 and drafted by the Leveller Wildman.

The Petition denounced the Protectorate, calling for a return to the 'Good Old Cause'. Those in the army opposed to the *Instrument* based their disagreement on the power given to the Protector, especially to oppose Parliament. They also noted that Cromwell's successor might use the army to totally destroy Parliaments. At this point, many of those close to the centre of power believed that the next Protector would be Lambert. The manuscript of *The Case of Colonel Matthew Alured*, unlike the printed version, accused Lambert of being 'the chiefest in modelizing the whole business' because of his ambition to be the next Protector.

The Baptist and Leveller sympathiser Admiral Lawson was in contact with the Three Colonels. A republican, Lawson encouraged a petition by his sailors at the time the Three Colonels were drafting their petition with Wildman. He had also secured the election of Wildman as MP for Scarborough and met with the Three Colonels and Wildman. At the time of Overton's arrest and incarceration in the Tower, Lawson was questioned but released. In 1656 Lawson was arrested. He was a leading figure in trying to establish an alliance between republicans and fifth monarchists. Also arrested were the republican Colonel Okey and Fifth Monarchists Colonel Nathaniel Rich and Thomas Venner.

Many Fifth Monarchists regarded the Protectorate as a betrayal of the godly and Cromwell as an apostate. Harrison was removed from the army and suffered periods of imprisonment. Vavasour Powell attacked Cromwell as 'the dissembleingst perjured villaine in the world'. Briefly imprisoned, Powell left London for Wales claiming he would raise 20,000 Welsh Saints. There was no rising, although Cromwell was attacked in print in 1655 in *A Word for God*. Others, notably Morgan Llwyd, were prepared to continue to support Cromwell, preferring to wait on God's direction.

The Army and Kingship

The most significant opposition to Cromwell taking the Crown came from the New Model, not only as the godly but as the chief political power. Their opposition was therefore not only a political threat to Cromwell but a reminder of the perspective of the 'saints' he respected. Typical of such emotional appeals to Cromwell was a letter he received from Captain William Bradford.

Activity

Talking point

Do the limits of royalist opposition to the Protectorate suggest that monarchy was unpopular with its traditional supporters?

Those that are for a crown, I fear you have little experience of them; the other [the army], most of them, have attended your greatest hazards. I am of that number, my Lord, that still loves you, and greatly desires to do so, I having gone along with you from Edge Hill to Dunbar. The experiences you have had of the power of God at these two places, and betwixt them, methinks, should often make you shrink, and be at a stand in this thwarting, threatening change.

5 *Captain William Bradford to Oliver Cromwell, 4 March 1657*

A more concerted campaign of army opposition led to a petition to Cromwell.

That they had hazarded their lives against the monarchy, and were still ready so to do in defence of the liberties of the nation; that having observed in some men great endeavours to bring the nation under the old servitude by pressing their General to take upon him the title and government of a king, in order to destroy him and weaken the hands of those who were faithful to the public, they therefore humbly desired that [he] would discountenance all such persons and endeavours, and continue steadfast to the good old cause, for the preservation of which they for their parts were most ready to lay down their lives.

6 *Officers' Petition of 1657 to Cromwell*

Activity

Source analysis

Why might the arguments put forward in Sources 5 and 6 be particularly persuasive with Cromwell?

Cromwell's indecision over whether to accept the title of king seems to have driven a final wedge between him and Lambert. This was not so much because of the title, but the 'civilian' basis of the Humble Petition which would replace his *Instrument*. As Little (2007) has argued, the Petition 'witnessed an unprecedented assertion of Parliament's powers within a written constitution'. While Cromwell did have serious religious objections to accepting the Crown, Lambert's leadership of the army's opposition to kingship was also a key practical factor in Cromwell's decision not to accept the Crown. Most at the time regarded Lambert as leading the opposition to kingship and the new constitution. While Fleetwood and Desborough accepted the *Humble Petition*, Lambert resigned.

Cromwell's own regiment remained a concern and especially the man who had in practice led it, from 1652, because of Cromwell's other duties: Major William Packer.

Key profile

William Packer, fl. 1644–62

Army officer and deputy major-general. Lieutenant in Cromwell's 'Ironsides'. Arrested in 1644 for disobedience to orders by Major-General Crawford, but more likely because the Presbyterian Crawford disapproved of his Particular Baptist views. Cromwell defended Packer as a 'Godly man', securing his release. Served in the numerous campaigns of the New Model and in charge of Cromwell's regiment from 1652. In July 1653 he received a licence from the council of state authorising him to preach in any pulpit in England. Allied with the London Fifth Monarchists he nevertheless supported the Protectorate. Having become an MP he became an opponent of the conservative civilian Cromwellians.

He was removed from his command after Cromwell failed to convince him of the errors of his position. He helped Lambert expel the Rump Parliament in 1659. When Lambert escaped from the Tower of London Packer was arrested and committed to prison. Packer suffered numerous incarcerations at the Restoration until in 1662 he was sent to be imprisoned in Dublin Castle. Packer was never put on trial; his date of death is unknown.

Cromwell, typically, confronted directly those in his regiment whose republicanism made them object to the recent constitutional changes. Cromwell took the time to argue with them over a number of days. In the end he removed Packer and five others who could not be persuaded to end their opposition.

Summary of opposition to the Protectorate

Despite the opposition it faced, Cromwell's regime was notable for the moderation in which it treated those who conspired against it. Only those who planned or took part in trying to overthrow the state were executed: eight in total.

Monarch	Reigned	Number of executions
Henry VII	1485–1509	6
Henry VIII	1509–47	38
Edward VI	1547–53	7
Mary I	1553–8	38
Elizabeth I	1558–1603	28

Cromwell's regime was secure; only his own army could realistically overthrow him. Furthermore, Cromwell had achieved the passive acceptance of the majority of the gentry. In practice they had accepted, as Hobbes outlined in *Leviathan*, that the regime by having de facto power, was a legitimate authority to be obeyed. In the context of the events of 1649 and English history, Cromwell's achievement of sustaining government without monarchy was remarkable.

 Activity

Revision exercise

Construct a chart outlining the strengths and weaknesses of the republican, royalist and army opposition.

Activity

Thinking point

Of the three types of opposition considered in this chapter which do you consider the most serious threat to the regime and why?

Summary questions

1 Explain why the *Instrument of Government* provoked opposition.

2 Explain why Cromwell refused the offer of the Crown.

3 To what extent was the limited opposition to Cromwell a sign of the general acceptance of the Protectorate?

5 Religious Radicalism, Toleration and the Major-Generals

Fig. 1 *Later depiction of a Puritan Roundhead, bible in hand and in the uniform of a New Model Army cavalry trooper*

The English Revolution spawned many of the religious groups that remain with us today such as the Baptists and the Quakers. Even some of the more radical and obscure groups that emerged from this period survived into the 20th century, with the last of the radical sect the Muggletonians dying in 1979. Religion was very much part of politics in the 17th century and this was most visibly illustrated when the case of the leading Quaker, James Nayler, provoked a political crisis at the heart of Cromwell's Protectorate. In October 1656 Nayler rode a donkey into Bristol with his women followers scattering flowers before him in a deliberate mimicking of Christ's entry into Jerusalem. The question as to what should be done with Nayler raised questions about the whole nature of settlement, illustrating how central religion was as politics in the 17th century and saw Cromwell shift from the attempt at godly rule through the major-generals to consider becoming King Oliver.

The influence of radical religious groupings, including the Fifth Monarchists and Quakers

There was nothing new about religious radicalism but, in the context of revolution, radical ideas could come to the surface and indeed were a key force of the revolution. For many, this fact provided a reason to retreat into monarchy. The Presbyterian Thomas Edwards, who initially welcomed the revolution, was horrified by the radical ideas it unleashed. In outlining these in his work *Gangraena* Edwards was concerned that the reformation of these years had led to a 'Deformation', i.e. the undermining of religious stability.

Fig. 2 *Pamphlet attacking the proliferation of radical religious groups*

The Fifth Monarchists under the Protectorate

The Fifth Monarchists opposed the Protectorate, but lacked enough support in the army or at the centre of power in London to really threaten Cromwell. In 1654 Major-General Thomas Harrison obeyed an order to return to his native Staffordshire and he remained a relatively passive figure until his gruesome execution at the Restoration.

In February 1656, members of John Roger's Fifth Monarchist church, based at Lambeth, approached Cromwell for the release of Rogers from his imprisonment. Typical of Cromwell, he invited Rogers and some of his followers to a meeting with some Councillors. Rogers turned up with 250 followers but would not accept Cromwell's call for a declaration that he would live peaceably. Later in the same day Cromwell was visited by other leading London Fifth Monarchists, including Harrison. Again Cromwell took time to talk to them. They failed, however, to respond to a further summons to discuss their differences. Eventually when they refused to give a declaration to live in peace, Cromwell placed them temporarily in various prisons.

Venner's rising

Rogers was eventually released in December 1656. The Fifth Monarchists planned a rising against the Protectorate but were only able to get very limited support; not even Harrison would support a rising. In the Fifth Monarchist stronghold of Morgan Llwyd and Vavasor Powell in South Wales there had been a shift from action to reflection. Focus therefore centred on Thomas Venner.

Venner was a cooper and lay preacher who had returned from Massachusetts. Venner had already tried to blow up the Tower of London.

> ### Cross-reference
>
> For the Fifth Monarchists before the Protectorate, see Chapter 3.

In *A Standard Set Up* the Fifth Monarchists denounced Cromwell and outlined how authority should be vested in the Saints. Venner's military rising in April 1657 was prevented by Thurloe's prior intelligence. Venner was placed in the Tower.

During the kingship crisis of 1657 Venner and Rogers were in the Tower. Another leading Fifth Monarchist, John Carew, suggested cooperating with Baptists to strengthen opposition to the regime, but this was rejected by others in the movement.

The limited Fifth Monarchist influence within the army and the incarceration of their leading figures meant that Fifth Monarchist influence over the direction of settlement was, apart from briefly in 1653, limited. While Cromwell had sympathy with much of the Fifth Monarchist position, ultimately he regarded its more radical proponents as a threat to order.

Activity

Thinking point

Explain why Fifth Monarchist political influence in this period was limited.

Baptists

Baptist beliefs:

- Practice of 'believers' adult baptism'.
- Church of England was not a true church and only true believers should commune together in a separate church.
- Strict Biblicism: they followed only biblical sacraments.
- Equality within a church structure of voluntary members.
- Millenarianism.
- Anti-Catholicism.

The Baptists derived their name as a form of abuse from their belief in adult baptism. They were derided as 'Dippers' because of their ritual of baptism by total immersion. Bell has outlined why adult baptism was regarded as threatening.

> Unable to find any scriptural support for infant baptism, the Baptists rejected this practice as papal innovation, viewing it as part of the Antichristian pall that had obscured true doctrine. Proper baptism required that the believer be capable of professing for him or herself faith in Christ and personal salvation. By aligning their practice with biblical standards, the Baptists were taking a theologically radical position that cut across many prevailing ideas with regard to Christian unity, for if children were not to be baptized the universality of the Church was denied. Most early modern Christians viewed baptism less as a sign of faith and more as a rite of entry into the Church and by extension society. As Baptists on the other hand required belief before baptism, it was irrational to baptise infants. They thus put forward a radically individual theology, in which baptism did not convey salvation, but was rather a proclamation of it.

1   *M. Bell, 'Freedom to form: the development of Baptist movements during the English Revolution', in C. Durston and J. Maltby (eds.), **Religion in Revolutionary England** (2006)*

Baptist development was helped by division between Presbyterians and Independents, which meant that the latter defended people like the Baptists. McGregor has argued that another reason for their development was that they 'were the first radical, popular movement able to take advantage of the freedom and relative cheapness of the printing press in the unique conditions of revolution to appeal to an increasingly literate population'. The Baptists were significant in providing examples for other movements or for those who moved through the Baptists into other movements, particularly in terms of propaganda and evangelical tours. As with the development of other ideas and movements during the English Revolution, the role of the New Model was significant. There were Baptists preaching in some regiments, a prominent example being Captain Paul Hobson who was protected by Colonel Charles Fleetwood. Other significant army figures who were Baptists were Major William Packer and Colonel Robert Bennet. Such men offered protection to others. The President of the Protectorate Council of State, Henry Lawrence, was also a Baptist.

There was never a single Baptist entity. There were, however, three main groups; the General and Particular Baptists and the Seven-Day Baptists. Both the General and Particular Baptists existed before 1640. The essential difference between them was that the Particular Baptists were more Calvinist in their belief that Christ had only died for the elect. The Seven-Day Baptists emerged in the 1650s and derived their name from their belief that Saturday was the true Sabbath.

Rather than seeking to undermine the state, most Baptists were loyal to the Protectorate. One Baptist referred to the *Instrument of Government* as a Magna Carta for the Saints and some Baptists acted as Triers. Cromwell certainly supported the toleration of the Baptists. There were attempts by the Fifth Monarchists to establish an alliance with the Baptists but this was resisted; an indication of the movement's desire for acceptance. By 1660 Baptist numbers had reached about 25,000.

> ▪ Activity
>
> **Could the Baptists be considered a threat in this period?**

Quakers

The Quakers were the most significant radical group because of the numbers they attracted and the subsequent impact of the conservative political reaction against them that made some accept the Restoration.

The Society of Friends, as they referred to themselves, emerged from the north of England in the late 1640s. The conversion to Quakerism of Margaret Fell, who was later to be the wife of post-1660 Quaker leader George Fox, saw her family residence, Swarthmoor Hall in Cumbria, become the headquarters of a movement that sought to spread its message. It proved remarkably successful in doing so.

Key features of Quakerism:

▪ Rejected formalism of most religions, no ceremony or structure of ministers.
▪ Rejected predestination.
▪ Inner light: all carried this within them and was more reliable than any ministers or the Bible.
▪ Worship was informal 'meetings' at which individuals spoke when they were moved to.
▪ Role of women was prominent and seen as equal.
▪ Rejected social norms and formal addresses to those higher in society.
▪ Disrupted church services and publicly rebuked ministers.
▪ Literal interpretation of Jesus' teachings during the Sermon on the Mount.

The Quakers sent missionaries south in 1654 and 1655 and the movement's numbers exploded, reaching perhaps as many 60,000. There is evidence to suggest that as they entered new areas they sometimes took with them lists of known separatists who might be receptive to their message.

Their beliefs and actions made them a revolutionary group, even though most were from the 'middling sort', as they challenged the hierarchy of society. This was reinforced by the fact that many Quakers, for example James Nayler, had served in the New Model and during 1658–1660 many Quakers were enthusiastically prepared to serve the Interregnum regime and use force to protect it. In particular many rallied to support Lambert. In doing so they created a 'Quaker fear' that drove a conservative reaction. It was only after 1660 that Quakers repositioned themselves as pacifists.

General Monck in particular was fearful of the Quakers, purging religious radicals from the New Model in Scotland and supporting Charles Stuart as a bulwark against radicalism.

■ A closer look

The impact of Quakerism

A feature of the radicalism of Quakerism was the alienation of others who had been regarded as religious radicals in the 1630s and early 1640s. The case of the Norfolk Independent John Money is typical of how the revolution moved quickly and why some who were persecuted in the 1630s felt uncomfortable in the 1650s and were passive at the Restoration.

In the context of the forces unleashed by the English Revolution, especially Quakerism, John Money's Independent radicalism of the 1630s was relative. Persecuted in the 1630s, with the civil war he became the minister of his town, Wymondham, in the 1640s. A leading Quaker, Richard Hubberthorn spoke in Money's Wymondham steeplehouse 'at which the priest, whose name was John Mony' was offended. Imprisoned in Norwich Castle Hubberthorn later gave more details of the incident: 'That he that preached, viz: Mr. John Money was a deluder of the people....to the Light of Christ I speak, that with it John Money may see himself to be out of Doctrine of Christ, holding up those things that Christ cryed wo against.'

In the 1630s Laudianism had marginalised people like Money. By the 1650s his independency had become the establishment. Money found himself under attack by much more militant religious forces such as the Quakers.

■ Activity

Thinking point

Why did the Quakers appear so threatening to the traditional elite?

Seekers

Thomas Edwards' *Gangraena* (1646) established the idea of a Seeker movement. His work was key in producing a negative image of all religious radical groups. Seekers were not a movement or group but more a mentality, those that were seeking where they belonged, specifically religious truth. Having rejected the established church they studied the Bible. Some even rejected this for reliance on revelation through the Holy Spirit. McGregor argued that there:

... was no sect of Seekers in revolutionary England. There were, however, alienated individuals in plenty for whom we have no better general category than the heresiographers' definition of the Seeker as a lost, wandering soul, finding no solace in the discipline of church or sect, anticipating wondrous events in the last days, vulnerable to the charisma of a crackpot messiah or the solipsism of the divine inner light.

2   *J.F. McGregor, 'Seekers and Ranters', in J.F. McGregor and B. Reay (eds.), **Radical Religion in the English Revolution** (1984)*

Those labelled as Seekers, such as William Erbery, did not accept the label. In light of McGregor's definition, others such as John Milton and even Cromwell have been termed Seekers by historians.

Seekers can be seen as illustrative of the personal spiritual journey of many in these years which illustrates the fluid nature of these movements and their shared ideas. Given the breakdown of confidence in their own salvation in the light of **predestination** many came to **antinomianism** now that they were free from the Church of England and exposed to more radical preachers.

Hill has argued that 'it is hardly surprising that men and women, faced with an unprecedented freedom of choice, passed rapidly from sect to sect, trying all things, finding all of them wanting'. Spiritual autobiographies of the time show some passing through Presbyterianism, Independency and Anabaptistry before ending as Seekers, Ranters or Quakers.

Key terms

Predestination: at its most radical this was the belief that salvation was already decided by God and was not dependent on leading a good life.

Antinomianism: a belief that those destined to achieve salvation could not sin and as a result had been freed from normal moral law.

A closer look

The spiritual journey of Laurence Clarkson, 1615–67

Having reacted against the Laudianism of the 1630s, Clarkson became a Presbyterian, seeking out the ministry of a leading Presbyterian, Edmund Calamy. From this he moved to the preaching of John Goodwin and Independency. It was from this point that Clarkson moved into antinomian ideas. In 1644 he was a preacher to the company of Captain Paul Hobson in Fleetwood's regiment in the Eastern Association Army and, like Hobson, became a Baptist.

In 1645 he spent six months confined due to allegations of 'having dipped six Sisters one night naked' and then 'that which of them you liked best, you lay with her in the water'. Visited by William Erbery, Clarkson renounced the Baptists and was released having become a 'Seeker'. In 1649 Clarkson made contact with a group of pantheistic (theory by which God and the world were one) antinomians who were labelled Ranters. It was probably Clarkson who published the pamphlet *A Single Eye* in June 1650 which Davis argued did 'much to unleash the whole Ranter sensation'. In the mid-1650s it was claimed he had moved into Muggletonianism and following the death of John Reeve in 1658 he tried to establish himself as the leader of the group but submitted to Muggleton's leadership in 1661.

Fig. 3 *A contemporary image of* The World Turned Upside Down *portraying the idea that the forces unleashed as a result of the revolution had led to a subverting of the natural order*

Muggletonians

During the revolutionary period, there were even people who claimed to be the reincarnation of Christ, such as John Robins. Two associates of Robins, John Reeve and his cousin Lodowicke Muggleton, claimed they were the witnesses from Revelation 11:3 – 'And I will give power unto my two witnesses, and they shall prophesy a thousand two hundred and threescore days, clothed in sackcloth'. From this they established the Muggletonians.

As messengers sent to prepare for Christ's second coming, the Muggletonians were millenarians, like the Seekers and Fifth Monarchists. As divine prophets, they claimed they were armed with the keys to Heaven and Hell. From 1652 these two men developed a support base, mainly in London and the south, of artisans and shopkeepers that numbered in the hundreds. An underground organisation about which it is difficult to be precise, the Muggletonians had little, if any, political influence. Both men were briefly imprisoned in 1653.

In 1656 Reeve dedicated his *Divine Looking-Glass* to Cromwell, believing that God would make him an instrument of good. By 1658 the Ranter Laurence Clarkson had met Reeve, also a former Ranter. Clarkson was convinced that Reeve was God's last prophet. With Reeve's death in 1658 there ensued a power struggle between Clarkson and Muggleton over who was the true heir of Reeve's authority. Clarkson took to print and in *Look about you* and *The Lost Sheep Found* claimed that he wrote with direct revelation from God and that he was the 'only' true prophet now living. Muggleton counter-attacked, excommunicating Clarkson and stopping his salary. Clarkson was forbidden to write again. This, much as with other radical movements of the time, allowed Muggleton to rewrite the history of Muggletonianism. In doing this he wrote Clarkson out of its history and placed himself as an equal to Reeve, hence Muggletonianism.

No matter the focus on radical groups by historians such as Hill, another expert on religious radicalism, Reay, has stressed that 'the sectaries never triumphed, despite the fears of many an Anglican and a Presbyterian. Their main effect was to terrify the men of property and to reinforce religious conservatism. In 1642, in 1648, in 1653, in 1657, and most important of all in 1659, radicalism stimulated reaction'.

Ideas of religious toleration

In addressing his first Protectorate Parliament in September 1654, Cromwell reflected on the issue of religious toleration outlining 'fundamentals'. From the *Instrument* he saw 'government by a single person and a Parliament' as fundamental. He asked the question – 'Is not liberty of conscience a fundamental?' Cromwell stated that 'Liberty of conscience is a natural right; and he that would have it ought to give it'. The implication of this would appear to be that Cromwell supported liberty of conscience and thereby religious toleration.

It was in the context of the breakdown of the authority of the Church of England, civil war and revolution that, as with Cromwell, others engaged with ideas for, and against, toleration in what has been termed 'the toleration controversy'. The question of the extent of toleration first became a major issue in 1644. Fundamentally it remained an

Activity

Talking point

Why did groups like the Muggletonians attract followers in this period?

Activity

Group activity

Consider the material in this chapter in light of the consideration of the Ranters in Chapter 3. Either prepare a class presentation or devise a newsbook front page focusing on the threat of religious radicals in this period.

Activity

Thinking point

Explain why Cromwell supported greater toleration.

argument for the non-royalists and, although broad generalisations, three groups can be isolated:

Group	Position on toleration
Anti-tolerationists	Wanted uniformity, discipline and order. This was predominantly the position of the Presbyterians and the Scots.
Conservative tolerationists	Wanted limited toleration for orthodox Protestants. This was the stance of Independents.
Radical tolerationists	Questioned the role of the magistrate in setting boundaries and advocated a very broad or complete toleration. This was the position of a small minority of radicals.

The position of the anti-tolerationists is clearest. The Scots in particular wanted Presbyterianism in a national church structure with an organised form of discipline. For Presbyterians and anti-tolerationists the civil war and parliamentarian armies had led to the dangerous proliferation of 'heresies'. Most vividly outlined, for propaganda purposes, in the work of two leading anti-tolerationists Thomas Edwards and William Prynne, the spread of radicalism was exactly why there needed to be a limit to toleration.

Through their military and political alliance with the English Parliament of 1643, the Solemn League and Covenant, the Scots hoped to control religious radicalism. Indeed the final outcome of the Westminster Assembly of Divines codified in 1647 as the Westminster Confession of Faith and an ordinance of May 1648 for 'the Punishing of Blasphemies and Heresies' seemed, on the surface, to be in line with what they wanted. Leading Scots Presbyterians in England such as Robert Baillie were clear, however, that what had actually been established by Parliament was 'a lame Erastian Presbytery'. Furthermore, by the time it came to be enacted, power was seized by the Independents through Pride's Purge and it was not put into practice.

The conservative tolerationists, men like Cromwell, would accept an established church but wanted toleration for the gathered churches. The argument of the conservative tolerations was put forward by leading independent ministers such as John Owen. They wanted toleration for those who they regarded as the 'Saints'. While this would have included Independents, Presbyterians and Baptists it would not have included Socinians and Catholics. Legislation from 1650, the Toleration Act, had essentially made the conservative Independent position of toleration the official position. The act, passed by the Rump, removed the requirement of attendance at the parish church. With the growth of radicalism in the 1650s many conservative tolerationists retreated to a more anti-tolerationist position. Owen certainly sought to modify the toleration enshrined in the *Instrument of Government*.

The radical tolerationist position was only advocated by a small minority, whether radical Independents, Quakers, Levellers or other radical individuals. The leading proponents were men like Henry Vane. They regarded Christianity as being non-coercive and by allowing freedom of ideas a return could be made to what they felt 'primitive Christianity' would have been. They also argued their position from Natural Law contract theory, where magistrates' authority came from popular consent, not God. God had not given men the power to legislate with regard to others' religious views. From this they argued that the magistrate's power was limited only to secular things.

Exploring the detail
William Prynne's Ears

In the 1630s William Prynne was twice mutilated for his religious pamphlets attacking Henrietta Maria and Laudianism. As punishment Prynne publicly had parts of his ears sliced off.

Cross-reference

For the Solemn League and Covenant see Chapter 1 and for Pride's Purge see Chapter 2.

As Protector Cromwell's position with regard to toleration is fundamental. In many ways he fell between the two broad groupings classed Conservative tolerationists and Radical tolerationists. Clauses 35 to 37 of Lambert's *Instrument* dealt specifically with religion. Clause 37 stated:

> [S]uch as profess faith in God by Jesus Christ (though differing in judgement from the doctrine, worship or discipline publicly held forth) shall not be restrained from, but shall be protected in, the profession of the faith and exercise of their religion; so as they abuse not this liberty to the civil injury of others and to the actual disturbance of the public peace on their parts: provided this liberty be not extended to Popery or Prelacy, nor to such as, under the profession of Christ, hold forth and practice licentiousness.

3

The *Instrument* formalised a broad toleration that many radicals had called for.

What Cromwell also faced, however, by 1653 was that some freed by the breakdown of the authority of the Church of England and the spirit of the English Revolution had gone further than he could countenance. This dilemma for Cromwell, between religious freedom and order, was visible in the cases of Biddle, and most notably Nayler. While he was uneasy about the authority of Parliament to discipline these individuals he was also uneasy about the actions of the Socinian and the Quaker. The *Humble Petition and Advice* (1657) not only saw a more conservative constitutional settlement but also a more conservative religious settlement.

In considering Cromwell's attitude, some historians have suggested that it was shaped by pragmatism. For Worden, Cromwell's concern was not toleration but unity. He had sympathy for those he regarded as within the godly, Independents, Presbyterians and Baptists, but was unsympathetic to Quakers, Socinians, Anglicans and Catholics. Pragmatism shaped extensions of toleration.

Hutton (2004) has painted a more negative picture of Cromwell's attitude, seeing him as a representative of a small interest group, a 'faction' of the godly. Hutton has argued that 'Cromwell did not believe in toleration as a virtue in itself'. Davis (2001) regards the examples of Cromwell's intervention on behalf of various persecuted individuals as part of the evidence for a 'broader tolerance of attitude' than suggested by Worden, and certainly than Hutton allows Cromwell. It was this context that allowed Cromwell to keep contact with a range of individuals of very different religious persuasions but whom he regarded as all having something of faith. His providence made him believe that God would provide answers rather than man. Cromwell's Protectorate allowed more religious freedom for individuals than any regime before and for a long time after.

Cromwell and Catholics

It may be somewhat surprising, certainly in the context of the military campaign in Ireland and traditional English anti-Catholicism, but there were moves, with Cromwell prominent, for some form of toleration for Catholics during the Protectorate. This derived from the same reconsideration of the relationship between an individual's faith and the state that allowed so much freedom for groups like the Fifth Monarchists, Baptists and Quakers that would have been unthinkable before 1640.

After the civil war there had been some discussion by Charles I and the New Model with Catholics which would have led to Catholics achieving a similar position to that of Protestant dissenters. Under Cromwell's Protectorate there was a more systematic consideration of the relationship between Catholics and the state.

Two Paris-based English Catholics, Henry Holden and Thomas White (known as Blacklo), sought to shape an English Catholic church loyal to the Protectorate and with a looser relationship with the Papacy. In 1655 White outlined his argument in *Grounds of Obedience and Government*. This consisted of:

- accepting Cromwell as Protector
- Parliamentary Oath of Allegiance for all English Catholics
- six English Catholic bishops appointed by the Pope with limited powers.

Those who sought accommodation with the Protectorate became known as the Blackloists, and gained control over the political direction of English Catholicism in this period.

These Catholics were no doubt encouraged by the fact that Cromwell himself sought liberty of conscience, but not toleration, for Catholics. While Catholic priests would not be able to seek to convert others they would be able to act in a pastoral fashion.

There are a number of examples of Cromwell's favour to individual Catholics, preventing either their persecution or allowing them some individual freedom. Cromwell also allowed attendance of the mass at the chapel in the Venetian embassy. He also protested at the execution of a Jesuit priest in 1654.

Cromwell's death and the Restoration ended the influence of the Blackloists.

Cromwell and the Jews

An Amsterdam Jew, Manasseh ben Israel, produced a petition for the Jews to be allowed to live in England and practise their worship and trades freely. It was Cromwell who insisted that this proposal was put before the Protectoral Council. Cromwell then pushed for a conference to discuss the proposal. The conference was between four Protectoral Councillors, church ministers and lawyers at Westminster Hall in December 1655. During the two weeks of this conference, Cromwell attended every session. Cromwell strongly supported the readmission of the Jews. Despite this the Protectorate Council refused, indicating the constitutional balance of powers at work. Cromwell ensured, however, that in the months to follow the Jews were unofficially allowed back into England. Cromwell's desire for the Jews to be readmitted to England was rooted in his millenarianism. For Cromwell, if the millennium was to be established, the Jews need to be converted as prophesied in the Bible.

 Activity

Talking point

Use the material in Chapter 3 on Cromwell's campaign in Ireland and the information in this chapter on Cromwell and the Catholics. Was Cromwell anti-Catholic?

Did you know?

The Jesuit John Southworth who was executed in 1654 was hanged, drawn and quartered. Cromwell, who disapproved of his execution, made sure that his body was sewn back together and then sent for burial abroad.

Did you know?

The Jews had been expelled from England in 1290 by Edward I.

 Activity

Revision exercise

Explain the extent and limits of toleration in this period.

Fig. 4 *Oliver Cromwell (1599–1658) preaching to a Puritan congregation*

The rule of the major-generals, 1655–7

Four reasons can be isolated in the decision to resort to the rule of the major-generals:

- **Reformation:** A priority for Cromwell, especially after his disillusionment with the First Protectorate Parliament.
- **Failure:** Specifically the failure of the Western Design. For Cromwell this suggested that reformation was needed.
- **Finance:** The regime was increasingly financially exposed. The Decimation Tax which accompanied the major-generals was an attempt to reduce the army to a militia.
- **Royalism:** Penruddock's Rising of March 1655 indicated the continuing potential threat of royalism and royalists who refused to accept defeat.

The introduction of the major-generals was, to a degree, a result of Cromwell and Lambert's over-reaction to the failure of the first Protectorate Parliament, the Western Design and, more directly, the apparent renewed royalist threat. Perception was more important than the reality. The wording of 'A Proclamation Prohibiting Delinquents to bear Office' (September 1655) hints at the mentality which the spectre of royalist insurrection had reawakened. It referred to:

> the inveterate and restless malice of that Party to involve these Nations in blood and confusion; who have avowedly, and with open face professed their end was, and still is (though in the utter ruin and desolation of these Nations) to set up that Power and Interest which Almighty God hath so eminently appeared against.

4   *The Saints Guide (1653)*

The Western Design's failure and Cromwell's illness added to the sense of crisis. Coward (2002) refers to a 'siege mentality' at this point 'at the heart of the Protectorate'. In his speech dismissing the first Protectorate Parliament Cromwell made clear his frustration, now heightened by the

Exploring the detail

The Decimation Tax

The Decimation Tax was a fine of 10 per cent of annual income imposed on wealthy royalists from 1655 to fund local militias.

rumours of royalist plotting. The final straw was MPs' failure to provide for the army.

Lambert was prominent in the introduction of the original and the additional instructions of August and October 1655 and June 1656. In the debates surrounding the major-generals, the reason for Lambert's support of the scheme and the general drift of his thinking towards military rule are clear - self-preservation against the royalists.

Negative terms associated with the major generals:

 Obvious sign of military rule.

 Lower social origins.

 Religious radicalism.

 Higher taxes.

 Interference in local government.

> I am as guilty of the Act of Oblivion as any man. I have laboured to oblige that party; to win them, as much as may be; but find it impossible till time wear out the memory. They are as careful to breed up their children in the memory of the quarrel as can be. They are, haply, now merry over their Christmas pies, drinking the King of Scots' health, or your confusion … If the Act of Oblivion was not reciprocal, and they be not tied to keep their part as well as we, it is an ill bargain for us.

Fig. 5 *The negative image of the major-generals*

5

The Instructions to the major-generals indicate the concern to prevent further rebellion. The first instruction stated that they were to 'endeavour the suppressing [of] all tumults, insurrections, rebellions or other unlawful assemblies'. Later instructions indicate the role of the major-generals in promoting reformation:

> 19 That all gaming houses and houses of evil fame [brothels] be industriously sought out and suppressed within the cities of London and Westminister and all the liberties thereof.
>
> 21 That all alehouses, taverns and victualling houses towards the outskirts of the said cities be suppressed, except such as are necessary and convenient to travellers; and that the number of alehouses in all other parts of the town be abated, and none continued but such as can lodge strangers and are of good repute.

6

England was split into 11 areas with major-generals assigned to each. What the major-generals actually did depended on the attitude of the individual Major-General. Edward Whalley made concerted efforts in his area to improve the lot of those at the bottom of society and the records indicate that even in his short time of influence he made an impact. Berry at the start of his work in Wales told the Fifth Monarchist Vavasour Powell that he 'came forth in this worke, as sent of God'. Durston's study of the major-generals (2001) has indicated the limits to their traditional image as 'kill joys' for their attempts to 'suppress or control the populace's traditional leisure pursuits' were 'at best sporadic and

	Activity

Source analysis

Read Lambert's opinion of the royalists in Source 5. Summarise his argument in point form.

Activity

Thinking point

To what extent was Cromwell's aim of godly reformation only achievable through military dictatorship?

uncoordinated'. In general, given the scope of the tasks assigned to them, and the very real limits of central and local government, it is no wonder that the major-generals failed to 'rule' and transform society.

Reactions to the rule of the major-generals

Some of the reaction to the major-generals from the traditional elite was part of their general concern at the military's influence. In any consideration of reactions to the rule of the major-generals, or the post-regicide regimes, particularly the Protectorate, it is useful to bear in mind the qualification made by Coward in his study of the Cromwellian Protectorate (2002). He has pointed out that it is difficult to make a clear assessment of reactions to the Protectorate because of the limited sources; many destroyed their records from the 1650s, and those who did write about it did so after the Restoration.

Furthermore, reaction to the major-generals should be set in context of the work of Reece on the military presence in the years 1649–1660. Reece has shown that such was the military presence throughout the whole period that the novelty of the major-generals can be exaggerated. Some general points can, however, be made with regard to the major-generals exacerbating concerns already held, especially concern at the role of the military. This manifested itself in a variety of ways.

Government

There was concern at the role of the military in the state, exemplified by the *Instrument* and the profile of men like Cromwell and Lambert. Of more concern for the gentry was the threat to their control of the localities. While they were not ousted, during the Protectorate there were no large scale purges of local government and rather than replace the local governors the major-generals sought to work with them; the gentry felt threatened by the greater role played by the lesser gentry, soldiers and merchants as a result of the revolution. In the provinces gentry concerns seemed to be confirmed when many of the major-generals found that they needed to remove men from the commissions of the peace to make their rule more effective.

Finance

There was concern that the high levels of taxation, necessary to support the army, were to be permanent. Figures for average annual taxation from 1558 illustrate the extra burden on the gentry.

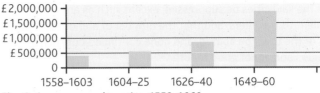

Fig. 6 *Average annual taxation: 1558–1660*

Concern at high taxation levels was also an issue for Protectorate MPs and the failure to achieve a parliamentary financial settlement became a central tension in the years 1656 to 1659.

This extra tax burden should, however, be set in the context of the development of the English state, and therefore its finances, under the later Stuarts.

The Decimation Tax under the major-generals hindered the acceptance of the regime by the defeated royalists. Although those subjected to the Tax

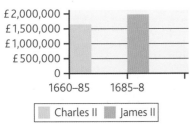

Fig. 7 *Average annual taxation: 1660–1685*

were a relatively small number, under 2,000, the process of examining their record did little for reconciliation. The Decimation Tax also failed financially in its main task to raise enough money to allow the regime to reduce the army and transfer security to a militia. Here we can see the contradictory impulses of the regime. Cromwell and many of his councillors wanted godly reform, a reduction of the financial burden and 'healing and settling'.

Religion

The New Model was invariably linked with religious radicalism in that many radicals had been, or were, soldiers. The army also prevented persecution of radicals. The threat of religious radicals also raised fears of the social, economic and political threat posed by religious radicalism. What heightened this fear the most was the apparent explosion of Quaker numbers in the 1650s.

Furthermore in aiming for a godly reformation in the provinces, the majority of the major-generals developed links with those the gentry regarded as radicals. While this reformation failed, it reinforced the negative connotations for many gentry of army rule and led to a reaction in the Second Protectorate Parliament.

Durston (2001) argued that the 'central feature of the rule of the major-generals was not that it was army rule, nor that it was London rule, but rather that it was godly rule, and it was as such that it was decisively rejected by the great majority of the people'. The major-generals simply did not have the means to force people to act in a godly manner. The reason for the collapse of the major-generals was not so much their alleged unpopularity but their practical failure.

Activity

Talking point

Could the major-generals scheme ever have succeeded?

Cromwell's reaction: the calling of the Second Protectorate Parliament, the Militia Bill and the end of the major-generals

The most important reaction to the rule of the major-generals was Cromwell's. Cromwell had shifted again to looking for 'healing and settling', having never lost his desire to secure a parliamentary settlement.

> The attachment to parliaments in principle explains Cromwell's underlying respect for constitutional propriety. He made great play of the fact that he always allowed his parliaments to deliberate free from Protectoral interference; and throughout his career he carefully distanced himself from the more flagrant breaches of parliamentary privilege, such as Pride's Purge or the exclusion of MPs from both the first and second Protectorate Parliaments. Although Cromwell probably approved of the motives which lay behind these episodes, he apparently did not wish to be associated with unconstitutional purges of parliament.
>
> When the interests of the godly and the interests of the nation, or of a national institution, came into collision, Cromwell usually drew back, waited and reflected. This trait was a symptom of a profound ambiguity at the very core of Cromwell's personality. The problem was that Cromwell was trying to use an institution which had evolved as the 'representative of the whole realm' to advance the cause of a godly minority. It was, however, a strategy based upon a profound belief in Parliament's importance.

7   *D.L. Smith, 'Oliver Cromwell: A Great Parliamentarian?',* **Cromwelliana (1995)**

Cromwell praised the major-generals at the opening of the Second Protectorate Parliament, but his opposition to the Decimation Tax, which in practical terms he had also helped some royalists circumvent, showed that he sought their removal. It was the Decimation tax that caused more resentment than the major-generals and it was generally finance that hampered settlement. The Decimation, as an extra-parliamentary tax, was unlikely to be the basis of long term stability. Cromwell was thus willing to pay the price of abandoning the major-generals and the architect of the Protectorate, Lambert.

While no one appears to have raised the issue of parliamentary approval of the Decimation in the first three months of Parliament's sitting, Desborough, by introducing the Militia Bill seeking to make it a permanent tax, sought to strengthen its legitimacy. It was clearly a deliberate ploy to introduce the bill to a sparsely attended house on Christmas Day 1656. After Desborough's typically forceful espousal of the Decimation and the Militia, Lambert starkly expounded the choice he felt they faced.

> I wish any man could propound an expedient to be secure against your common enemies, by another way than as the militia settled. The quarrel is now between light and darkness; not who shall rule, but whether we shall live, or be preserved, or no. Good words will not do with the Cavaliers.

8

Lambert's statements in Parliament in relation to the Decimation and Militia make clear his bitterness that the royalists had not been willing to accept the Protectorate. He openly stated that his thinking had shifted to more direct military solutions. As well as preserving themselves and their honour, by pressing the Decimation and Militia, Lambert and Desborough could, possibly, have been trying to incite some in Parliament and the army against Cromwell to breach the unstable 'civilian' alliance that some, such as Broghill, were trying to construct. The sub-text for the debates on Decimation, the Militia Bill and Nayler was the offer of the Crown to Cromwell.

Cromwell's opposition to Decimation and Militia severely undermined Lambert's position and that of the military. The Militia Bill debates were part of a factional power struggle at the heart of the Protectorate between the 'military' and 'civilians', increasingly personified by Lambert and Broghill. Egloff (1990) argues that the negative reaction of most MPs to the Militia Bill 'reinforced the Protector's own ambivalence and unease, and led him finally to abandon the Generals in favour of a new constitution', the *Humble Petition and Advice*.

At the same time as the tension over the Militia Bill Lambert and the military must have felt uneasy over Cromwell's failure to intervene on behalf of the leading Quaker James Nayler. As well as concern for his old quarter-master, Lambert was well aware of the constitutional implications of Parliament's proceedings against Nayler. Given judicial power, future parliaments could judge his and others' actions.

A significant reaction to the major-generals was from Broghill and the offer to Cromwell of a different path to settlement, the *Humble Petition and Advice* and kingship. In the debates on the Decimation and Militia, Cromwell was positioning himself to accept a revision of the *Instrument* through the adoption of the civilian *Humble Petition*.

■ **Cross-reference**

For more on James Nayler, see Chapter 5.

The voices of Cromwell's civilian clients against the Decimation and the parliamentary vote of £400,000 towards the Spanish war a day after the Militia Bill's defeat suggest that the Protector had sacrificed the major-generals for a new settlement. That Cromwell was willing to countenance this shift to more civilian forms and even kingship was part of his reaction to the major-generals.

Summary questions

1. What was Cromwell's position on toleration?

2. Explain why the major-generals were set up.

3. What was Cromwell's reaction to the failure of the major-generals?

Activity

Talking point

Using the information in this chapter and from pages 54–55 make a case for each of the two forms of settlement Cromwell was trying to decide between: 'civilian' and 'military'.

6 Foreign Policy, Division and Restoration

In this chapter you will learn about:

- Cromwell's foreign policy
- divisions within the regime after Cromwell's death
- the Restoration Settlement.

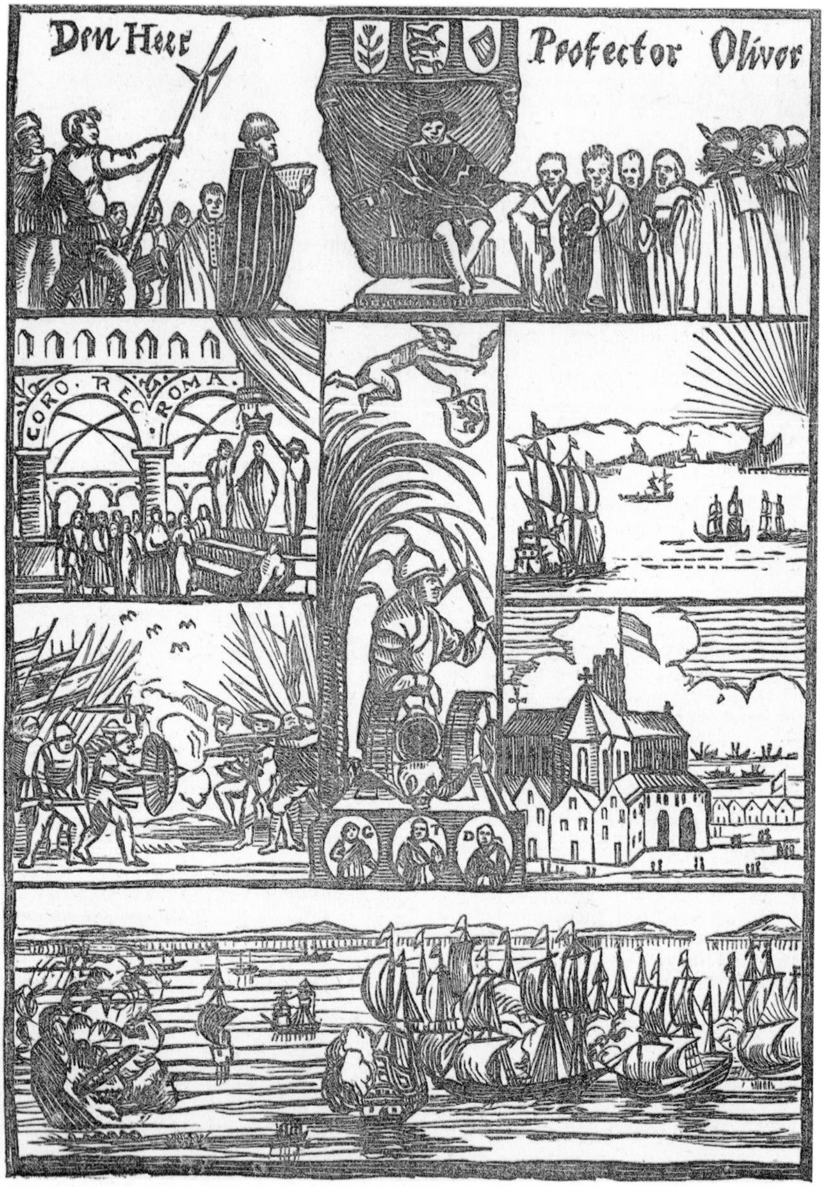

Fig. 1 *Page from a Dutch newspaper, Hollandsche Mercurius, of 1653, showing Oliver Cromwell as Lord Protector, a title he assumed on 16 December 1653. Cromwell sits holding a sword and above him are the arms of the Commonwealth*

Key dates

Apr 1654	Treaty of Westminster
Dec 1654	Western Design launched
Apr 1655	Defeat at San Domingo
May 1655	Landing in Jamaica
Oct 1655	Anglo-French Treaty heralds war against Spain in Europe
Sept 1656	Defeat of Spanish navy off Cadiz
May 1657	Blake captures Spanish treasure fleet at Santa Cruz; English troops land in Flanders
Oct 1657	New Model captures Spanish-Netherlands port of Mardyke
June 1658	Battle of Dunes; Jamaica secured; New Model occupies Spanish-Netherlands port of Dunkirk

Cromwell's foreign policy, including overseas trade and the use of sea power

Peace with the Dutch: Treaty of Westminster, April 1654

Cromwell, like many others in the army, had not been happy with the Rump's war against the Protestant Dutch. Even before the establishment of the Protectorate there had been moves to establish peace. Cromwell may well have thought in terms of shared Protestant interest against the forces of Catholicism. Peace enabled the English to begin trade in the Baltic again and allowed them to conclude a commercial treaty with Denmark which enabled them to compete on equal terms with the Dutch in the Baltic.

The treaty was also used to prevent the Stuarts exploiting their links with the Dutch House of Orange. This family was semi-royalty in the Netherlands having been a focal point in the military struggle for independence against Spain. William II of Orange had married Charles I's daughter, Mary (1631–1660). Although William II died in 1650 there was a danger that Charles Stuart could exploit the influence of the House of Orange to further his aim of returning as monarch. By the treaty the Dutch offered a guarantee that a member of the Orange family would never be Stadholder, nominal leader of the Netherlands.

War with Spain: the Western Design

The plan for an attack on Spain provides an example of division in the Protectorate Council, and suggests it was a forum in which genuine debate took place. Lambert disagreed with Cromwell over plans for an attack on Spain's American possessions. Lambert's opposition was based on a belief that France represented a more potent threat and the hard-headed realisation that the Protectorate was not financially stable enough to undertake such a design. Cromwell's arguments, which proved decisive, were rooted in the religious, Elizabethan and colonial contexts in which he viewed Spain. For Cromwell Spain led the forces of Antichrist which for a time had been countered by Elizabethan naval attacks.

William Penn was put in charge of the naval forces, comprising 30 ships. Robert Venables was put in charge of the land forces. Penn did not get on with Venables. The land force of 3,000 infantry and 100 cavalry was too small. It was also composed of small groups from regiments from all over the country that their commanders were glad to get rid of rather than men who had fought together as a group.

The force left in December 1654 but was defeated in April 1655 at San Domingo, now Haiti. From here the surviving forces retreated and secured the undefended island of Jamaica. In response Cromwell commented, 'We have cause to be humbled for the reproof God gave us at San Domingo, upon the occasion of our sins'. It was this response that led to the major-generals.

Relations with France

After Cromwell resisted French attempts to get him to hand back forts seized in North America, England seemed to be moving to war against France. Cromwell secured very generous terms from the Spanish who were trying to turn him against France:

- Free trade with the Spanish colonies.
- English protestants in Spain to worship freely in private.
- Dunkirk as a guarantee for Calais if this was seized in the war.
- £300,000 a year while the war lasted.

Another source of contention was the Vaudois Massacre (1655). This was the killing of Protestants, also known as Waldensians, in northern Italy by an ally of the French, the Duke of Savoy. In response to the massacre Milton wrote *On the Late Massacre in Piedmont*, proclaiming:

> Avenge, O Lord, thy slaughter'd saints, whose bones
>
> Lie scatter'd on the Alpine mountains cold.

Activity

Thinking point

Explain why peace was made with the Dutch.

Cross-reference

For Cromwell's reaction to the failure of the Western Design and the major-generals see Chapter 5.

Activity

Thinking point

Why did Cromwell's regime go to war against Spain?

Cromwell successfully used diplomatic pressure on France to force the Duke of Savoy to halt the persecution.

Activity

Thinking point

Construct a spider diagram to show the factors that shaped the regime's relationship with France.

Did you know?

Henrietta Maria's sister was the Duke of Savoy's mother. She took a major role in bringing about the Vaudois massacre.

Exploring the detail

The victories of Gustavus Adolphus and the power of Sweden

Gustavus Adolphus' victories saw Sweden emerge as a great European power in the 1630s and 1640s. Victory at Breitenfeld in 1631 left all of 'Germany' open to him. He advanced and took Erfurt, Wurzburg, Marienberg and Frankfurt. Adolphus then crossed the Rhine and took Worms and Mainz. He stood as the leader of Protestant Europe. For all of this Adolphus was lauded in England and seen as a model of Protestant kingship.

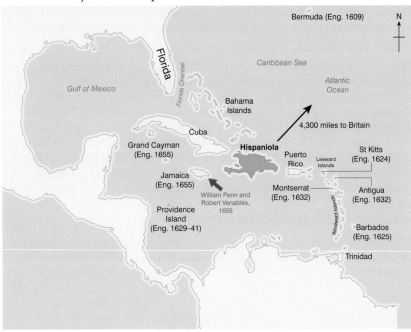

Fig. 2 *The Western Design 1655*

Thurloe's papers show that France was still chosen as an ally, however, because it was recognised as a danger, even in the 1650s. Part of this policy was also to ensure that conflict continued between France and Spain.

Baltic policy

For Cromwell, as for many of his generation, their hero had been the Swedish king Gustavus Adolphus who had not only stopped the advance of Catholicism in the Thirty Years War but, until his death in 1632, appeared to have them in retreat.

Fig. 3 *The Baltic in the 1650s*

Charles X of Sweden sought complete control in the Baltic. The result was a war with Denmark in 1657. Cromwell refused a full alliance with Sweden, settling for a commercial treaty. The main aim of English policy was to prevent any one power controlling the Baltic and thus be in position to prevent their merchants trading. The English ambassador in Sweden took a central role in bringing peace between Sweden and Denmark in February 1658 in the Treaty of Roskilde which did much to protect the interests of English trade in the Baltic.

The use of sea power

Cromwell continued the Commonwealth's activist foreign policy making use of the navy established under the Rump. Indeed Cromwell's personal motto, incorporated into the seal of the Protectorate, was 'Peace through war'. By 1653 the regime had 180 ships which put it ahead of its three main European naval rivals France, Spain and the Dutch. Under Cromwell this naval power was one of the reasons why both France and Spain bid for his aid.

Sea power was a vital part of the attack on Spain in the Caribbean. The Western Design fleet was, however, badly organised, with the sailors receiving limited training and supplies. The attack on Hispaniola was a failure and the subsequent capture of Jamaica was not well regarded at the time. There were, however, more successful elements of Cromwell's campaign against the Spanish, particularly in the Atlantic. In 1656 the English fleet captured the Spanish Plate Fleet securing £250,000. In 1657 they captured the Plate Fleet again; this time, however, there was no silver on it. In 1657 an English fleet supported the French allowing them to capture the Flemish town of Mardyke. Generally sea power supported the combined English-French land campaign in Flanders which ended with the English securing Dunkirk.

Sea power was also used against the French. Admiral Blake took extensive naval campaigns in the Atlantic and Mediterranean against the Spanish as well as the French. In late 1654 the French were planning to attack the heart of Spain's power in Italy, Naples. To do so they had to coordinate their two fleets, based at Brest and Toulon. Cromwell had secured from the Spanish the permission for Blake to use their Mediterranean ports and it was Blake's presence that prevented the French from launching their attack. The French were also forced to return the English merchant ships they had captured. The Pope saw Blake's presence as a sign that an attack on the Papal States was imminent. In fact Blake moved against the Barbary pirates.

In April 1655 Blake sailed into Porto Farino and destroyed the fort batteries and the nine warships of the Dey (leader) of Tunis who protected the pirates. As a result, the next month as he anchored off Algiers the Dey of Algiers negotiated the release of English captives who were being used as slaves.

In the Baltic, Cromwell also used sea power to achieve his aims. The main aim was to ensure that the area remained open to English merchants. To do this none of the main powers of the Baltic, Sweden, Denmark and the Dutch, could control the area. To reinforce this Cromwell threatened to send fleets into the Baltic to counter Dutch influence. In 1659 Richard Cromwell sent a fleet to protect English interests in the Baltic.

Sea power was also used to hamper the cause of Charles Stuart. Not only did a strong navy help to prevent a possible foreign-backed invasion of Charles Stuart, but it could be used to put pressure on the European powers not to support him. This had been the case in 1650 when the Commonwealth had Blake demonstrate English naval power off the Portuguese coast. In 1656 Cromwell ordered Blake to near the coast of Lisbon as a means by which to persuade John IV of Portugal to allow English merchants freedom to practise their Protestantism and trade with Portugal.

> ### Activity
> **Thinking point**
>
> Discuss and then prepare a class list of the factors that shaped policy in the Baltic.

> ### Did you know?
> It has been estimated that between 1 and 1.25 million Europeans were captured by Barbary pirates (pirates operating from the coast of North Africa) and sold as slaves to the Ottoman Empire and the states of north Africa between the sixteenth and eighteenth centuries.

Fig. 4 *Admiral Robert Blake, republican naval hero who was buried in Westminster Abbey only to be disinterred at the Restoration*

Did you know?

Naval vessels were ranked according to a system of 'rates'. First rate was the term for the largest battleships. Ratings then continued down in size to fourth rate.

Activity

Thinking point

Explain how sea power was used under Cromwell to exert the influence of the regime.

In 1654 the 'third-rate' *Tredagh* drew the Venetian ambassador to report that if they had such ships 'no naval power could stand against them'. In 1655 a new flagship, the 'first-rate' *Naseby*, was launched. This was the first 'first-rate' ship built since 1637 and was followed in 1658 by another, the *Richard*.

In the only significant study of Cromwell's navy, Capp has commented on the relative success of the navy through their:

> … sense of fighting for a cause, ideological as well as patriotic, [which] gave the officer corps a cohesion which the Stuart navy never matched, and Blake in particular exerted an authority none of the Restoration admirals could equal.

1

B. Capp, *Cromwell's Navy: The Fleet and the English Revolution 1648–1660* (1992)

Overseas trade

Chief trading companies

Trading company	Area of trade/influence
Levant Company	Mediterranean/Ottoman Empire
East India Company	Far East
Merchant Adventurers	Baltic, northern Europe
Russia/Muscovy Company	Russia
Bermudas Company	Caribbean/North America

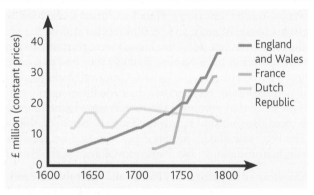

Fig. 5 *Overseas trade*

In the 1650s the basis of English overseas trade had much continuity with earlier periods, but there were also signs of future developments that would broaden England's interest as it developed into the world's major trading nation in the early 18th century.

Continuity in 1650s	Start of future developments
Exports predominantly based on woollen cloth	Greater diversity of exports
Majority of trade with Europe	More trade with Caribbean, America, Africa and Far East
London centre of trade	Development of other trade centres; for example, Bristol
European/colonial trade dominated by the Dutch	England emerges pre-eminent

Unlike the Rump politicians, Cromwell had few connections to the merchant community or the City generally. As a result, the regime relied heavily on a few individuals for cooperation and finance from the City.

The main priority was security. The state needed to make use of the agents of the trading companies for intelligence from abroad. Whereas Cromwell took only a limited interest in the concerns of the trading companies, they had to maintain their links with the state. The Levant Company were particularly successful with regard to this. Their chief concern was that Cromwell would succumb to the constant pressure from the Venetians to aid them in their struggle with the Ottoman Empire. On the point of losing their last foothold in Crete at Candia, the Venetians wanted to make use of English sea power. To protect their interests they could rely on one of Cromwell's chief city supporters, Andrew Riccard, who acted as governor of the Levant Company in 1655, 1656 and 1658. Riccard had been appointed by Cromwell to his Council of Trade in 1655, alongside men like Martin Noell, Thurloe's brother-in-law.

Even those who had access to the heart of the regime could not always rely on their mercantile interests being acted upon. Noell's proposed 'West Indies Company' to promote Caribbean trade was not acted on. They also proposed establishing trading and military links with an Indian Chief in Florida. Again this was not acted on.

Venning, in his *Cromwellian Foreign Policy* (1996), has been damning in his verdict on Cromwell's approach to overseas trade. He stated that 'when we glance at Cromwell's attitude to other companies and mercantile plans, it is clear that his lack of interest or initiative in these matters was total'. The limited consideration of the interests of overseas trade and the merchant consideration under the Protectorate should, however, be set in context. Given the nature of the regime, Cromwell had to put the interests of the army before that of merchants.

Assessment

In terms of sea power, Capp has argued that the period had a significant impact on future naval development. He has shown how a 'more professional outlook gradually developed, as war became a permanent condition and large fleets had to be set out each year. Increasingly appointments were filled by promoting men already in the service, not by recruiting outsiders. This process continued after the Restoration, with a largely separate caste of naval officers gradually evolving, and by 1688 the navy displayed a far more professional structure and mentality'. The royalist Clarendon commented that Cromwell's 'greatness at home was but a shadow of the glory he had abroad. It was hard to discover which feared him the most, France, Spain, or the Low Countries.'

Cromwell's foreign policy undoubtedly raised England's profile as a power in European affairs. William Lockhart, who served as ambassador to France under both Cromwell and Charles II, remarked on how he was treated with less respect when serving the monarch, reflecting the relatively limited influence of England after the Restoration.

The following could also be seen as foreign policy successes:

- Peace with the Dutch.
- Navy victory over the Spanish at Cadiz.
- Capture of the Spanish gold fleet.
- Capture of Mardyke.
- Commercial Treaty with Sweden.

Did you know?

Although Latin still formed a part of a university education, Latin was already something of an anachronism. The regimes of the 1650s relied on the language skills of the poet Milton who was appointed Secretary for Foreign Tongues. Even though Milton was the pre-eminent Latinist in England even he attacked the idea that Latin was useful preparation in educating ministers.

Activity

Group activity

Construct a chart showing examples of when foreign policy was influenced by religious concerns and examples of when it was influenced by other concerns.

After completing this chart, half the group should prepare a presentation that argues that Cromwell's foreign policy was predominantly influenced by religious concerns, and the other half prepare one that suggests it was shaped by other concerns.

Fig. 7 *Report of the death of Oliver Cromwell, 3 September 1658, the anniversary of his victories at Dunbar and Worcester*

■ Negotiating the Treaty of Roskilde between Sweden and Denmark.

■ Capture of Dunkirk.

■ Maintaining good relations with Venice and the Ottoman Empire.

■ Capture of Jamaica.

In the context of the problems he faced, Cromwell's achievement was remarkable. England was a country divided and drained by a civil war and facing unrest in Scotland and Ireland. Only a few of the leading figures of the 1650s had experienced living in Europe or had a grasp of Latin, the main language of diplomacy.

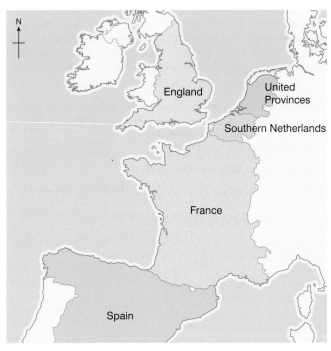

Fig. 6 *North west Europe in the 1650s*

The Rump and Cromwell earned the respect and fear of their neighbours that was not to be repeated until the next century.

■ Republican divisions, 1658–60

In 1659 there was a marked lack of enthusiasm when an attempt was made to restore Charles Stuart. Yet in 1660 monarchy was restored. After Cromwell's death the power groups of the Interregnum failed to produce a workable settlement and by December 1659 many feared a slide into anarchy. At this point the intervention of Monck, who saw the return of monarchy as a safeguard of stability, proved decisive. It was republican division, and in particular divisions in the New Model, that was to prove more influential than any support for monarchy.

The different groups

Following Cromwell's death there were a range of groups and individuals who sought settlement, but crucially, had different approaches.

Civilian Cromwellians/Presbyterians

The *Humble Petition* marked a shift to the 'civilian Cromwellian' position, although the fact that the constitution was without kingship was a problem for men like Broghill. Others who might be seen as part of this loose political grouping were Thurloe and Cromwell's second son, Henry. They wished to see a more traditional parliamentary settlement and a reduction of the army's influence.

Key profile

Henry Cromwell, 1628–74

Henry Cromwell served in Harrison's regiment in the second civil war, but was not involved in army politics. In 1649 Cromwell was given command as colonel in Ireland. On return to England he became active in politics as a representative of Ireland in the Nominated Assembly. He briefly returned to Ireland to report on the state of the loyalty of the army there before serving as an MP in the first Protectorate Parliament. In 1654 Henry became, in effect, ruler of Ireland. Linked with the civilian Cromwellians, notably Broghill, Henry nevertheless wrote to his father suggesting he refuse the offer of the Crown while approving of the more traditional form of the rest of the *Humble Petition*. With the removal of Richard Cromwell as Protector and the political turmoil of 1659, Henry removed himself from politics and lived the rest of his life quietly.

Commonwealthsmen/Republicans

Republicans like Haselrig remained opposed to the Protectorate. The emergence of the 'civilian Cromwellians' as well as the offer of the Crown to Cromwell had heightened their concern. Like the 'civilians' they wanted a weakening of army influence. They saw a one chamber parliament as the ideal.

Army grandees

The leading figures in the army were Fleetwood and Desborough. They wanted Richard's Protectorate to continue.

Key profile

Charles Fleetwood c.1618–92

Fleetwood's regiments in the Eastern Association and New Model were noted for their religious radicals. Fleetwood disappears from the historical record for much of 1647 to 1649 before joining Cromwell in invading Scotland. He went to Ireland after Ireton's death, actually having married Ireton's widow, Cromwell's daughter. He supported religious radicals in Ireland. Regarded as politically weak, he gave little direction to the army despite the meetings of the officers at his residence, Wallingford House. Avoided exception from the Act of Indemnity through the intervention of some in the Lords.

Lambert, despite his forced resignation over kingship in 1657, remained a figure of influence. When the Third Protectorate Parliament assembled in January 1659, Lambert entered the House as an MP and re-entered politics, establishing a working relationship with Republicans. This could only be an unsteady alliance given the disparate nature of the Republicans as a whole. Lambert seems to have been most closely linked with Henry Vane.

Monck

Monck had remodelled the Scottish forces to remove religious radicals, especially Quakers. In doing this Monck effectively created an army

Key dates 1658–60

1658
3 September — Oliver Cromwell dies

1659
January — Third Protectorate Parliament
May — Rump reinstated
August — Booth's Rising
October — Lambert dissolved Rump
October — Committee of Safety established
December — Three regiments reinstate Rump

1660
1 January — Monck entered England
3 February — Monck enters London; readmission of purged 1648 MPs
16 March — Long Parliament dissolved itself
4 April — Declaration of Breda
April — Meeting of Convention Parliament
8 May — Convention Parliament declared for Charles Stuart
29 May — Charles II entered London

Activity

Revision exercise

Write a report for the Republicans outlining why they should not trust Lambert. Refer to information in Chapters 3 to 6.

politically distinct from the New Model in England. A conservative, Monck was concerned at the breakdown of order. He had at his disposal a force with which to take action and established communication with Charles Stuart.

■ **Key profile**

George Monck, 1608–70

Monck had served as a mercenary during the Thirty Years War. When civil war broke out he returned to fight for Charles I. In 1644 Lambert captured him in battle. Imprisoned, it was Cromwell who persuaded Monck to use his talents for the parliamentary cause, eventually securing the command of the New Model in Scotland in the 1650s. At heart a conservative he purged this force, most notably of Quakers. Loyal to Richard Cromwell he began to establish links with Charles Stuart due to his concerns about the actions of the army grandees in England and in particular Lambert. His, or rather his army's intervention into English politics in 1659, was crucial in bringing about the Restoration. After the Restoration Charles II made Monck the Duke of Albemarle.

Soldiers, junior officers

In 1659 agitation among the junior officers and soldiers resurfaced over their arrears and growing concern that the grandees were doing little to protect their interests. Some of this stemmed from a feeling, played upon by Republicans, that leading grandees had profited from the Revolution. The grandees hoped to control the army, as, partly, in 1647, they were now faced with junior officers who were more determined to be a force in themselves and work with the republicans. On 6 April the junior officers, led by Colonel Robert Lilburne, with other Republicans, presented their demands to Richard Cromwell.

Quakers

By 1659 the Quakers had emerged as the most numerous of the sects spawned by the Revolution. They were significant in terms of the Restoration because of the reaction they provoked among the conservative gentry and men like Monck. The fear of Quakers was partly a reaction to what some saw as the undermining of political, religious, social and economic order. For many only monarchy could restore order.

Charles Stuart

Despite royalist hopes at Cromwell's death, Charles Stuart was of little initial significance. The regime did not immediately collapse and Richard Cromwell's Protectorate initially appeared viable. Charles Stuart could do little to aid his return from his exile on the continent. Royalist plotting had proved feeble.

■ **Key profile**

Richard Cromwell, 1626–1712

Richard may have served briefly in the army in 1647 but he was essentially a civilian until he was nominated by his father, as his eldest surviving son, as next Protector. Richard was initially accepted positively but his apparent favour to civilian Cromwellians saw him eventually removed by the army. At the Restoration Richard went to the continent, returning to England in 1680.

The Third Protectorate Parliament and Richard's alienation of the Army

Despite royalist hopes, the accession of Richard was generally accepted by many gentry who had tolerated his father's Protectorate. Indeed there was a feeling that the new Protector, because of his apparently non-aligned background, was more in tune with the traditional gentry. Smith (2007), in the most recent study of Richard's Protectorate, argues that 'his fall in 1659 was by no means a foregone conclusion'. Initially the army response was also favourable. Many hoped Richard would support the army, while others may have believed he would be easier to manipulate than his father. What soon became clear, however, was that the judgment of the 'civilians' was a more accurate reflection of Richard's character and intended policies. Richard was supported by the similar stance of Henry Cromwell and, more importantly, Monck.

There appeared scope for something similar to Broghill's 'civilian' strategy of 1656/7. Richard needed the cooperation of Parliament as adequate finance remained a problem. There was no power, however, for Richard's Council to sanction exclusions for the Third Protectorate Parliament.

In Parliament, Richard was met with opposition from Republicans, who were against a Protectorate, and Lambert, who distrusted the 'civilian Cromwellians'. As a result of Richard's reliance on his civilian advisors, Fleetwood and Desborough established a political forum based around John Owen's congregation at Fleetwood's Wallingford House. This forum came to include Lambert, who at the same time was still trying to work with Republicans and maintain links with the junior officers based at St James's, in line with Vane's ideas of a broad alliance.

■ Did you know?

In Richard Cromwell's Parliament there were a large number of new MPs. In February 1659 it was found that they had been joined by a 'madman' who had been sitting among them undetected for three days.

■ Key profile

John Owen, 1616–83

Theologian and independent minister. In 1648 Owen ministered to the parliamentary army besieging Colchester. In print Owen argued that God always had instruments to destroy his enemies and relieve the Church from oppression. It was in this context that he supported the regicide. Oliver Cromwell appointed Owen as chaplain to the New Model for the Irish and Scottish campaigns. In 1652 Owen preached at the funeral of Ireton.

A conservative tolerationist, Owen advised Cromwell on the establishment of the commission for the approbation of public preachers (March 1654) and subsequently served as a Trier. In December 1655 he was on a committee that discussed readmitting Jews to England. After a request from Pride and Desborough, Owen drafted a petition against the offer of the Crown to Cromwell in May 1657. In 1659 his gathered congregation had developed into something of an army political forum. At the Restoration he refused to conform but was allowed to live peaceably.

Republicans refused to recognise Richard as Protector. Measures to restrict religious toleration provoked the army. The army, triggered by Parliament discussing settling the army as a militia, forced Richard to dissolve Parliament which saw the end of his Protectorate in May 1659.

Division of the New Model

The army was not, however, a united force. Not only did Monck in Scotland have very different ideas about the direction of settlement, but the army in England was divided. The grandees, Fleetwood and Desborough, were not ideologically opposed to the concept of a Protectorate and were much more inclined to support Richard than Lambert was. In part they had been forced into removing the Protectorate by their juniors.

With the removal of the Protectorate, power, in the short term, was in the hands of the Council of Officers. After dismissing those officers loyal to Richard, as well as his essentially civilian advisors, the Council recalled radical officers like John Okey. The most prominent recalled officer was, however, Lambert. Lambert's return added to rumours about his role in recent events but also about what the future held. For many concern at what a Lambertian Protectorate might entail prompted a reluctance to oppose Monck or Charles Stuart.

The junior officers had been subjected to republican propaganda campaign designed to exploit their concern over their material grievances, directing them to blame the grandees. Pressure from the rank and file and junior officers now forced the grandees to reluctantly recall the Rump in May 1659.

The failure of republicanism

Failure of the Rump

Vane hosted conferences between the leading Republicans, particularly Haselrig and a delegation from the Council of Officers, which included Lambert, but not Desborough or Fleetwood. There was tension between Haselrig and Vane. Vane was noted as being especially close to Lambert, being strongly in favour of a Senate and religious toleration. Vane and Lambert appear to have acted as agents of alliance between army and Republicans. Unlike the inflexible Haselrig Vane was more realistic in being willing to compromise with the army.

With a new Council of State of 21 MPs and 10 non-MPs, who were all elected by the House, Lambert felt the army needed some protection. Haselrig and Lambert were the personification of conflicting strands of political direction. Hutton (1993) has argued, in relation to this relationship and Lambert specifically, that 'the men who had most firmly striven for the unfettered power of the Commons were now in harness with the man who had most successfully fettered them in the soldiers' interests'. Haselrig and the leading republican politicians of the Rump did not, however, recognise their dependence on the army and sought to assert their political authority. Furthermore they showed no real inclination to satisfy the soldiers' material grievances.

On 13 May Lambert presented the *Humble Petition and Address of the Officers* to the recalled Rump. It included fifteen articles of 'the Fundamentals of our Good Old Cause'. The thirteenth called for 'a select Senate, Co-ordinate in Power, of able and faithful persons, eminent for Godliness, and such as continue adhering to this Cause' to protect the army. Given his own *A Healing Question* it is not inconceivable that Vane discussed the *Address* with Lambert.

The main opponent of the *Address*, and the army, was Haselrig. Haselrig would accept no reduction of the Commons' authority. Haselrig's grouping in the Rump ignored the controversial aspects of the *Address* of 13 May. Haselrig and the Rump, in effect, committed political suicide by alienating the army. On the point of collapse the fragile alliance of republicans and army was saved, as in 1649–1651, by a military threat.

George Booth's Rising, August 1659

That Haselrig was all too willing to countenance Lambert's command of the force to counter Booth's Rising in Cheshire illustrates how seriously it was taken. The failure of this projected national rising should not distort the potential mushrooming of any opposition.

With the failure of a national rising and facing the imminent prospect of being overwhelmed by Lambert's forces, the conservative Presbyterian Booth, with between 2,500 to 4,000 men, sought negotiation. Lambert demanded surrender. Falling back before Lambert's forces, final resistance was ended in a brief, but intense, encounter at Winnington Bridge.

Fear of the Quakers

Reports of Lambert's troops espousing the 'Quakers' cause' scared many in London, as well as Monck. In defence the army had become more radical. This, coupled with the general Quaker fear, made the regime very unstable. Part of Lambert's relationship with Vane had been based on his willingness to accept religious toleration. Doubts over the nature of Lambert's own faith were clearly widespread and few seemed to regard him as anything but a danger to moderate political and religious sensibilities. The crisis of late 1659-60, with the increased rumours of the possibility of an attempted Lambertian Protectorate with Quaker support, simply brought these fears to a head.

In 1659 there was a national panic about radical groups and the Quakers, with the greatest support, symbolised this fear. The pamphlet literature of 1659 exaggerated the extent of their threat but, combined with apparent political and economic anarchy of the period, conservatives felt that their world was unravelling.

A closer look

Lambert, the Quakers and the Restoration

The perception of Lambert's troops as a radical force was, in part, true. During the 1659 campaign a local minister noted how Lambert's soldiers espoused the Quakers' cause. The Quakers before the Restoration were not averse to political action and Lambert was seen by many Quakers as the most favourable of those in power. The Quakers were taking up positions in civil and military affairs aided by the change of rule in London. Quaker support for Lambert also went as far as to organise support for him in parliamentary elections. It is no wonder that for many Lambert was equated with the Quaker cause and that some thought that through them he would seek to emerge as the new Protector. His relationship with Quakers and other religious radicals was not a direct reflection of his own religious stance. He saw them as no substantial threat to his main priority, the establishment of a civil government based around the concepts that had been evident in his *Instrument*.

By 1659–60 Lambert had been pushed to the political fringes. Lambert's main remaining constituency lay with groups, such as the Quakers, that alienated the nation's traditional elite. The problem for Lambert was that the increasingly radical shift in the nature of his potential support base brought a greater reaction against him.

The belief in the radical religious nature of Lambert's support, with its implied threat of social revolution, contributed to the apathetic reaction of many to the actions of Monck and the Restoration.

Lambert's removal of the Rump

On their return march from Cheshire, Lambert's army drew up the *Derby Petition*, expressing anger at the Rump's failure. Lambert returned to London in September and seized the initiative, determined to secure the army's position that the Rump had recently been undermining. By 13 October, Lambert's troops surrounded Westminster and removed the Rump.

The defection of Monck

With power in its hands, as in 1653, the army once more showed its limited political thinking. While Lambert, and indeed Vane, might have accepted a small ruling elite, it appears that they were not willing to establish a blatant military regime. Both probably realised the difficulties in achieving such an end. The army would still have to accept rule through some form of parliament. That Vane was to remain as part of the structure of government hints that the army leaders wished to work with sympathetic republicans.

The Committee of Safety (October to late December 1659) was set up by the Council of Officers as a provisional government. It was not the hub of a truly revolutionary regime. Indeed the range of opinion deliberately incorporated meant agreement was difficult. Such moderation was not, however, to stop the defection of Monck who declared for the removed Rump.

The seriousness of the situation facing the Committee was shown by the decision to send a force under Lambert towards Monck. That Lambert was chosen rather than Fleetwood was taken by some as a sign that real fighting was intended. Yet Lambert sought to avoid fighting. For Monck's part he also appears to have wished to avoid fighting because he believed that time was on his side. He had significantly reorganised his officer corps, and with his troops recently paid he could afford to wait longer than Lambert's unpaid force. Monck's reorganisation of his forces had been helped by the fact that those of his officers favouring Lambert had left his army.

The delays in the north brought further opposition to the Committee of Safety from other parts of the country, most notably Portsmouth and London, probably just as Monck intended. At this point Lambert's position in the north deteriorated further when his old commander, Fairfax, decided to act against him. When Lambert decided he needed to return to London his unpaid, ill-supplied and now demoralised force disintegrated on the march southwards.

The return of the Rump and Long Parliament

On 26 December 1659, the Rump was reinstated by three regiments of the army. It was only with the collapse of the Committee of Safety (17 December) in London, Portsmouth's declaration for the Rump and Fairfax's action that Monck moved into England on 1 January 1660, reaching London on 3 February.

From Ireland in December 1659 was more evidence of the breakdown of the authority of those who wished to prevent a return of monarchy. Conservatives in the army seized Dublin Castle and brought about the Irish Convention which declared for Charles Stuart.

Activity

Thinking point

Produce a republican pamphlet portraying Lambert as a potential military dictator. Use information in this chapter and Chapters 3 and 4.

Did you know?

After resigning as commander-in-chief of the New Model in 1650, Fairfax spent most of his time on his Yorkshire estate, Nun Appleton. Two of his chief pursuits were gardening and poetry. He employed Andrew Marvell as tutor to his daughter Mary. Marvell's poem Upon Nun Appleton could be read as a veiled attack on Cromwell.

Activity

Class debate

Which of the following individuals was most responsible for the failure of republican rule after Oliver Cromwell's death: Richard Cromwell, Lambert, Haselrig or Monck?

In England, Monck remodelled the armed forces to remove radicals. With the dismissal of Fleetwood, Desborough and Lambert, as well as a general purge of the army, Monck became commander-in-chief. Monck had a couple of meetings with Fairfax who, probably, made clear his desire for stability through Restoration. When Monck was in London, apparently supporting the Rump, further pressure was placed on him by Fairfax, alongside county petitions, calling for a free Parliament. The traditional gentry were determined to seize the chance to reassert themselves for the first time since 1648.

Monck and his officers also wanted political and religious stability. When the yet again restored Rump did not offer this Monck began the process of Restoration. In London Monck forced the inclusion back into the Rump of the purged MPs from 1648, in effect reforming the Long Parliament which, on 16 March 1660, dissolved itself to allow 'free elections'.

Fig. 8 *Procession of Charles II between the Tower of London and Westminster on 22 April 1661, the eve of his coronation. Charles is on the white horse*

It was at this point, on 4 April 1660, that Charles Stuart, with Monck's prompting, produced the *Declaration of Breda* to appeal to those who sought stability. Drafted by Clarendon the *Declaration* outlined that if he was restored Charles would rule as a traditional monarch through Parliament. He promised the army its arrears, a pardon to all his subjects apart from a few individuals and even 'liberty to tender consciences'.

The return of Charles Stuart

Free elections produced the Convention Parliament that assembled on 25 April. Half of the Convention was made up of Parliamentarians, but of many different political and religious views, if mostly moderate Presbyterians. Many of these aimed to restrict the King's power before he returned, while others resisted imposing limits on the returning monarch. For them the Restoration was a way of seeking the King's favour and thereby office. There were also royalists who had got into the Convention gradually through by-elections and disputed elections. These were naturally opposed to limitations on the returning monarch. On 8 May the Convention declared Charles Stuart king and he returned to London at the end of the month.

The Restoration Settlement, 1660–7

The Restoration Settlement was the work of two bodies, the Convention and the Cavalier Parliament, and was to lay the foundation for the early years of Charles II's reign.

Activity

Class discussion

Which of the following factors was the most important in bringing about the restoration of monarchy:

Religion, political divisions, the role of individuals, the appeal of royalism, the economy?

Did you know?

In the 17th century 'revolution' meant different things:

1 Revolution of planets and thus the Restoration as a revolution in the sense of a return.

2 Revolution in terms of unexpected change. Most contemporaries viewed the Restoration in this context of the word.

The Convention

Measures were aimed, in an ad hoc rather than planned fashion, to restore order and constitutional monarchy. The Convention had to address the following issues:

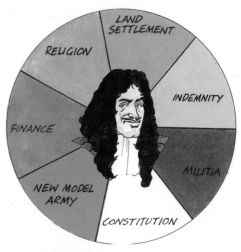

- Indemnity.
- Land settlement.
- Disbanding the army.
- Constitution/Prerogative.
- Finance.
- Religion.
- Militia.

Fig. 9 *The issues for Charles II at the Restoration*

Indemnity

Charles had promised in the *Declaration of Breda* a general pardon, with Parliament deciding who should be excluded. In the Indemnity debates royalists called for widespread vengeance. In the end thirty men were excluded. The Indemnity Act was a pragmatic necessity for Charles and passed on 29 August 1660. It was crucial for Charles as he needed:

- the army to disband
- money from the City of London
- support of the political elite, many of whom were Parliamentarians.

Despite the Indemnity Act the Restoration was accompanied by a range of blood-letting and persecution.

Land settlement

As a result of the revolution of 1649, the lands of bishops, royalists, Catholics and the Crown were sold off. The purchasers had a vested interest in the previous regimes and as some were powerful and had also helped bring about the Restoration, Charles needed to be careful about upsetting them. He left the matter to Parliament. The complexity of the land issue saw Parliament fail to legislate a solution. In the absence of statute ad hoc measures were taken. Church and crown land was reclaimed. A commission was set to consider compensation. The land question was settled partly because the most substantial purchasers were excluded from the Indemnity Act and their land seized. Others had recouped their outlay before 1660 and many royalists had already taken measures to reclaim their estates or protect them before 1660.

Disbanding the army

In the *Declaration of Breda*, Charles had promised the army its arrears. With the Indemnity Act passed and arrears voted by the Convention the army was peaceably disbanded.

Constitution

A key question was whether the limits put on monarchy by the legislation of 1640 were to remain. A number of bills were designed to limit the powers of Charles Stuart and implement his promises in the *Declaration of Breda*. These attempts at restricting the power of the

Cross-reference

For an explanation of the persecution that accompanied the Restoration, see Chapter 7.

monarch failed given the short time available for enacting them and royalist obstruction.

With Charles Stuart's return without conditions, those who had wished to limit his powers were in too weak a position to do anything. A bill to confirm parliamentary privileges and fundamental laws became becalmed in the Lords through the influence of Charles Stuart. It would have confirmed *Magna Carta*, the legislation of 1641 and in theory that passed by the Long Parliament as a whole. Charles became king without any limitations imposed on him.

Finance

Initially the Convention kept finance in its own hands and it paid off the army. In terms of a settlement for the monarch it was decided to abolish feudal tenures, but provide compensation. Charles was granted tonnage and poundage for life. Customs were granted to the King, but only those specified in a parliamentary bill. These were the means by which the King should 'live off his own'. Charles was finally granted £1.2 million a year for government costs in peacetime. This would come from customs and excise. As this was almost double Charles I's income it appeared generous but, in practice, only about a £400,000 could be raised from these means. In 1662 a Hearth Tax was introduced to try and bridge the gap.

This itself proved insufficient and Charles II's finances were to come under even greater pressure because of his wars with the Dutch. The chief consequence of the limits of the Crown's finances was that Charles II was dependent on parliamentary grants of finance and therefore had to call Parliament every year between 1660 and 1681.

Religion

Another key question in 1660 was what kind of church should be restored? What was to be done in relation to the numerous non-conformists that had been free to worship during the Interregnum, let alone radicals like the Quakers? The *Declaration of Breda* had promised an Indulgence for nonconformists. This did not materialise. About 700 of England's 9,000 ministers were removed as the Church of England was restored without it being broadened to encompass any nonconformists, not even Presbyterians. A conference at Hyde's London house produced the Worcester House Declaration (October 1660). This stated that bishops and presbyters would ordain and censure clergy. Ministers would be left to decide what of the Prayer Book they used. It was not ratified by the Convention Parliament due to the opposition of Episcopalians.

Militia

The Convention passed no bill in relation to the militia but there was no challenge to Charles's control of it. In 1661 and 1662 two Militia Acts gave Charles sole control of all armed forces. In July 1661 a bill gave Charles control of the Militia, reinforced in May 1662 when Charles was given the power to raise up to £70,000 a year for three years through a militia rate to support the forces raised.

Charles announced the dissolution of the Convention on 20 November, probably in annoyance at the lack of legislation with regard to the Militia and problems with the religious settlement.

Exploring the detail

The Hearth Tax was a wealth tax, as it was a tax paid on each fireplace in a building. The bigger the building the more fireplaces it would have had.

Activity

Thinking point

How difficult would it be to instigate a 'Restoration' after the events of 1649 to 1660? How might Charles II deal with the ideas unleashed by the years 1649 to 1660?

The Cavalier Parliament

A royalist backlash saw a 'Cavalier' Parliament elected in May 1661. The typical cavalier county squire had no desire to be in government. MPs were concerned with local issues. They wished for a return to normal and the Crown, not them, was government. Any who wanted power could enter the King's service. They did not want, however, the King to be absolute. Seaward, in his study of *The Cavalier Parliament and the Reconstruction of the Old Regime, 1661–1667* (1988), has argued that their conservatism 'prevented them from wanting to build on parliament's Civil War achievements, made them equally suspicious of attempts to strengthen the monarchy too far'. In the end 'the conservatism of parliament, and the government's recognition of that conservatism, set bounds both to the government's intentions and its achievements'.

In June 1661 the Commons introduced a bill that would allow them, through commissioners, to remove men from the 1640s and 1650s and appoint 'loyal' or 'well-affected' men. The Commons' commissioners carried out a sweeping purge. Local government returned to the hands of the traditional ruling elite. The Act for the Safety and Preservation of His Majesty's Person and Government cancelled all ordinances; that is, any acts of Parliament that had not received the royal assent. This did mean, however, that some of the parliamentary legislation of 1641 that had sought to limit the Crown's powers was to stand:

- **Abolition of Star Chamber:** Star Chamber was a prerogative court that had been used by Charles I to try some of his leading critics.
- **Abolition of high commission:** Church court used by Charles I to enforce anti-Calvinism.
- **Abolition of ship money (and other financial reforms):** Charles I had raised money on his prerogative through 11 years of rule without parliament, 1629 to 1640.
- **The Triennial Act:** Passed in 1641 to ensure the monarch called a parliament at least every three years.
- **Exclusion of bishops from Lords:** This was to prevent a core group of support for the monarch.

Soon, however, the Act excluding the bishops was repealed. The presence of the bishops in the Lords gave the Crown an influential group of supporters. Some church courts, but not the High Commission, were brought back. In 1664 a remodelled Triennial Act removed the compulsory element of the Crown calling a Parliament every three years, replacing it with the hope he would call a Parliament *at least* every three years. Sessions were also not to have a specified minimum duration. Even the Convention's Indemnity Act and land settlement were reviewed by the Cavalier Parliament. Only the intervention of Charles, who realised the unrest this might create, stopped the Cavalier Parliament proceeding.

The Cavalier Parliament strengthened the position of Charles II:

- **Press:** Press censorship formalised by the 1662 Licensing Act. 1660 proclamation to burn Milton's *Defence of the People of England* (1650) justifying regicide. Printer of the 1663 tract *Mene Tekel* that argued that there was nothing in the Bible that prevented resistance to a tyrant was hanged, disembowelled and quartered.
- **Petitioning:** An act to prevent mass petitioning. Three JPs or a county grand jury were needed to authorise any petition with only 20 or more signatures. Furthermore only 10 people could present the petition.

- **Popery:** The Act for the Safety and Preservation of His Majesty made it punishable to accuse the King of trying to bring in popery or stirring up hatred of the monarch.
- **Parliament:** Parliament could not legislate without the monarch.

Parliament did not retreat on the financial measures of 1641, recognising that Parliament's real power over the Crown was financial. The reinforcement of Charles's annual income of £1.2 million per annum with the Hearth Tax (1662) still did not prove enough, especially under the pressures of the Dutch Wars. The limited financial settlement made Charles reliant on Parliament.

The failures of the Restoration settlement were the basis for continuing problems in Charles's attempts to consolidate his rule to 1667 and arguably for the Stuarts until their removal in 1688.

> It is difficult to see what the Restoration actually settled, beyond the fact that the English state was to be headed by a monarchy. Not only were the tensions between the Crown and Parliament or Church and Dissent unresolved, but the fact that no-one could feel that they had come out on top meant that all the key protagonists had everything to contend for. In such a situation, it was inevitable that political and religious strife would develop.

2

*T. Harris, **Politics under the Later Stuarts: Party Conflict in a Divided Society 1660–1715** (1993)*

Did you know?

The most obvious sign of the Restoration settlement as an attempt to wipe out the Interregnum was the dating of the start of Charles II's reign to the execution of his father in January 1649. Technically, therefore, Charles reigned for 36 years. A further qualification can be added to this – England's calendar still ran from 25 March to 25 March. Charles I had been executed by this reckoning in January 1648.

Summary questions

1. Was Cromwell's foreign policy shaped by religious considerations?
2. What was the main weakness of Richard Cromwell's position as Lord Protector?
3. To what extent was the Restoration more a failure of republicanism than a sign of support for Charles Stuart?

Charles II, 1660–7

Fig. 1 *Anglo-Dutch naval battle, 1667*

In this chapter you will learn about:

■ the personality of Charles II

■ the role of Clarendon

■ Charles II's relations with France and the Netherlands to 1667

■ the religious policies of Charles II to 1667

■ why opposition to Charles II failed.

In 1660 Charles II returned to England amid general public rejoicing. There rapidly followed a number of high profile trials, executions and imprisonments. A rigid Anglican church was reimposed, taking no account of the range of dissent that had flourished since 1640. Charles's court was decadent and this became reflected in the culture of court and elements of society. Charles's government came under increasing financial strain. In 1665 plague raged through England to be followed by the Great Fire of London. In June 1667, the Dutch sailed up the Thames to destroy the flagship of Charles's navy and humiliate England's pretensions to be a major European or colonial power. For many God seemed to have judged Charles's regime.

Charles II and royal government to 1667

Charles II's popular image as a 'merry monarch' was corrected by academic studies of the King by Ronald Hutton (1989) and John Miller (1991). Hutton has referred to Charles II as an opportunist, inconsistent and reckless. He has stressed that with regard to the reign its 'brutality, dishonesty and cynicism of its politics' took its character from Charles. Miller sees Charles II, at least until his later years, as a weaker and more vacillating monarch than Hutton. Yet, in the context of how he came to the throne Charles, eventually, proved a remarkably successful monarch.

Charles's aims

Royal government was underpinned by Charles's desire not to 'go on his travels again' and dominated by one man besides the King, the Earl of

Clarendon. The Restoration Settlement did not solve the ambiguity of the unwritten constitution and in particular there was no means of solving a clash of interests between crown and political nation or people. Miller has argued that everything 'depended on Charles's skills as king and politician and his willingness to confine himself to the politically feasible'.

Charles wished to emulate Louis XIV and while Miller has argued there was the potential for absolutism in England it would have been different to French absolutism. Charles was too reliant on the political nation who governed the counties.

Fig. 2 *A pamphlet of 1660 setting the execution of Charles I over an image of the revenge exacted on the surviving regicides*

 Key profile

Louis XIV, 1638–1715

The French monarchy reached the pinnacle of its power under Louis, the model of absolutism. Known as the 'Sun King' Louis' Versailles palace was a visible symbol of his power. In a series of seven wars between 1661 and 1715 Louis extended French control across what is essentially France today. In contrast Charles's two wars against the Dutch highlighted the weaknesses of England as a European power and when he signed an alliance with Louis in 1670 he became, in effect, his client.

Activity

Revision exercise

As you read this chapter, note down the evidence which would support the view that by 1667, Charles II had shown himself to be untrustworthy.

Charles did not, however, understand his subjects. He had been away from England since 1642, apart from a brief failed invasion in 1651 that ended in defeat at the hands of Cromwell. One characteristic Charles shared with his father was a propensity to see criticism as disaffection. Miller argued that 'Charles was not disposed to trust' the political nation. By 1667 many of the political nation would have felt little reason to trust Charles.

The court of Charles II

Miller has referred to Charles's court as 'frivolous, promiscuous and chaotically informal'. Charles's court, as with his political pragmatism, mirrored that of his grandfather James I. The Restoration court was debauched, led by Charles II himself. In 1665 the courtiers were described as 'nasty and beastly… Rude, rough, whoremongers; vain, empty, careless'. Charles's debauchery was mirrored in leading courtiers like Buckingham and most notably the Earl of Rochester who died aged 33 from alcoholism and syphilis. Rochester wrote of Charles II:

> 'Restless he rolls from whore to whore,
>
> A merry monarch, scandalous and poor.'

The behaviour of the King thus undermined the image of divine right monarchy.

One aspect of Charles II's court that he shared with that of his prudish father was not a positive one; the number of high-profile Catholics at court. These merely reinforced the idea of a Popish conspiracy and doubt about the King's own religious beliefs.

Leading Catholics at court:

- Charles's mother, Henrietta Maria.
- Charles's wife, Catherine of Braganza.
- Charles's brother, James, Duke of York.
- George Digby, the Earl of Bristol.

Key profiles

Henrietta Maria, 1606–69

Daughter of Henry IV of France she married Charles I in 1625. Henrietta Maria was regarded as influencing Charles I towards Catholicism and absolutism. Her advice to Charles I during the crisis of 1637 to 1642 was invariably to take a hard line. She spent the years of exile at the French court, establishing a royalist faction known as 'the Louvre'. She returned to England at the Restoration and was prominent in calls for retribution. Henrietta Maria continued to meddle in politics, notably being hostile to Clarendon, but generally Charles II was pragmatic enough to limit her role.

Catherine of Braganza, 1638–1705

Portuguese princess and wife of Charles II. A marriage treaty of 1661 was followed by a marriage by proxy in Lisbon in 1662. When Catherine actually arrived in England there were two marriage ceremonies. The first was Catholic and held in secret. The second Anglican ceremony was the public marriage of Charles and Catherine. As part of the dowry Charles received the ports of Tangier and Bombay from Portugal. Catherine and Charles never had any children but Charles resisted calls from parliament to divorce Catherine. She remained in England until 1692 when the anti-Catholicism at William's court saw her return to Portugal.

Fig. 3 *Charles II's wife, Catherine of Braganza, Princess of Portugal*

Cross-reference

To find out more about the Earl of Clarendon, see pages 105–107.

Did you know?

Charles II had no children with his wife. As a result his brother, James, remained as the heir to the throne. Charles had, however, at least 14 illegitimate children.

The dominant minister until 1667 was Edward Hyde, the Earl of Clarendon. The leading ministers of the Cabal, post-1667, were, however, an issue as Clifford was a Catholic and Arlington a Catholic sympathiser.

Many of Charles's mistresses were Catholics. For example, Barbara Villiers, Countess of Castlemaine, later Duchess of Cleveland, had five children with Charles that he acknowledged. Another Catholic mistress was the Scottish Catholic, Frances Stuart. The most prominent, and perhaps the most influential, was the French Catholic Louise de Kerouaille, who became the Duchess of Portsmouth. Charles actually went through a mock wedding ceremony with Portsmouth in 1671.

The role of Charles's mistresses must also be set in an appropriate context, being another example of where reality belies Charles's 'merry monarch' popular image. Hutton gives the example of Louise de Kerouaille. She was in effect pressurised into becoming another royal mistress by Charles, his minister Arlington and Louis XIV, who saw the advantages of the English king having a French mistress. Charles made her illegitimate son, born in 1672, the Duke of Richmond and Lennox.

The regime's failings were seen as a result of Charles's moral failings. In short Hutton has referred to the 'brutality, dishonesty and cynicism' of the court and is clear that this came from the character of the King. Like Charles I the style of the court under Charles II reinforced the impression of Catholic influences being adopted. Charles mimicked the French style of his cousin Louis XIV at Versailles with architecture, painting and music being essentially **baroque**.

This decadence was also reflected in Restoration drama.

Key terms

Baroque: highly ornate and extravagant in style and, in the case of Louis XIV and Charles II, designed to give prestige to their courts and impress other powers.

A closer look

The projection of court style

Alan Marshall in his *Age of Faction* (1999) provided an overview of 'Court style' under Charles II:

> From 1660 to 1702 the cultural language of the court represented a world of extravagance, a baroque splendor with absolutist overtones. This cultural environment was a living one in which all the day-to-day activities of the court took place and were given public expression. All societies, particularly elite ones, require a framework of reference within which to operate. This framework, or culture, enables them to define themselves and their aims, to justify their existence or order their actions. It is a form of 'political ideology'. In this ideology, cultural artefacts and modes of expression have a functional use: they become part of the means of social control created to inspire, amaze, instruct, entertain or suppress both the elite who view them and the outsiders to whom they are projected. Royal edifices, ceremony and artefacts were always intended to 'speak' to a wide audience. They were part of a conscious system of power projection – expressions of the monarch's political power, material wealth and artistic taste.

This court style manifested itself in:

- following the examples of the French court of Louis XIV in terms of ideas and fashions
- reassembling the art collection of his father which had been sold off during the Interregnum
- a number of courtiers who were debauched drunkards, the most notable being the Earl of Rochester.

Unlike his father, Charles II had no real interests in the arts and even his supposed interest in the science of the day was superficial. The court reflected this superficiality.

For Smith 'the Court reinforced all the Country's worst fears about the Crown's authoritarian ambitions'. The court was positive in that it did perform the function of 'point of contact' being, initially, open to a wide range of opinion and more to the public. Every Friday Charles II conducted the ceremony of 'touching' for the 'King's Evil', the disease scrofula, a form of tuberculosis.

Did you know?

In the ceremony Charles II did not literally touch the victims of scrofula but ran his hand over them. Between April 1669 and December 1684 Charles II 'touched' 28,983 of his subjects for scrofula. Between May 1682 and April 1683 Charles 'touched' 8,577 people.

The role of Clarendon

Hyde, the Earl of Clarendon, was the Lord Chancellor and Charles II's principal adviser from the Restoration to 1667. Clarendon's position was based on his role in Charles II's government in exile and his capacity for work. His willingness to consider everything in detail was a perfect counterpoint to a monarch for whom the details of government held no real interest.

There were, however, fundamental weaknesses in Clarendon's seemingly pre-eminent position.

- **Personality:** Clarendon's business-like approach to everything and power over government made him arrogant and dismissive of others. He came across as self-righteous. Not only did these traits stop him building up a political network; more importantly, they increasingly alienated the King.
- **Privy Council:** These personality traits meant he did not manage the Privy Council to his advantage as a support base.
- **Parliament:** Similarly Clarendon did not manage Parliament and thus allowed opposition to develop.

His failures to take account of the politics of the Privy Council and Parliament can be seen to be because of his passive approach to managing them. Despite his pre-eminence his failure allowed his rivals to outmanoeuvre him. The real weakness in Clarendon's position was, however, his relationship with the King. While Charles II may have recognised Clarendon's skills he did not like him. It was therefore easier for Charles to use Clarendon as a scapegoat.

What Clarendon was blamed for:

Point of blame	Details
No heir to the throne	Clarendon had negotiated, with the support of the Council, the marriage of Charles II to the Portuguese princess Catherine of Braganza. The failure of this union to produce children was turned against Clarendon.
The sale of Dunkirk	Cromwell had secured the first English control of French land since the English had lost all French lands, apart from Calais which was held until 1558, in 1453. Clarendon sold Dunkirk for £300,000.
The Clarendon Code	The imposition of religious conformity.
Jealousy	Political rivals were jealous of his influence.
Daughter's marriage	Clarendon's daughter Anne married Charles's brother James who was next in line to the throne. Clarendon thus appeared to be exploiting his influence to secure further power.
The Dutch War	Clarendon had tried to prevent a war against the Dutch, but was blamed for how badly it went.

It was the disasters in the Dutch War that saw Charles II make Clarendon a scapegoat. Clarendon's rivals, in particular Buckingham, Arlington and Coventry, put pressure on Charles II to sacrifice Clarendon. Charles was more than happy to oblige. By this stage he had more than had enough of Clarendon who himself was ill. In August he was forced to resign. Clarendon's rivals pushed, however, for his impeachment, claiming treason. The House of Lords refused to put Clarendon in the Tower. His enemies then attempted to set up a special court of 24 Lords to proceed against him. Clarendon knew by this stage that Charles II was not a man to be trusted to protect a minister and went into exile in France.

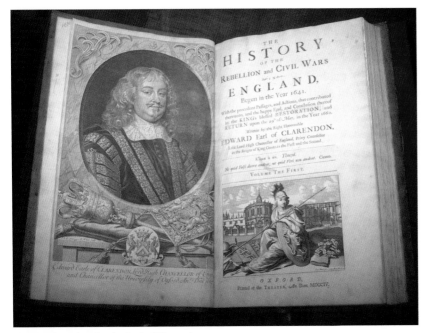

Fig. 4 *Edward Hyde, the Earl of Clarendon*

Exploring the detail

Clarendon's *History of the Rebellion*

Clarendon began his *History* while with royalists on Scilly and Jersey in 1646–8. At this point he had got to 1644 in his narrative. While in Montpellier between 1668 and 1671 he constructed his *Life*. The following year when at Moulins he received his original manuscript of the *History* and over the next few years used material from the *Life* to construct the *History of the Rebellion*.

Miller has written that while 'the Commons showed only a limited interest in Clarendon's impeachment, Charles canvassed the Lords, urging them to condemn his most loyal servant. Rarely does one see so clearly the self-centred ruthlessness behind Charles's affable façade: to save his skin, he would sacrifice anyone, no matter how innocent'. This assessment is mirrored by Hutton who saw the treatment of Clarendon as 'wholly in character for a ruler who had always turned with absolute ruthlessness and petty spite upon anybody who defied him or crossed his will and then became vulnerable to his malice'.

Assessment of Clarendon

Clarendon pursued a Constitutional Royalist agenda of strengthening the Crown's military, financial and constitutional position, but respecting the liberty of the subject. Clarendon managed the underlying tensions of the differing perspectives of what would become known as 'Court and Country', between the Anglicans and the Dissenters and anti-Catholicism. These tensions were to emerge in the post-Clarendon world.

Executions and persecution

Local records indicate a range of negative responses to the Restoration. Charles was referred to as a 'rogue' who 'none that loves him but drunk whores'. Some stated publicly a desire to kill the King. A fundamental part of the Restoration settlement was securing the monarchy from the threat of those who it most readily perceived as posing a threat.

On 15 May 1660, the Convention Parliament ordered that justice be meted out on the regicides Oliver Cromwell, Henry Ireton, John Bradshaw and Thomas Pride. For a parliament that had welcomed monarchy back there was nothing surprising about initiating revenge against those who had committed the act that had led to 11 years of republican rule. What of course was different was that all four men were already dead. For the justice required by this parliament to be enacted their bodies would have to be dug up, taken to Tyburn, the traditional place for the execution of traitors, hung, decapitated and disembowelled before being publicly displayed.

Activity

Thinking point

Write a speech for Clarendon defending his record.

Activity

Thinking point

To what extent was Clarendon's fall more a consequence of the actions of Charles II than the failure of policies?

The horror of such a process is only heightened by the length of time these men had been dead. Cromwell died in September 1658; Pride in October 1658; Bradshaw in October 1659. Ireton had died in 1651. As Howard Nenner has pointed out Charles 'needed to react to the 'murder' of a parent while at the same time fashioning his response to the dictates of political necessity'. Others who had survived to see the Restoration were subjected to punishment as part of the Restoration Settlement.

The trials of October 1660

The speech of the Speaker of the Lords in August 1660 to the King presenting the Indemnity Bill indicates the atmosphere in which the surviving regicides and others came to trial:

> [L]ooking over a long, black, prodigious, dismall roll and catalogue of malefactors, we there meet not with men but monsters, guilty of blood, precious blood, precious royal blood, never to be remembered without tears; incomparable in all the kinds of villainy that ever was acted by the worst of miscreants, perverters of religion; subverters of government; false to God; disloyal to the best of kings: and perfidious to their country: and therefore we found an absolute and indispensible necessity incumbent upon us, to except and set some apart for trial, to expel the poison of sin and rebellion out of others, and that they might be made sacrifices to appease God's wrath, and satisfy divine justice.

1

The trial of the regicides, according to Hutton, 'breached custom by requiring only one witness for each act of treason' and the comments at the proceedings indicate that guilty verdicts were foregone conclusions. All who proceeded to trial had to be found guilty; their fate was then left to the dictates of Charles's will. Those listed as present as part of the new regime were the Restoration establishment, but this included some who may have been uncomfortable with some of the arguments raised during the proceedings, particularly Monck and Denzil Holles.

Charles clearly saw that to reimpose monarchy there needed to be some accommodation with elements of the Interregnum regimes. In doing so the act of regicide was isolated in the overall context of the years 1642 to 1660. In a letter of May 1660 the Commons had sought to repudiate Parliament's responsibility for regicide stating that it had been 'the Act of some few ambitious and bloody Persons'. As well as the politically pragmatic reasons for such a view it also acted as a salve for men like Holles and Monck who played a prominent role in the tribunals of 1660. Post-regicide accommodation was then made with those from the Interregnum regimes who were not regicides to make non-monarchical rule viable.

The man selected as the first regicide to be brought to trial was Major-General Thomas Harrison. He offered

■ Regicides: Thomas Harrison
■ Republicans: Thomas Venner
■ Religious radicals: Henry Vane

Fig. 5 *Persecution of potential opposition*

a justification by the authority of Parliament which was dismissed by the court. Harrison declared the religious basis for the regicide:

> [It] was not a thing done in a corner. I believe the sound of it hath been in most nations. I believe the hearts of some have felt the terrors of that presence of God that was with his servants in those days, (however it seemeth good to him to suffer this turn to come on us) and are witnesses that the things done were not done in a corner.

2

There was little chance that Harrison would not be found guilty and the court ordered that he suffer the traditional death for treason:

> That you be led back to the place from whence you came, and from thence to be drawn upon an hurdle to the place of execution; and there you shall be hanged by the neck, and being alive shall be cut down, and your privy members to be cut off, your entrails to be taken out of your body, and, you living, the same to be burnt before your eyes, and your head to be cut off, your body to be divided into four quarters, and head and quarters to be disposed of at the pleasure of the king's majesty, and the Lord have mercy upon your soul.

3

A contemporary royalist pamphlet recounted that as Harrison was going to suffer this punishment, someone in the crowd called in 'derision to him, and said, Where is your *Good Old Cause*? He with a chearfull smile clapt his hand on his Brest, and said, *Here it is, and I am going to seal it with my blood*'.

In 1662 there were high profile show trials of the non-regicides, Henry Vane and John Lambert. Vane's refusal to seek mercy saw Charles demand his death. The jury in the trial were kept without food and water until they returned a guilty verdict and musicians played under the scaffold as he was about to be executed to ensure no one could hear Vane's last words. In contrast Lambert requested mercy and, perhaps in the context of growing concern at the impact of continued executions, he was imprisoned for the next 22 years until his death in 1684.

Alongside these high profile show trials and executions there was daily persecution of other minor figures of the Interregnum. The Harringtonian republican Adam Baynes suffered a series of imprisonments until his death in 1671.

Charles II's relations with France and the Netherlands

Charles's attitude towards foreign policy was shaped by insecurity prompted by Dutch economic strength and French absolutism.

Charles's relations with France

In contrast to relations with the Dutch, Charles's attitude to France and his cousin Louis XIV was positive. The brief French intervention in the Dutch war in 1666 was an opportunistic attempt to take

Did you know?

William Goffe, regicide and major-general, fled to America with his father-in-law and fellow regicide Edward Whalley. Tradition has it that they lived in a cave in the woods outside New Haven for three years to avoid English agents sent to hunt them down. The sympathy of the colonists protected them and in 1675 when they had moved to Hadley, Massachusetts, Goffe organised the settlers to prevent the town being overrun by a Native American attack. Goffe died in 1679 being buried in Hadley next to Whalley who had died in 1675.

advantage of English weakness. Charles managed to regain the territories lost to France in the West Indies but had to cede Nova Scotia to them. He was, however, naturally inclined to see himself as an ally of France and in fact after 1670 he became merely a client of Louis XIV. This had serious domestic consequences because it was France that became the central Catholic absolutist threat in the minds of Charles's subjects. Charles's subjects equated the strengthening relationship between the two states as a sign of Charles's drift to Catholicism and absolutism.

Charles's relations with the Netherlands

As well as economic rivalry with the Dutch Republic, the Dutch were also linked to religious radicalism and republicanism. There were a number of reasons for increasing tension between the English and Dutch during the 1660s:

- **The 1660 Navigation Act:** This was much more aggressive than the 1651 act. By the terms of the 1660 Act only English ships could carry certain listed goods. All goods imported from colonies in West Africa, the West Indies and Asia had to be carried in English ships.
- **The 1663 Staple Act:** Colonists had to import European goods from England in English ships.
- **Anglican Royalists:** The Dutch Calvinist republic was the antithesis of everything they held dear.
- **Charles II:** He felt that the war could be profitable.

The Second Dutch War

In June 1665 James, Duke of York, the Lord Admiral, won a victory over the Dutch off Lowestoft. In July 1666 the English won the St James's Day battle in the mouth of the Thames. These two victories were outweighed, however, by a number of failures:

- **August 1665:** A failed attack on the Dutch fleet at Bergen.
- **Start of 1666:** France and Denmark entered the war against England.
- **June 1666:** The Four Days' Battle with the Dutch in the Channel saw the death of 8,000 English and the sinking of 20 ships.

Opinion moved against the war; in particular the trading companies complained of economic losses. Others were becoming increasingly aware of the threat of Louis XIV, the epitome of Catholic absolutism. In the spring of 1667 peace negotiations were begun. Then in the summer of 1667 the Dutch humiliated the English. The English fleet was laid up in the Medway near Chatham. Here it was attacked in June 1667. The Dutch sailed up the river and sank three ships and towed two others back to the Netherlands. One of those towed back was the flagship, the Royal Charles. Nothing appeared more symbolic of Charles II's failure.

The reverses in the Dutch War were in the wider context of what appeared to be evidence of mismanagement and divine displeasure. Harris has stated that 'Charles's foreign policy was the most inglorious – by any standard – and certainly appeared disastrous compared to what had been achieved under Cromwell in the 1650s'.

Key dates

1660–7: Anglo-Dutch relations

1660	
September	Navigation Act against Dutch carrying trade
1665	
March	Second Dutch War
June	Naval victory over the Dutch off Lowestoft
August	Failed assault on Dutch fleet at Bergen
1666	
June	Four Days' Battle – English naval defeat
July	St James's Day Battle – English naval victory
1667	
June	Dutch raid English fleet in Medway
July	Treaty of Breda

In 1665 Parliament had voted £3.75 million for the war but a year later the Admiralty was in chaos and appeared to have badly mismanaged the war.

Failure in foreign policy was seen in the context of what appeared to be God's judgement on England. In the summer and early autumn of 1665 the bubonic plague devastated London and other parts of the country. In May 1665, 43 plague deaths were recorded in London. In September, 26,219 deaths were recorded. In London in total there were about 70,000–100,000 deaths from the plague. The Derbyshire village of Eyam suffered an 80 per cent casualty rate. The plague had been brought to the village in some infected laundry. The death toll was so great because the village rector persuaded the villagers that they should remain in the village rather than risk spreading the plague to neighbouring areas.

Fig. 6 *The impact of the plague: a Bill of Mortality, listing deaths*

In response, Charles II and the court moved to Oxford where Parliament met. Back in London there was chaos and economic collapse. Then, on 2 September 1666, fire broke out. The Great Fire of London lasted five days, covering 395 acres of London. Its chief structural victim was St Paul's Cathedral. 250,000 people were made homeless.

As well as the physical impact of both the plague and the fire there was also a psychological impact. People wondered 'was this God's judgement on Charles's rule?' Paul Seaward has seen 1667 as a turning point for the regime:

> In 1667, all their (gentry) worries rose rapidly to the surface. The war and an agricultural crisis had accelerated their decline and shown up the corruptions of the City and the court, a court so viciously perverted that it had rather rule by an army than face justice in parliament. Those who had fought for the king, no less than those who had fought for parliament, were incensed. Far from restoring the old relationship of the Crown and the gentry, and far from conforming the alliance of the Crown and the royalists, the court seemed intent on ignoring and insulting them. The year 1667 appeared to mark not just the end of an administration, or of a policy, but also the limits to the reconstruction of the old regime.

4   *P. Seaward, **The Cavalier Parliament and the Reconstruction of the Old Regime, 1661–1667** (1989)*

Did you know?

In London, in an attempt to prevent the spread of the plague, 40,000 dogs and 80,000 cats were slaughtered. This actually made the situation worse as there were less natural predators to kill the rats that carried the plague.

Fig. 7 *The Great Fire of London*

Religious policies of Charles II, 1660–7

The Church of England was reimposed with the Restoration as part of the conservative reaction. It was another part of the failure of the Restoration settlement to come to terms with the forces unleashed by civil war and revolution.

Although nearly 2,000 ministers were expelled at the Restoration large scale nonconformity was still a reality. The Church of England could not even now claim to represent the nation. The Church also had less power to enforce its will because of the removal of the Court of High Commission and the decline of diocesan (an area administered by a bishop) courts. It was therefore the local elite who had to enforce conformity, but some JPs and Deputy Lieutenants were themselves non-conformists or sympathetic to those who would not conform to the Church of England. Generally nonconformity was stronger in urban settings whereas the rural gentry remained more conservative, more typically Anglican. Settlement was a reflection of cavalier/royalist gentry control over the Church. With their control they removed non-Anglicans and persecuted Dissenters.

Charles and Clarendon sought a broader church than the one they got. As a result of the Worcester House Declaration the Savoy House Conference was held. This showed that the Presbyterians were divided and that the bishops had little willingness to compromise in any religious settlement. The Cavalier Parliament reimposed a rigid church. The Cavalier Parliament ordered MPs to take communion by Anglican rite.

Miller has written of Charles's 'concerted attempt to secure toleration for Catholics'. There was a Lords' bill to repeal some of the laws against them, allowing priests to register with the secretary of state. According to Miller 'Charles strongly supported it'. The bill failed in the Lords but it would not have got through Commons and the public was against any toleration for Catholics. Charles's attitude was certainly different towards the Quakers. Hutton has seen Charles as particularly vindictive in his repression of Quakers, referring to his 'personal malice' in urging their persecution.

Charles's policy towards Dissenters fluctuated with apparent threats. There were repressive measures after the regime came under threat:

- 1663 Northern Rising led to the 1664 Conventicle Act.
- Second Dutch War led to the 1665 Five Mile Act.

By the Conventicle Act, religious meetings of five persons or more were forbidden. The initial punishment of a fine could, on the third occasion, result in transportation. The Five Mile Act meant that any preacher or teacher who refused the compulsory oaths that were part of the Act of Uniformity could not go within five miles of any corporate town or parish where they had taught. In 1670 a second Conventicle Act reinforced the persecution of Dissenters and Charles even removed some JPs who were judged too lenient in acting against conventicles.

Fig. 8 Christopher Wren, architect of the rebuilding of St Paul's Cathedral after the Great Fire of London

Did you know?

Sir Christopher Wren, architect of St Paul's, was employed at this time to seal up the meeting houses of non-conformists in London. He also designed 53 churches across London as well as being a Professor of Astronomy at Oxford.

Harris has pointed to the contradiction in the Restoration religious persecution:

> [M]ost English nonconformists were not political subversives. The biggest group by far, the Presbyterians, had opposed the regicide and actively welcomed the restoration of monarchy, and most Independents, Baptists and Quakers were prepared to make their peace with the restored monarchy and merely wanted to be allowed liberty of conscience they had been promised in Charles's Declaration of Breda. The trouble was, pursuing a policy of religious intolerance out of a fear of political subversives ran the risk of making the potentially loyal disloyal and creating the very real problem that such a policy was designed to prevent.

5   *T. Harris, **Restoration: Charles II and His Kingdoms** (2005)*

Although Clarendon wanted a broader church settlement the restoration religious settlement paradoxically became known as the Clarendon Code, the principal measures of which were:

- Corporation Act 1661
- Act of Uniformity 1662
- Conventicle Act 1664
- Five Mile Act 1665.

> **Activity**
>
> **Revision exercise**
>
> What were the strengths and weaknesses of the Restoration religious settlement?

The failure of opposition to Charles II, 1660–7

The work of Richard Greaves in a series of books on the radical underground in Britain in the late Stuart period has illustrated the range of potential, if limited, opposition to Charles II.

Lambert's Rising

One of the first entries in Pepys' Diary concerns Lambert's escape out of the Tower of London in April 1660. Lambert's only chance of success was support from the army. Unfortunately for Lambert many republicans waited upon events only, if they were not executed by Charles II, to rue their inaction later. The force Lambert gathered at Daventry disintegrated when faced by government forces. Lambert was captured and returned to the Tower. Others who had supported Lambert were rounded up.

Lambert's Rising failed because of the practical difficulties he faced. There was widespread discontent in the army but Lambert was recaptured before he could take advantage of this. To a large degree he was also hampered by what Reece has referred to as 'Repeated purges since summer 1659' which 'had shattered army unity'.

The New Model Army

The army found itself in different circumstances from 1647–9. It was essentially defensive in its posture in the late 1650s. According to Hutton (1993) the 'resources for a second English Revolution were present'. Ultimately this was never put to the test because of Monck's intervention and the collapse of control in London. Hutton (1993) argues that the officers 'possessed an ideological limitation which posed severe problems. The officers of the English army did not want government solely to themselves, but by 1659–60 they had no natural allies. They believed, like almost every Englishman of the age, that ultimate authority must rest in a parliament. Yet every parliament, even purged to a radical minority, had shown suspicion of them and their ideals'. Those who opposed monarchy were divided and unable to form a united front of opposition at the point, late in the day, when it became clear that Monck's actions were paving the way for a Restoration.

Venner's Rising, 1661

Perhaps the most visible attempt to overthrow Charles II was the Fifth Monarchist rising of Thomas Venner. Thomas Venner was a Fifth Monarchist who returned from New England in the 1650s. His attempted rising against Cromwell in 1657 was defeated and he had been imprisoned until February 1659. In *A Door of Hope* (1661) Venner denounced Charles II as an 'enemy, a rebel and a traitor to Christ'. The rising by Venner and his small number of supporters, no more than fifty, in London in January 1661 took three days to suppress. Their battle cry was 'King Jesus, and the heads upon the gates', references to their Fifth Monarchism and the displayed heads of those regicides who had been executed by the Restoration regime, mostly notably the Fifth Monarchist Major-General Thomas Harrison, set on a pole at Westminster Hall. Already there were the heads of Cromwell and Ireton. That the regime took three days to crush the small number of fanatics increased the panic in London. By the time Venner's men were finally crushed the regime had actually dispatched the Duke of York, Monck, the Earls of Oxford and Northampton and Lord Fairfax with 700 horses to deal with the rising.

Mass arrests followed as well as the persecution of nonconformists in London. The leading figures in the rising refused to give any information to the authorities. On 19 January 1661 Venner was hanged, drawn and quartered. Other executions followed. There were few other attempts to overthrow the government. In late 1662 six alleged plotters were hanged and others were given to Louis XIV as galley slaves.

Northern/Yorkshire plot, 1663

In 1663 there was the more serious 'Northern' or 'Yorkshire plot'. Fifty men gathered at Farnley Wood and others organised across Yorkshire. There were plans to coordinate with rebels from Ireland and Scotland. The numbers remained limited, however, and the lack of any immediate success against the organised forces of the state prevented others joining and any coordination of those rebels who had been prepared to act. Again the Northern Rising was more limited than it first appeared and Charles exaggerated the extent of the threat, according to Hutton, to 'rally support for his increasingly unpopular rule'.

Other failed risings of these early years of the reign also proved limited:

- Yarrington/Packington plot.
- Tong plot.
- Dublin plot.
- Rathbone plot.

There is little doubt that a chief problem for opposition was the persecution and action taken by the regime. Miller has stressed that Charles II was 'the first English king to have even a small standing army in peacetime'. The following measures helped to prevent opposition:

- Purging of Corporations weakened dissenters and potential opposition – many more changes than during the Interregnum.
- Summer of 1662: In preparation for the imposition of the intolerant Church Settlement in August, the regime prepared its forces.

> ### ■ Did you know?
> The diarist Samuel Pepys recorded seeing the heads of Cromwell, Ireton and Bradshaw when he was at Westminster on 5 February 1661. There were reports that the heads were still there in the 1680s.

- September: Five army regiments ordered to be raised.
- December: Under the May 1662 Militia Act Lord Lieutenants levied £70,000 for the year to support troops.
- 1663 Act allowed each Militia unit to be kept up for 14 days at a time, in effect allowing the Militia to be in constant readiness.
- Charles had about 8,000 soldiers at his disposal alongside the militia.

These measures, coupled with the disheartening impact of the Restoration, the treatment meted out to the regicides in 1660 and the changing nature of nonconformity to be more introspective meant that opposition to the regime can be seen, in hindsight, as ineffective and limited.

The changed nature of Republicanism also limited opposition. For Miller the 'lack of republican activism after 1660 might seem strange, but doctrinaire republicans had never been numerous and many with such sympathies, conditioned to see earthly events as the workings of God's Providence, reacted to the Restoration with either perplexity or fatalism'. Milton's response was *Paradise Lost*. David Norbrook has illustrated that the poem's 'overall intellectual and generic structures' were imbued with republicanism. The poem adopts a range of classical references which were characteristic of the English republican tradition. Keeble has concluded that Paradise Lost 'articulates a republican discourse' but ultimately it was an introspective personal response. Harris has argued that:

> In the changed context of the Restoration, seeking the abolition of monarchy made little practical sense. Yet there were still many who continued to promote the cause of greater political, religious and economic liberty and justice, and who challenged the authority structures in both Church and state, even if they accommodated themselves to working within a monarchical framework. In other words, the champions of the 'Good Old Cause' might have come to favour a republic in the 1650s, whereas after 1660 support for a republic might have all but disappeared, but this should not lead us to conclude that support for the 'Good Old Cause' had necessarily all but disappeared.

6   *T. Harris, **Restoration: Charles II and His Kingdoms** (2005)*

 Activity

Thinking point

List the weaknesses of the opposition to Charles II. Which weakness was the most important?

Learning outcomes

From this section you will have gained an understanding of Cromwell as Lord Protector, including theories of government as well as the Republican, royalist and military opposition to the Protectorate. You will also consider the influence of radical religious groupings, particularly the Fifth Monarchists and Quakers, but also the wider context of ideas of religious toleration. You will also have gained an understanding of reactions to the Major-Generals and how this was part of a crisis of 1657 about the direction of settlement. You have examined the main features of Cromwell's foreign policy, including overseas trade and the use of sea power. You will also have gained an understanding of republican divisions, 1658–60, the failure of republicanism and the Restoration Settlement, 1658–67. This consideration of the Restoration Settlement has also provided you with a context for considering Charles II and royal government to 1667, the role of Clarendon, Charles II's relations with France and the Netherlands, Charles II's religious policies to 1667 and the failure of opposition to Charles II to 1667.

AQA Examination-style questions

Why did the governments of the Interregnum fail to find an acceptable settlement in politics and religion?

As with all essays a clear structure will help you convey your argument clearly. One approach is a thematic structure. This is particularly useful given that there is only a limited amount that you can write under exam conditions. You should isolate the key themes that made it difficult for the Interregnum regimes to achieve an 'acceptable settlement' such as:

- internal instability/division
- radicalism
- economic and social breakdown
- conservative reaction.

The main themes should also be broken down in examples of precise evidence selected to illustrate and explain the theme.

For example, the Quakers are a key group to explain the radicalism of the period which hampered settlement, not only in that they threatened the new rulers but also were the group that most unsettled the traditional elite who saw their emergence as a consequence of the revolution. Fear of the Quakers grew and became particularly intense in the period 1658-60. In illustrating the threat of the Quakers reference could be made to the following evidence:

- Ideas a threat to the established order.
- Increasing numbers/movement across the country.
- Nayler incident.
- Impact on Monck, 1658–60.

The Consolidation of Charles II's Rule, 1667–78

Division and Persecution

Fig. 1 *A 17th century coffee house*

In this chapter you will learn about:

- the key ministers of Charles II
- the relationship between Crown and Parliament, including issues of finance
- the emergence of Tories and Whigs
- the continuing support for Republicanism.

Fig. 2 *Charles II, the King who returned monarchy to Britain*

The role of key personalities: Charles II and his ministers

The Cabal, 1667–74

For Seaward (1989) the dismissal of Clarendon in 1667 marked 'the end of an administration and of a policy'. Clarendon's fall allowed the rise of a new group of advisors that became known as the Cabal:

C – Clifford, Sir Thomas: Treasurer of the Household.

A – Ashley, Baron: Chancellor of the Exchequer.

B – Buckingham: the Duke.

A – Arlington, Lord: Secretary of State.

L – Lauderdale: Charles's Commissioner in Scotland.

A closer look

Profiles of the Cabal

Clifford – Thomas Clifford, first Baron Clifford of Chudleigh, 1630–73

Catholic royalist promoted through favour of Arlington, became a Privy Councillor in 1666. Pro-French and anti-Dutch, he helped to negotiate the Secret Treaty of Dover. Advised Charles to stop the Exchequer and publish the Declaration of Indulgence.

Made Lord Treasurer in 1672. Opposed the Test Act of 1673, resigning from office.

Ashley – Anthony Ashley Cooper, first Earl of Shaftesbury, 1621–83

Initially a royalist but changed sides in 1644. Member of Council of State in 1653 but then joined opposition. Part of the delegation to the Hague to invite Charles to England in 1660. Made Lord Ashley in 1661 and appointed Chancellor of the Exchequer. In 1672 made Lord Chancellor and Lord Shaftesbury. Supported Declaration of Indulgence and Test Act. After fall of Cabal became involved with Monmouth. Attempt to impeach the Duke of York as recusant but took a leading role in the Exclusion Crisis. Planned a rising in 1682 but fled into exile.

Buckingham – Villiers, George, second Duke of Buckingham, 1628–87

His father was the favourite of both James I and Charles I but was assassinated in 1628. He was educated with Charles II and James II as boys at the court of Charles I. Fought in second civil war and at Worcester. Returned to England in 1657 and married Mary Fairfax, but imprisoned until 1660. Appointed to Privy Council in 1662 and chief opponent of Hyde, with whom he had fallen out during the years of exile in the 1650s. Supported Declaration of Indulgence. Commons pressured Charles into dismissing him in 1674 and Arlington had also turned against him. Joined Shaftesbury in opposition but did not support Exclusion and withdrew from politics.

Arlington – Bennet, Henry, first earl of Arlington, 1618–85

Catholic who fought in civil war and advisor to Charles II during exile. Supported Dutch War in 1660s and created Lord Arlington in 1665. Opposed Clarendon. Constructed Triple Alliance with Dutch and Sweden in 1668 but he was also the main force in securing the Treaty of Dover. The Test Act forced his chief ally, Clifford, to resign. Arlington lost influence with the rise of Danby.

Lauderdale – Maitland, John, second Earl and first Duke of Lauderdale, 1616–82

Scottish Presbyterian who supported the Covenant in rebellion against Charles I after 1638 but then promoted the Engagement from December 1647 whereby the Scots invaded England in an attempt to restore Charles I's authority in England. After the regicide he supported Charles Stuart. Captured at Worcester and imprisoned until 1660. Appointed Secretary of State for Scotland at the Restoration. Persecuted Conventicles in Scotland. Resigned in 1680.

Fig. 3 *Anthony Ashley Cooper, the Earl of Shaftesbury*

■ Key terms

Crypto-Catholics: those Catholics who kept their Catholicism as secret or 'closet' to maintain their political roles or position at court.

Freethinkers: those who were outside the Church of England and did not believe in the literal truth of the Bible. They believed that the world could be understood through examining nature.

If the Cabal had anything in common it was that they were not Anglicans.

■ Clifford was a **crypto-Catholic**.

■ Arlington was a Catholic sympathiser.

■ Lauderdale supported the Scottish compromise of the Presbyterian Church with episcopacy.

■ Ashley and Buckingham have been described as '**Freethinkers**'.

The Cabal had no coordinated policy. There were a number of reasons for this:

- The differences between them.
- The approach of Charles II.
- The very nature of having government in the hands of a range of men.
- The removal of the dominance of Clarendon.

Only Clifford and Ashley worked closely together in trying to improve finances. Lauderdale was based in Scotland, Arlington and Buckingham hated each other. Arlington probably, through his hard work, did most to shape policy. In contrast Buckingham was a debauched dilettante, but, because of this, was closest to the King.

Charles, like many skilful rulers, used the differences between his ministers to his advantage. By playing them off against each other, he strengthened his own position. All were aware of their reliance on the favour of the King. Charles was very much a pragmatist with his main aim being the maintenance of his authority.

There were two general aims in this period:

- Extend religious toleration to Catholics and Dissenters.
- An alliance with France.

The Cabal had led to the development of what have been labelled 'court' and 'country' and the emergence of a more defined division that was to come to a head after 1678. It was to be the end of the Third Dutch war and the fall of Buckingham and Arlington in 1674 that marked the end of the attempt to broaden toleration and the Cabal.

Sir Thomas Osborne, Earl of Danby

The emergence of Danby symbolised the shift to Anglican policies, the support for Crown and Church. He could build on a Court grouping established in the Commons, notably by Arlington. Through patronage, Arlington became known as the 'Bribe Master General'. Charles did not like Danby, but recognised his political talent. In the end, however, Danby's position was weakened by the limits of Charles's support. Hutton (2004) found that in the 1670s and 1680s Charles became even less guiding with his ministers. Charles was a weak director of his ministers, but this approach allowed him to use them as scapegoats.

There was an interrelation between foreign policy, religious policy and finance, all shaping the relationship between Crown and Parliament. In turn any consideration of these issues by parliament would have a constitutional subtext.

Relations between Crown and Parliament, including issues of finance

Initially domestic politics took place in the context of the disasters of the Dutch war, the plague and the Great Fire of London. All seemed a judgement on the decadence of Charles's kingship.

Finance was, as ever, an issue between Crown and Parliament. In 1665 royal income was £820,000; by 1666–7 it had fallen to £647,000. The perspective of MPs was that the problems were due to crown mismanagement rather than structural problems with the financial system.

Cross-reference

For Charles's relations with France see Chapters 7 and 9.

Cross-reference

For the post-1678 political division see Chapter 10.

Fig. 4 *Thomas Osborne, Earl of Danby*

Key dates

Danby's rise to power:

1665 MP
1668 Treasurer of the Navy
1672 Privy Councillor
1673 Lord Treasurer
1674 Created Earl of Danby

■ A closer look

Problems of financial reform

The lack of fundamental reform to the Crown's finances was not just a problem for Charles II, but had been a problem that had bedevilled all early modern monarchs. Elizabeth I (1558–1603) had not updated the sources of income and with a sustained period of inflation the weakness in crown income was exacerbated. Major reform was needed but it was safer politically for monarchs to organise their finances in the short-term than undertake financial reforms which, by definition, would mean challenging the interests of the political nation represented in Parliament.

That the situation was so bad was recognised by James I's first chief minister, who had also been chief minister under Elizabeth I, Robert Cecil. In 1610 he started negotiating with Parliament a major reform of the Crown's finances, the Great Contract. In return for an annual grant from Parliament of £200,000 and the removal of debts of about £600,000, the Crown would give up some prerogative income. Both crown and parliament felt they had too much to lose in such an agreement and reform was never attempted again under James. It took civil war and the establishment of republican rule (1649–60) after the execution of Charles I in 1649 for real changes to the finances of the state to take place.

With the restoration of monarchy under Charles II, the Crown finances essentially resorted to their traditional short-term methods. It took another revolution, the Glorious Revolution of 1688–9 when James II was removed because of his Catholicism and absolutist tendencies and replaced with the Dutch, William of Orange (William III), before real reform of the Crown's finances took place that made the monarch reliant on parliament. It is in this context of 1558 to 1689 that Charles II's failure to reform the financial system should be considered. The financial restrictions he had to work under and his unwillingness to give power to parliament, or indeed parliament's failure to appreciate the need for reform, help to explain his reliance on Louis XIV for finance. It should also be noted, however, that there was an increased tax burden under Charles II compared to his father and his grandfather.

Corruption was certainly rife. In late 1666, the Commons began to investigate the accounts of the navy. In February 1667 Parliament appointed Commissioners to examine the public accounts when it gave a parliamentary grant of £1,800,000. Parliament used finance to try to restrict the greater religious freedom that Charles wanted to allow. In 1667 the Treasury Commission reduced expenditure and made credit easier to secure by instituting a system whereby the Crown's loans were repaid in the sequence in which they had been granted.

In 1669 the Commons used its financial influence in response to concerns about Charles's decision to allow the Conventicle Act to expire in 1668. Their refusal to grant £300,000 forced Charles to issue a much more rigid Conventicle Act in 1670.

Post 1672 – the emergence of division

The next session in 1672 marked a watershed in Charles's relationship with Parliament. The rest of the reign saw a focus on the threat of popery and arbitrary government with little trust between the 'court' and the political nation, the 'country'. Fundamental to this were the:

- Anglo-French attack on the Dutch
- Declaration of Indulgence
- Duke of York being a Catholic.

An attack on the Dutch Republic was planned for the spring of 1672 in coordination with the French. This would, naturally, require finance. With all the repayments of loans, the Crown would only have an income of about £400,000 in 1672. In light of this, on 20 January 1672 Charles II proclaimed the 'Stop of the Exchequer'. This suspended repayment of any more loans. This effectively meant that Charles was declaring the Crown bankrupt. It had an immediate effect on all those who had loaned the Crown money and also meant it would be very hard for Charles to secure any future loans. He needed money from parliament more than ever. Parliament gave the Crown £1.2 million to fund the attack on the Dutch.

When Parliament met again on 4 February 1673 they focused on Charles's Declaration of Indulgence. By a Commons vote of 168 to 116 on 24 February Parliament declared that only they could suspend the penal laws. This became a constitutional issue. Charles's response was that he had no desire to suspend any laws. In reaction the Commons declared that the King had 'no such power' to suspend laws and that power was never claimed by any previous monarch.

To get money from Parliament Charles had to withdraw the Declaration and issue a Test Act. Parliament voted Charles £1,126,000 in 18 monthly assessments and Charles adjourned Parliament on 29 March.

The next session of Parliament (January to February 1674) was marked by an attack on Arlington and Buckingham which Charles II did little to hinder. Buckingham was removed from all of his offices. Parliament refused to vote money and this forced Charles to end the Dutch war by the February 1674 Treaty of Westminster. The end of the Dutch war and the fall of Buckingham and Arlington in 1674 marked the end of the attempt to broaden toleration and the Cabal.

Danby and Parliament

Danby's emergence initially strengthened the position of the Crown in Parliament because he stood for policies in tune with the views of most MPs:

- No toleration but a rigid Church of England.
- An anti-French pro-Dutch foreign policy.

More important in influencing Parliament were Danby's efforts in building on Arlington's construction of a royalist grouping in Parliament through **crown patronage**.

By late 1675 Danby had 30 MPs receiving substantial crown pensions. Before parliamentary sessions, selected MPs received personalised letters directing them to support the Crown. Danby's political management reinforced for some that there was a design to impose Catholicism and absolutism on the country. Such fears were skilfully exploited by Shaftsbury and Buckingham.

Charles II declared at the meeting of Parliament in April 1675 that he would 'leave nothing undone that may show any zeal to the Protestant religion, as it is established in the Church of England, from which I will never depart'. A Test Bill was introduced by which all office-holders and MPs had to swear that the taking up of arms was unlawful and

Activity

Revision exercise

Explain the main sources of dispute between Crown and Parliament in this period.

Key terms

Crown patronage: the power of a monarch or leading crown ministers to bestow jobs or offices as a means to bind the recipient as a loyal client.

they should not seek to alter the government of the Church and state. This Bill was defeated by Shaftesbury and Arlington's opposition who portrayed it as an attempt to impose absolute government. With the defeat of the bill in April 1675 there was an attempt to impeach Danby.

In November 1675 Parliament only voted £300,000 for the navy and added to this a clause appropriating all customs revenues to support the navy rather than other areas of crown expenses. Danby had, however, improved the financial position of Charles II through restraint in his role as Lord Treasurer. More significantly the withdrawal from the Dutch War and a boom in trade cut costs and raised income. Between 1674 and 1677 royal income was an average of £1.4 million a year. Almost half of this came from customs revenue. Despite this Danby could not control Charles II's spending. The crown debt actually increased by £750,000 between 1674 and 1679. This meant that finance was to remain a crucial issue in shaping the relationship between Crown and Parliament.

In February 1677, Parliament reassembled. Shaftesbury and Buckingham were placed in the Tower for five months for claiming that as the Parliament had not met for 15 months new elections for a new Parliament should be held.

With continuing French success against the Dutch £600,000 was voted for the navy by Parliament. Any further money was conditional on an alliance against France. The constitutional dimension of this vote is clear from Charles's response. He argued that if 'I suffer this fundamental power of making peace and war to be so invaded' by Parliament then no other state 'would any longer believe that the sovereignty of England rests in the Crown'.

By the subsequent December 1677 Anglo-Dutch treaty Charles agreed to impose peace terms on Louis, by force if needed. Consequently in January 1678 Parliament voted to raise an army of 30,000 men and money of £1 million, although only £300,000 was raised by a Poll Tax.

■ The clash between Court and Country – the emergence of Tories and Whigs

Seaward, in his study of the *Cavalier Parliament* (1989), has argued that the impact of more regular sessions of parliament in the 1660s was the attempt to manage it more, particularly under Danby, and this produced the erosion of shared interest between court and country and led to mutual mistrust and the emergence of division in the period 1673–8. This was to come to a head with the attempt to exclude James, Duke of York, from the throne after 1678.

Charles's general aim of toleration for Dissenters and Catholics, while strengthening ties with Catholic absolutist France, was not popular. Opinion in the 'country' was generally opposition to the 'court'. England remained, on the whole, an anti-Catholic country with an elite wedded to an Anglican intolerant church. Coupled to these emotional political indexes the 'country' had a natural distrust of government, believing it corrupt and wasteful. The 'country' opposition was not, however, a defined political party. The 'country' position was to:

- defend the privileges or rights of Parliament against the Crown's prerogative
- defend Protestantism, domestically and abroad – thus hostility to Dissenters, Catholics and France.

In short, opposition to Catholicism and absolutism.

■ **Cross-reference**

For the Exclusion Crisis, see Chapter 10.

A closer look

Key opposition politicians

William Coventry, 1627–78

A self-confessed 'trimmer' (one who sought consensus) he was prominent in the attack on Clarendon in 1667 after which he removed himself from the service of the Duke of York. In 1669 he was imprisoned in the Tower for sending a challenge to the Duke of Buckingham who had caricatured him in the play *The Country Gentleman*. When released he abandoned the court and became prominent in the parliamentary attacks on Danby. He would not support Exclusion and went into self-imposed political retirement after the dissolution of July 1679.

Sir Thomas Meres, 1634–1715

Bitter at not receiving office, Meres was a critic of Danby and supported Exclusion. Gradually his fear of popery softened his attitude to dissent.

William Cavendish, 1641–1707

In the 1670s moved towards a 'country' position because of fear of popery, the French and distrust of the Stuarts. In 1673 and 1674 he made frequent parliamentary attacks on the Cabal. Played an active role in the attempt to impeach Danby. More moderate in relation to Exclusion Cavendish actually voted against it in 1679. Resigned with other Whigs from the Privy Council in 1680. Supported Exclusion in October 1680 but never Monmouth. Cavendish distanced himself from the more aggressive Whigs. An opponent of James II he had established contact with William of Orange's emissary, Dykvelt. One of seven men who invited William to England he fully supported the regime of William III.

William Russell, 1639–83

Insignificant until 1673, he emerged as a leading opponent of the popery and absolutism of the Stuarts. Russell became a chief ally of Shaftesbury. Supported Exclusion. Resigned from the Privy Council with other Whigs in 1680. In 1683 arrested in relation to the Rye House Plot and executed.

William Sacheverell, 1637–91

A leading critic of the court and supporter of Exclusion. After the defeat of the Exclusion Bill in the Lords in November 1680, however, Sacheverell moved to become part of the Tory reaction to the extent that he was regarded as a 'collaborator' of James II. He did not take any role in the revolution of 1688.

The Cabal had led to the development of what have been labelled 'Court' and 'Country'. By the collapse of the Cabal in 1674 the 'Country' grouping had added to its number Buckingham and Shaftesbury. There was clearly some coordination of parliamentary strategy by the 'Country' grouping in 1673–4. The 1674 founding of the Green Ribbon Club in a London tavern can be seen as a more formal organisation of an 'opposition' grouping.

Danby's emergence and a more Anglican pro-Dutch policy did not ease the Court/Country division. Danby's policies were portrayed, particularly by Buckingham, as another attempt to impose arbitrary government. In trying to create a government body of MPs, Danby could be seen as trying to subvert the role of Parliament. In November 1675, the pamphlet *A Letter from a Person of Quality to his Friend in the Country* was published. Probably written by Shaftesbury, this pamphlet argued that there was a conspiracy to impose absolutism by a 'distinct party' of 'high episcopal' and 'cavalier' men through a standing army. They sought to turn Parliament into a body that merely supplied money to the Crown.

Although MPs did not know it, there was some foundation to claims that Danby was a threat to parliament in Charles's ties to Louis XIV, especially the financial aid the Catholic absolutist king provided in order that Charles would not keep Parliament in session. Country opposition pushed Charles into keeping Parliament prorogued between November 1675 and February 1677. In December 1677 Andrew Marvell's *An Account of the Growth of Popery and Arbitrary Government* argued that for some years there had been a 'design' to establish England 'into an absolute tyranny, and to convert the established Protestant religion into downright Popery'.

Key profile

Andrew Marvell (1621–78)

Poet and politician. In 1650 produced *An Horatian Ode upon Cromwell's return from Ireland*. At this time he became tutor in languages to Fairfax's daughter, Mary, later to marry the second Duke of Buckingham. While in Fairfax's employment he produced *Upon Nun Appleton House*, read by some as a veiled attack on Cromwell, although in 1655 Marvell's *First Anniversary of Government under Oliver Cromwell* was published. In 1657 Marvell became a Latin Secretary in Thurloe's office. Elected an MP for Hull in the Convention Marvell gradually became disillusioned with Charles II finally producing *An Account of the Growth of Popery and Arbitrary Government*.

Activity

Revision exercise

In what ways did Danby and the royal policies he represented create concern for MPs?

After the Dutch and French signed the Peace of Nijmegen in 1678, Charles prorogued Parliament but kept his 30,000 troops and thus raised the spectre of the imposition of absolutism through a standing army. When it came into the open that Danby had gone along with Charles's continuing links with the French while getting money from Parliament and raising troops it totally undermined his position in Parliament and he was sacrificed in 1678.

Harris (2005) has argued that 'over the period 1660–78 the Crown experienced a considerable loss of prestige'. His judgement is based on the following criteria:

Activity

Challenge your thinking

To what extent was it fear of Charles's intentions rather than his actual policies that was more responsible for the breakdown of Crown and Parliament relations?

■ A monarch was supposed to be majestic.
■ A monarch was expected to achieve glory for his nation through foreign policy.
■ An English monarch was supposed to defend the Protestant faith.
■ A monarch was supposed to protect the subjects in lawful rights.

For Harris in 'all these respects the Restoration regime proved a bitter disappointment' and it was this that provoked a 'country' or 'Whig' reaction and the Exclusion Crisis. The terms Whig and Tory themselves became widely used by 1681. Smith in his study of *The Stuart Parliaments* (1999) argued that both the Whigs and Tories derived from the 'country' and 'court'.

There developed a social segregation based around taverns, coffee-houses and clubs aligned to Whigs or Tories. Whigs saw Tories as promoting popery; Tories saw Whigs as Republicans.

Tories believed in:

- divine right
- civil authority that came from God
- no right of resistance, even against tyranny
- the threat of absolutism from nonconformists, republicans and Parliament
- Church of England.

Whigs believed in:

- civil authority from people
- right of resistance against tyranny – contract of government
- threat of absolutism linked to Catholicism
- Parliament representative of people and protector of Protestantism, liberty
- being more favourable towards dissent.

The political division under Charles II was reflected in the absolutist writings of Filmer and anti-absolutism responses. It has been argued by Smith (1998) that it is 'from these contrasting outlooks that the political ideologies associated with Whigs and Tories gradually emerged'.

> ### Did you know?
> 'Whig' and 'Tory' came from terms of abuse. A Whig was a Scottish Presbyterian of the late 1640s whereas a Tory was an Irish Catholic cattle thief.

A closer look

Robert Filmer, author of *Patriarcha*

Although it was not published until 1680 Filmer actually tried to get *Patriarcha* published in 1632. The request for a licence to print was passed to Charles I himself. He refused permission to publish it. The subtitle of Filmer's work is indicative of his argument – 'The naturall power of kings defended against the unnatural liberty of the people'. It was published in 1680 through the influence of Archbishop Sancroft to promote the Tory cause. It provoked its main written response from John Locke in his *Treatise of Two Governments*, which itself was not published until 1690.

There were three main parts to *Patriarcha*:

1 Refuted arguments that people were originally free and that political authority originated in the consent of these people.

2 In contrast Filmer identified political authority with patriarchal authority – no one was ever free as all royal-patriarchal authority descended from Adam. While some kings may have been elected by their people, the origin of the monarch's power was divinely instituted at creation.

3 From these he interpreted the development of the English Constitution.

For Filmer, Parliament was only called from the time of Henry I (1100–35) and therefore the people had no right to representation.

It was to be out of the politics of the Exclusion Crisis (the attempt to prevent the Catholic James Duke of York succeeding to the throne) that the terms Whigs and Tories became more common. Yet this division was rooted in the Court/Country division of these years.

■ Key profile

John Locke (1632–1704)

Philosopher. It was probably Shaftesbury and Locke who produced the attack on Danby in *A Letter from a Person of quality to his Friend in the Country*, in part explaining the three and a half years Locke spent in France from November 1675. He returned to England in 1679, but retreated to Rotterdam on account of his acquaintance with some of those involved in the Rye House Plot. Locke was to remain in the Netherlands until the revolution of 1689, when his most famous work, *Two Treatises of Government*, was finally published, albeit anonymously.

The edition of the *Treatises* edited by Peter Laslett (1988) firmly placed Locke's *Two Treatises* in the context of the early 1680s when it was written as an anti-absolutist response to Filmer's *Patriarcha* (published in 1680). John Dunn (1983) has shown that the *Two Treatises* provoked little response at its publication. Only in the 18th century did Locke's work become more widely read. John Marshall has even questioned how far Locke was 'revolutionary' seeing his work as essentially part of conservative Whig country-gentry culture. *The Two Treatises* was only reprinted once between 1714 and 1763. Locke's work acquired new significance and more readers as a result of America's struggle for independence, being published in America for the first time in 1773.

■ Continuing support for Republicanism

The apparent threat of Catholicism and absolutism saw a growth of republicanism in the mid-1670s. In London, in particular, republican literature was circulated in manuscript form. Taverns and coffee-houses acted as centres of information.

Care is needed in defining the nature of republicanism in the 17th century as well as in its post-Restoration incarnation compared to the years of the Interregnum. There is some debate about the nature of Republicanism and who the republicans were under Charles II. Smith (1998) has suggested that in this period Republicanism was 'less an ideological commitment to republican forms of government than a growing disillusionment with Charles'. Increasingly the experience of Charles's rule and the threat of his Catholic heir made monarchy seem a threat.

It was probably this form of popular Republicanism that was more widely significant at the time than the works of the leading republican theorists Henry Neville or Algernon Sidney. Neville was a Republican and friend of Harrington. In 1679 he produced his major work *Plato redivivus*. In response to the threat of Stuart absolutism, Neville argued along the lines of a Harringtonian rotation of power strongly limiting the powers of the Crown. Sidney, in his Court Maxims of 1665–1666, argued for rebellion against the Stuarts. In his *Discourses Concerning Government* in 1683 Sidney attacked Filmer's *Patriarcha* and defended the principles of liberty, reason and virtue within the context of Greek Christian humanism as well as Machiavellian and Roman militarism.

■ Activity

Thinking point

Why was there continuing support for Republicanism? How was Republicanism in the post-Restoration period different from that in the years of revolution?

Other republicans, like John Ayloffe, used pamphlets to argue for a Venetian-style republic. In 1672 in *Nostradamus's Prophecy* he attacked Charles II's subservience to the French. During the Third Dutch War Ayloffe, with his close friend Andrew Marvell, worked for the Dutch to undermine the French. In his poem of 1678, 'Marvell's Ghost', he portrayed the poet coming back from the dead to prophesy the end of the Stuarts. Ayloffe did much to link in the popular imagination Charles II's French alliance with the threat of popery in England through his pamphlet, *Englands Appeale from the Private Caballe at Whitehall* (1673).

As the economic and therefore political balance between king, lords and commons had shifted there was a need for a new form of government. Such socio-economic arguments can be seen as the basis of Harrington's republican text of 1656, *Oceana*. For Houston, in *A Nation Transformed* (2001), economic developments were at the root of some thinking about the nature of representation in this period and considering republicanism as a reflection of changing political, social and economic networks in England.

Republicanism was one response to the obvious dangers of a royal prerogative that was still left undefined by the ancient constitution at the Restoration.

 Activity

Stretch and challenge

Was post-Restoration republicanism fundamentally weakened by the experience of 1649 to 1660?

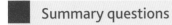 **Summary questions**

1. How did Danby try to manage Parliament?
2. How much of a threat was republicanism in the years 1667 to 1678?

9 Domestic and Foreign Divisions

Key terms

Comprehension: the aim of broadening the established Church of England to allow a greater range of non-conformists to conform to and come within the Church of England.

Cross-reference

For the Clarendon Code see Chapter 7.

Divisions between Anglicans and Dissenters

The restored Church of England was a broader church than Charles I's Laudian dominated church. Some Presbyterians were absorbed into the Restoration church. What was also different about the Restoration church was that it was, in effect, under the control of Parliament rather than the King. Thus in the years 1660 to 1688 the Cavalier and Tory Anglicanism of many MPs led to the persecution of dissent. Both in 1667 and 1668 **comprehension** bills were drafted by MPs only to be not presented to the Commons which was predominantly against broadening the church settlement to include more non-conformists.

Charles II, who wanted a more comprehensive Church, did not seek to have the Conventicle Act renewed and therefore it expired in 1668. Nonconformists could now meet freely. Generally Dissent was stronger in urban areas where there was more likely to be a ruling elite with shared ideas or some sympathy. In such areas JPs and local magistrates were less prone to impose the full weight of the harsh Clarendon Code than the more conservative rural elite. For some non-conformity was a link to the recent Interregnum where the New Model protected non-conformists from persecution. Against this greater freedom for Dissenters were the majority of country gentry who not only had power in the localities but were also represented in Parliament. They worked with the sympathetic bishops who also had a power base in Parliament through their seats in the Lords.

In 1669, as a reaction to the lapsing of the Conventicle Act, the Commons refused to grant a subsidy of £300,000. This had the desired effect for in 1670 Charles allowed a more rigid Conventicle Act in return for parliamentary funds:

- Extraordinary taxation.
- Grants of new duties on imported wines for eight years.
- Additional excise for nine years.

On 15 March 1672 Charles issued a second Declaration of Indulgence in England. In this Charles stated his **suspending power** in relation to all the penal laws against Catholics and nonconformists. As a consequence, if the preacher had a royal licence nonconformists could worship in public. Protestant Dissenters and Catholics could however never form a bond together and the general anti-Catholic hatred of the bulk of the population remained strong. Many were suspicious of Charles's intentions with regard to Catholics, reinforced by the alliance with Catholic France against the Dutch.

Parliament protested against the Declaration as being unconstitutional. To get money from Parliament Charles had to withdraw the Declaration and issue a Test Act. The emergence of Danby after the collapse of the Cabal in 1674 led to a reversion to a more rigid religious policy focusing on support for the Church of England and no moves towards toleration as a means to increase the influence of the Crown. As Miller (2000) has stressed, the Commons became more hostile to Dissent as they sought to protect what they regarded as the 'Cavalier' regime from the increasing threat of Dissent, an absolutist France and the threat of absolutism and Catholicism at home. In this context Dissent and the Declaration had a significant impact on the politics of the Exclusion Crisis and the subsequent Tory reaction.

Key terms

Suspending power: prerogative to suspend operation of any law. Used by Charles and James to suspend penal laws against Catholics.

Fig. 1 *Anti-Catholicism would be a long-standing issue in British politics. Here King William III and Queen Mary are pressing the Pope's nose to the grindstone (engraving c.1690)*

> The Declaration had directly challenged the very being of the established church. Having been made brutally aware that they could not trust the king to protect their interests, those who loved the Church realized that they had to stand up and fight, in the political arena and using the machinery of government and law. The Declaration, far from calming religious animosities, had enflamed them.

 J. Miller, *After the Civil Wars: English Politics and Government in the Reign of Charles II* (2000)

Activity

Revision exercise

Construct a chart with three columns, listing in the first the religious measures enacted in this period, in the second a summary of what they said and in the third, their significance.

Persecution of non-conformity was certainly more the hallmark of Charles's regime than toleration, especially when compared to the 1650s. Baptists and Quakers suffered more persecution than other groups. In 1662 the Quaker Act had outlined a series of punishments for Quakers, ranging from fines to transportation. At least 450 Quakers died in prison under Charles's regime and at least 15,000 suffered some form of punishment, whether fines, imprisonment or transportation. The height of persecution was the early 1670s and early 1680s. Several thousand Dissenters died as a result of persecution.

Exploring the detail

The role of women in the early modern period, was, traditionally, not an area of extensive study. Given the roles assigned to women in the early modern period a gender based study can be problematic because the surviving sources can be limited. Over recent decades there have increasingly been more studies of the role of women in history and such gender history adds a fuller picture to our understanding of the past. An example of a study with focus on women but within the broader framework of the early modern period is Amy Louise Erickson's *Women and Property in Early Modern England* (1993).

Nature of nonconformity

Dissenter numbers come from the Compton Census, named after Bishop Henry Compton. Ordered by Danby in 1676, it suggested 100,000 nonconformists out of an adult population of 2.25 million in England and Wales. These numbers only included those regarded as hard line non-conformists and therefore it has been estimated that the actual figure of nonconformists was between 200,000 and 300,000. Much of the Anglican reaction to nonconformity was an overreaction to the fear that derived from the knowledge that Dissent was widespread and would be impossible to wipe out.

Women were fundamental in the survival of Dissent. Women played a crucial role in the Quaker movement. Forty-five per cent of the Quakers sent as missionary ministers to America in the period 1656 to 1663 were women. Patricia Crawford has indicated that women outnumbered men two to one in separatist churches and stressed the importance of 'household religion and female piety'. It was mothers 'who taught their children on a daily basis about the importance of their faith' that 'ensured the perpetuation of Nonconformity'.

The impact of the Interregnum and the Restoration had actually made nonconformity, in general, less militant. For all nonconformists introspection became a chief feature rather than public faith. For many the Restoration was interpreted as God's judgement on their cause.

A closer look

John Milton's experience of defeat

The poet John Milton was not alone in the despair he felt at the Restoration. His last three poems dealt with the experience of defeat. *Paradise Lost*, started in 1658, was finished in 1665. His next work, *Paradise Regained* and then *Samson Agonistes*, were both formed by his experience of the defeat of the revolution. Milton was also reflecting on the Restoration and the immediate revenge wrought against the regicides and the disinterment from their Westminster Abbey tombs, and public exhibition on gallows, of the bodies of Cromwell, Bradshaw and Ireton.

In *Samson Agonistes* there was a message for readers and Milton specifically referred to the work as 'exemplary to a Nation'. Milton's message was that God had judged them unworthy of the liberty they had and had returned them to bondage. Republican thinkers had made errors, had been too proud but had also failed to act to protect the republic, especially in 1658–9. Yet Milton's political purpose in *Samson Agonistes* was to give hope to those who continued to support the 'Good Old Cause' as the means of eventual delivery from the evils of monarchy. They must, like Samson, face their current persecution with godly strength, aware of their ultimate victory.

The experience of defeat made nonconformists more passive. The most obvious and extreme example of this was the Quaker movement which had moved from countenancing armed struggle in 1659–1660 to being an essentially pacifist movement in the 1660s.

With the removal of James Nayler, the Quaker movement came increasingly under the influence of the other leading Quaker, George Fox. Between August 1659 and the beginning of 1660 Fox withdrew from all activity undergoing something close to a spiritual nervous breakdown. In 1661 came the first official Quaker declaration of 'absolute pacifism' as a result of disillusion with the lack of impact of their political action and self-preservation in the face of the Restoration. Fox's position was helped by the deaths of the other leading figures of the movement from the 1650s, not just Nayler. Fox rewrote Quaker history in his *Journal*, taking care to ignore Nayler's role.

Fig. 2 *The sufferings of Quakers under Charles II: imprisonment, fines and transportation*

Dissent also had a limited appeal after the Restoration:

- It needed a level of spiritual commitment only some could manage.
- The emphasis on the Bible tended to exclude the illiterate.
- Sermons could last hours.

In contrast Anglicanism was less demanding, the physical element to service and repetitive nature being more accessible. As with the nonconformists there was a similar retreat from religious fervour by Anglicans that was part of the development of **Latitudinarianism**. Such men were more in favour of a wider toleration than the majority Anglican view that still held sway in the Church and more markedly across the gentry.

Another factor limiting the impact of Dissent was the division among Dissenters. Miller (2000) has stressed that although the relationship between the Church and Dissent was a major issue into the next century, the differing non-conformist groups were not fused into one entity called Dissent. There were significant differences which led to a continuing polemical battle between Presbyterians, Independents, Baptists and Quakers.

A key part of the continuing importance of religion was the struggle between the Church and Dissent. For Harris (2005) the failure of the Restoration religious settlement meant that the political divisions were rooted in religious divisions. For Knights in *Representation* (2006) 'Controversy over religion was seldom solely about private belief, but also or mainly about public practice and the ideal relationship between civil and religious power. We can therefore call most of the arguments about religion consciously political in some form or other'.

Key terms

Latitudinarianism: a belief that reason and personal judgement are more useful than church doctrine.

Activity

Revision exercise

Summarise the weakness in the position of the following groups:

- Republicans.
- Dissenters.
- Quakers.

The impact of the Test Act

March 1673 – First Test Act

Imposes oaths designed to exclude Catholics from public office.

The 1673 Test Act required all office holders to swear the Oaths of Supremacy and Allegiance as well as take a declaration against the

Catholic doctrine of transubstantiation. Office holders would also need to provide documents proving they had recently received Communion in the Church of England.

An immediate impact of the Test Act was Parliament's 1673 vote of £1,126,000 in 18 monthly assessments for Charles. The most important impact of the Test Act was that James, Duke of York, who would be the next king, went public with his Catholicism when he failed to take communion in Easter 1673. James had probably converted to Catholicism as early as 1668. As a result of the Test Act in June 1673 James had to resign as Lord High Admiral and Clifford had to resign as Lord Treasurer.

The Dutch played upon the anti-Catholicism of the English and the fears provoked by public knowledge of James's Catholicism. The English agent of William of Orange produced the pamphlet *England's Appeal from the Private Cabal at Whitehall to the Great Council of the Nation* in February 1673. The key theme of this work was the link between France, popery and absolutism. The English had traditionally linked absolutism and Catholicism and so this propaganda was pushing at an open door. Furthermore from Charles I's reign there had been a fear of a Popish plot at court and this was now revived by such pamphlets in terms of the court working with France to establish absolutism in England.

The threat posed appeared greater when in September 1673 James married again to the Catholic princess, Mary of Modena, whose family were clients of Louis XIV. The exposure of James's Catholicism and the threat of a line of catholic monarchs was a key factor in what was to become the Exclusion Crisis of 1678-83. In response to James's marriage the Commons actually demanded that the marriage should not be consummated. Anti-Catholicism was still a significant political force. In November 1678 a Second Test Act to exclude Catholics from both Houses of Parliament, with a special exemption for James, Duke of York, was passed.

■ Charles II's relations with France and the Netherlands, 1667–78

Fig. 3 *Departure of William of Orange and Princess Mary for Holland, 19 November 1677 (National Maritime Museum, Greenwich, London)*

■ **Activity**

Write a definition of Dissent.

How were the Dissenters persecuted in this period?

■ **Key dates**

1667 Second Dutch War ended by Treaty of Breda

1668 Formation of the Triple Alliance between England, Dutch Republic and Sweden

1670 Secret Treaty of Dover

1672 Start of the Third Dutch War

1674 Treaty of Westminster

1676 Louis promises Charles more subsidies to keep Parliament prorogued

1677 Alliance with Dutch against France

1678 Peace of Nijmegen

Louis XIV was Charles II's cousin and Charles's experience of the power of the French monarchy during his time on the continent seems to have made an impression on him. Under Louis XIV, who became king in 1643 at the age of four, France had emerged as the most powerful European state. Relations with France dominated Charles's foreign policy.

The 1667–1668 War of Devolution centred on Louis XIV's claim that his wife, the Spanish Infanta Maria, was the rightful heir to 14 provinces in the Spanish Netherlands. With a lightening war against Spain he secured twelve fortified places within the Spanish Netherlands. The cost, however, was the end of the traditional alliance with the Dutch Republic. In January 1668, a Triple Alliance between England, the Dutch Republic and Sweden was formed. Louis' response was to seek an alliance with his cousin, Charles II. Using his ambassador Croissy he began negotiations with Charles II that ended in three different versions of a treaty, the most important being the Secret Treaty of Dover of 1670.

The different versions of the Treaty of Dover

	Public Treaty	The Secret Treaty of London	The Secret Treaty of Dover
Known to	Public	All of the Cabal and all of the Privy Council within a year of its signing	Charles; Arlington; Clifford; James, Duke of York
Signed	February 1672	21 December 1670	22 May 1670
Term: Attack on the Dutch	Naval and military attack on Dutch by England and France	Naval and military attack on Dutch by England and France	Naval and military attack on Dutch by England and France. France would provide 6,000 men and £150,000
Term: the future of the Dutch Republic	Parts of the Dutch Republic (more than stated in the Secret Treaty) would be taken by the English and French with the rest ruled by Charles II's nephew, William of Orange	Parts of the Dutch Republic (more than stated in the Secret Treaty) would be taken by the English and French with the rest ruled by Charles II's nephew, William of Orange	Parts of the Dutch Republic would be taken by the English and French with the rest ruled by Charles II's nephew, William of Orange
Term: French aid to Charles II			France would pay Charles £225,000 a year
Term: Charles II's Catholicism			Charles II was to declare himself Catholic when he could

Public knowledge of the Secret Treaty of Dover would have destroyed Charles II. No definitive answer can be given as to why Charles signed it.

For Hill (1961) it represents Charles's true beliefs, but which he was sensible enough to recognise that he could not pursue. Miller (1991) has seen it more as a product of a burst of pro-Catholic enthusiasm that did not last. It could also be seen as a means for Charles to make the alliance more attractive to Louis. Jones (1987) has seen the Catholicity clause as the only way that Charles could put pressure on Louis after a successful war against the Dutch. By delaying any conversion he could try to ensure that Louis did not abandon him as a fellow Catholic who by doing so would also imperil the survival of English Catholicism.

It could also be argued that the Catholicity clause was opportunistic, that Charles never had any intention of acting on it and his aims were essentially diplomatic. These other factors were probably more important in Charles's signing of the Treaty. Smith (1998) has stressed Charles's impulse to emulate Louis XIV whilst Charles's desire for revenge against the Dutch for the humiliations of the previous decades was also a factor in his signing of the alliance with the French. The financial aspects of the treaty would also give Charles freedom in his dealings with Parliament.

The Secret Treaty of Dover was followed by two other secret agreements with Louis XIV of August 1675 and February 1676. Charles was promised £112,000 if he kept Parliament prorogued (suspended). For France an English Parliament posed a threat as most MPs were anti-French, regarding the French state as the height of absolutism and Catholicism and therefore a threat to English liberties. From 22 November 1675 to 15 February 1677, Charles kept Parliament prorogued. In the context of his pragmatism and his problems, finance, to free him from Parliament, and Charles's feeling of a personal bond to Louis was probably at the root of his pro-French stance. His death-bed conversion to Catholicism may also suggest that this is where his religious sympathies had long resided, if he had the sense not to act on them. It is likely that all of these considerations, finance, religion, revenge against the Dutch and a possible means to put pressure on Louis were all part of Charles's thinking with regard to the Treaty of Dover. With no statement from Charles himself there can be no definitive answer. More acutely, as Spurr in his consideration of *England in the 1670s* (2001) has remarked, the treaty was a 'watershed – for the rest of his life Charles II would be a French client and prey to constant anxiety that Louis would leak the details of their agreement'.

The Third Dutch War

On 17 March 1672, two days after his Declaration of Indulgence, Charles II declared war on the Dutch. The main attack was by Louis XIV leading 120,000 troops into the Republic. Charles's naval support of the French was, like his previous conflict with the Dutch, a failure. The English failed to capture a Dutch fleet returning from Smyrna, on the Aegean coast, and a battle off Southwold was inconclusive.

Despite English failure, French numbers proved decisive. In June they occupied Utrecht and this led to the assassination of the Dutch Grand Pensionary, the republican Johan De Witt. He was replaced by Charles II's relation, William of Orange as Stadholder. The success of Catholic France was of deep concern in England and made the war very unpopular.

■ **Did you know?**

The details of the Secret Treaty did not become public until the 1770s when they were of no issue.

Fig. 4 *A Dutch warship. Charles II was humiliated in his two conflicts with the Dutch in the 1660s*

Continued failure only made the war against the Dutch even more unpopular. In the summer of 1673 there were two more failed naval engagements against the Dutch. In August 1673, Spain and the Holy Roman Empire entered the war against England. At this point Parliament refused to vote money and this forced Charles to end the Dutch war by the February 1674 Treaty of Westminster.

The Dutch War became increasingly unpopular in the context of the growing fear of the strength of France. From 1667 it was France that appeared to have pretensions to **universal monarchy**.

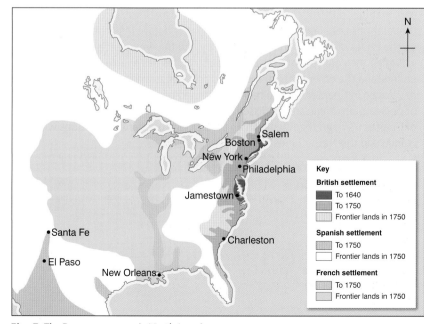

Fig. 5 *The European powers in North America*

Exploring the detail

The Holy Roman Empire

Less influential than in the 16th or early 17th century, the Empire covered a large area of central Europe from the Baltic to the Alps and from France to Poland. This Empire was covered by a mix of princedoms and states, some of whom in theory elected the Emperor but in reality by the 17th century the title was controlled by the Habsburg family. The Habsburgs were rulers of both Spain and 'Austria' but as Spain declined, influence in the Empire shifted more to the Austrian Habsburgs.

Did you know?

As part of the wars between England and the Dutch their North American colonies were drawn into the conflict. The city of New Amsterdam was in Dutch hands until 1664. It was then seized by the English until it was recovered by the Dutch in 1673. Then by the terms of the Treaty of Westminster the Dutch ceded the territory. Under the English New Amsterdam was renamed New York, after the Duke of York who was granted the territory by his brother.

Key terms

Universal monarchy: the concept of one monarchy having world power, or striving for world power. In the 16th century the English saw this threat coming from Spain. In the 1660s some Anglican Royalists saw the threat coming from Dutch republicanism with its commercial and colonial success. The military success of France under Louis XIV made the French the latest pretender to universal dominion.

Activity

Class discussion

To what extent was Charles II's French policy a success and his Dutch policy a failure?

Charles's Destruction of Danby's pro-Dutch policy

A symbol of Danby's pro-Dutch policy was his management of the marriage of James Duke of York's Protestant eldest daughter, Mary, to Prince William of Orange, the new Dutch Stadholder, in November 1677. In December 1677 by an Anglo-Dutch treaty, England agreed to impose peace terms on Louis, by force if needed. In relation to this, in January 1678 Parliament voted to raise an army of 30,000 men and £1 million. The subsequent Poll Tax, however, only brought in £300,000.

Despite Danby's public policy, the King sought to maintain his links with Louis XIV and it was this that was to bring Danby's fall and the crisis of the regime. In August 1677 the English Ambassador in Paris, Ralph Montagu with Danby's knowledge, had carried out secret negotiations with the French that led to them granting two million livres if Parliament remained prorogued and England refrained from going to war with France. In May 1678 Charles conducted another secret treaty with the French. In return for more money he would prorogue Parliament and disband the army Parliament had voted to raise at the start of the year. Charles prorogued Parliament but did not disband his 30,000 troops. Neither the Dutch nor the French, with good reason, trusted Charles. In July 1678 the two countries ended their war with the Peace of Nijmegen.

Spurr (2001) has delivered a damning verdict on these years and indicated the link between foreign policy failure and the developing domestic crisis. For Spurr 'throughout these years the brute facts of political life were simple. England was a client of France and France terrified the English. Most diplomacy and any war meant trusting Charles with money and troops that he might misuse. England was a society of several religions. The Duke of York was a Catholic. And, finally, Charles II's dissembling and reversals of policy, never mind his private life, eroded his subjects' trust in him'.

Learning outcomes

From this section you have gained an understanding of the role of key personalities, particularly Charles II and his ministers. You have examined the relations between Crown and Parliament and have in particular focused on the issues of finance, the part of Danby and the emergence of division, including the concepts of Court and Country. This has enabled you to understand the emergence of the Tories and Whigs whose importance will be developed in Chapter 10. You have also gained an understanding of the nature of persecution, Anglicanism, dissent and republicanism in the later stages of Charles II's reign together with an assessment of Charles's relations with France and the Netherlands.

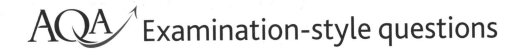 Examination-style questions

Were the difficulties faced by Charles II due more to financial concerns than foreign policy in the years 1667 to 1678?

Both factors should be addressed and an argument constructed leading to a judgement as to whether finance or foreign policy caused the greater difficulties for Charles II.

Some consideration of the inter-relationship between the specified factors in the question should form part of the essay. Foreign policy was always a financial issue but Charles's relationship with France should particularly be considered given how the financial aspect of it shaped Charles's relationship with Parliament.

Other factors should also be considered; for example, the role of religion.

Again this factor can be considered in relation to foreign policy and finance. Religion, specifically anti-Catholicism, remained very much a factor in attitudes toward foreign policy. Finance was also used by Parliament to prevent Charles establishing a broader church.

The Solemn Mock Procession of the POPE Cardinals, Jesuits, Friars, &c.
Through the CITY OF LONDON November 17.th 1679.

London Published January 1828 by William Miller Albemarle Street.

In this chapter you will learn about:

■ the Exclusion crisis

■ why Exclusion failed

■ the growing absolutism of Charles II.

In 1669, James Duke of York's Catholicism became public knowledge. With his brother Charles II having no legitimate children, the prospect was raised that a deeply anti-Catholic English nation could have the first Catholic monarch since 'Bloody Mary' (1555–8). Charles II was, however, only three years older than his brother James. In 1670 Charles was 40 and James 37. There was the prospect, as the 1670s progressed, that James could die before his brother. James's two daughters, who were next in line to the throne, Mary (b.1662) and Anne (b.1665) were both Protestants. In 1673, however, James married for the second time to the 15 year old Catholic princess and client of Louis XIV, Mary of Modena. With this marriage there now loomed the very real prospect of a Catholic line of succession and this threat underpinned what was to become the Exclusion Crisis. It was not, however, until June 1688 that James and Mary had their first child, a son, James Edward. This was to bring the growing crisis of James's reign to revolution.

Charles II, 1678–85: the Exclusion Crisis and reasons for its failure

Shaftesbury had been dismissed as Lord Chancellor in November 1673 when he had urged the King to divorce Catherine of Braganza in order to marry again and have a legitimate Protestant heir. He also urged Charles to annul James's marriage to Mary of Modena. By the spring of 1674 Shaftesbury was removed from the **Privy Council** and became an 'opponent' who aimed to exclude James, Duke of York, from the succession. The Exclusion Crisis was the attempt by men like Shaftesbury to 'exclude' and thereby prevent Charles's heir, James, becoming king. A fear of absolutism and Catholicism underpinned the Exclusion Crisis.

James was feared not only as a Catholic, but in the context of the apparent growing threat of absolutism under Charles II. Fundamentally the Exclusion Crisis was based on long-standing opposition to Catholicism and absolutism. This anti-Catholicism became more overt as the 1670s progressed. In November 1673 began what became regular pope effigy-burning processions in London. As early as February 1674 the Earl of Carlisle proposed that any prince married to a Catholic should be excluded from the succession.

Out of the politics of the Exclusion crisis, the terms Whigs and Tories, rooted in the Court/Country division, became common usage. While the Exclusion Crisis saw Whigs and Tories become more defined groups they were not political parties in the modern sense. Scott (2000) stresses that the crisis of 1679-81 did not bring about the development of parties but competing factions and that these factions were tied together ideologically if not in organisation. For Scott the idea of parties developing from the Exclusion Crisis is 'another case of the **long 18th century** giving premature birth to itself from the depths of a different period'.

Both Knights (2004) and Miller (2000) have stressed the importance of the process of political division both centrally and in the localities as part of the crisis. There developed a social segregation based around taverns, coffee-houses and clubs aligned to Whigs or Tories. Zook (1999) has singled out the influence of an underground network of radical conspirators and propagandists. Their aim was to ensure a Protestant succession but in doing she has argued their ideas became more radical and helped to lay the basis for liberal political thought as well influencing the later Rye House (1683) conspirators, the Monmouth rebels and the 'revolutionaries' of 1688. For Zook ideas were forged as much by action and debate, particularly in the London taverns, coffeehouses and streets, as by the pen of philosophers. For Zook more influential than philosophers like Locke were activists such as the lawyers Thomas Hunt and William Atwood, the Anglican vicar Samuel Johnson and the independent preacher Robert Ferguson (*M. Zook, Radical Whigs and Conspiratorial Politics in Late Stuart England*, 1999). Others like Knights (1994) and Ashcraft (1986) have also indicated how Locke's ideas had been prefigured by pamphleteers.

For Knights in *Representation* (2006), religion was a fundamental part of politics.

Key terms

Privy Council: the King's selected advisers who met in private to shape the monarch's wishes into policy and oversee its implementation.

Long 18th century: the term used by some historians who, with regard to the periodisation of History, believe that the period 1688–1832 merits study as a whole because of themes that run through it.

Cross-reference

For more on definitions of Whigs and Tories see Chapter 8.

[P]olitical views were shaped by religious ones and only by recovering their religious context can we fully understand them; we should see political and religious concerns as entwined. But to neglect the politics of religion, or deny change, would be to miss what was obvious to most contemporaries, that religion, as opposed to private faith, was a tool in a partisan, political contest.

1

*M. Knights, **Representation and Misrepresentation** in Later Stuart Britain (2006)*

Activity

Revision exercise

Write two paragraphs explaining the emergence and beliefs of the Whigs and the Tories.

Such an emphasis on religion is also clearly stressed in Harris's work linking the crisis to the failures of the Restoration religious settlement. Scott (2000) has also pointed out the continuity between the early and late Stuart period with regard to the fear of popery and absolutism but also stresses the impact of England's relationship with France.

Concerns about James as heir became a full blown political crisis with the revelation of the 'Popish plot'.

The Popish plot

The clergyman Israel Tonge produced a document which he claimed proved there was a Popish plot by which the Jesuits had planned the assassination of Charles II, so that he could be replaced by his catholic brother, supported by an invasion from France and a Catholic rebellion in Ireland.

Tonge obsessed about the Jesuit threat. In 1677 Tonge met Titus Oates, who filled Tonge with tales of Jesuit plotting. Tonge came to live in the house of one Christopher Kirkby, a former assistant in Charles II's scientific experiments. Through this connection Tonge related a tale of an assassination plot to Charles II himself in August 1678.

Fig. 1 *Titus Oates, the originator of the Popish plot*

A disbelieving Charles II left Danby to investigate. Danby came to believe that Tonge, who would not reveal Oates as his source, was merely deranged. At this point Oates invented correspondence to support the plot to keep Danby interested. This was posted to the Duke of York's confessor Father Bedingfield with the intention that they would be intercepted by Danby. They weren't and Bedingfield took them to James and it was actually he who demanded an investigation, the actual original intention of Oates. Tonge was brought before the Privy Council. At this point Tonge revealed that his information came from Oates.

The Popish plot was essentially based on Oates' fabrications. He was believed because of the hysterical anti-Catholicism that had long been part of the English political consciousness. Anti-Catholicism intensified in 1670s because of the expansion of France under Louis XIV who the English now saw as aiming at universal monarchy. A 1679 pamphlet *An Appeal from the Country to the City* was typical of the popular imagery of the consequences of Catholic invasion and rebellion. It referred to 'troops of Papists ravishing your wives and daughters, dashing your little children's brains out against the walls, plundering your houses and cutting your own throats, by the name of heretic dogs'. Such hysteria was reinforced by the unexplained murder of the magistrate Godfrey who had taken Oates' first sworn statement, confirming for many that there was a Catholic conspiracy.

The development of anti-Catholicism from the Reformation of the 1530s was shaped by some key events:

- **The return of Catholicism under Mary I, 1553–8:** With the death of Henry VIII's only son, Edward VI, the first daughter of Henry VIII came to the throne. Mary was Henry's daughter from his first marriage to the Spanish princess Katherine of Aragon. It was Henry's divorce from Katherine that had been one of the precursors of the Reformation and the establishment of Protestantism. Mary returned England to Catholicism and under her many Protestants were burnt at the stake.
- **John Foxe's *Book of Martyrs*:** This account of Mary's burning of Protestants became the second most read book in England after the Bible and resulted in anti-Catholicism becoming part of the English identity.
- **The Spanish War:** Under Elizabeth I the Spanish threat heightened anti-Catholicism, notably at times such as the attempted Spanish invasion of 1588, the Spanish Armada.
- **The Gunpowder Plot, 1605:** The attempt by a group of Catholics to blow up King James I and Parliament vividly illustrated the real threat from English Catholics no matter how small their numbers.
- **The Thirty Years War, 1618–48:** The religious war in Europe had some impact on English opinion. The major defeat for the Protestants in 1620 at the Battle of the White Mountain raised the spectre of Catholic invasion which was repeated at various times throughout the war and reinforced by the Irish Rebellion of 1641.

Edward Coleman, one of those implicated in the Popish plot, had been secretary to James. A search of his house revealed letters to Jesuits and one to Louis XIV's Jesuit confessor. Some of the letters indicate that James trusted Coleman and was well aware of what contacts he had. The parliament of 1678 did not have access, however, to all of the letters and thus it was not clear to MPs the level of James's complicity.

At the start of November Parliament declared that:

> … there hath been and still is damnable and hellish plot contrived and carried on by the popish recusants for the assassinating and murdering the King, and for subverting the government, and rooting out and destroying the Protestant religion.

2

Investigations into the plot lasted into 1681 and resulted in the execution of 35 men. By 1683 the plot had collapsed.

The Popish plot was significant, however, because it heightened the concerns that already existed over the growing power of the Crown and James as a Catholic heir to the throne. In November it was proposed in the Commons that James should not be allowed in the presence of the King or in his counsels. Charles had to accept a second Test Act in 1678 which excluded Catholics from Parliament. An exemption in the case of James was only passed by two votes. Alongside the Test Act Charles agreed to prosecute the penal laws with more rigour. In the short term attention passed away from James as focus turned to the chief minister, and the apparent architect of Charles's drive to absolutism, Danby.

Exploring the detail

English anti-Catholicism

Suspicion of the papacy pre-dated the Reformation, for example the criticism of Wyclif's 14th century *De Papa, Concerning the Pope*. In the 14th century Acts of Parliament, Praemunire and Provisors restricted the Pope's rights over the church in England. By the Reformation England broke completely with the Catholic Church and anti-Catholicism and anti-popery became more entrenched in the English identity over the next 100 years.

Activity

Challenge your thinking

To what extent was the Popish plot an example of perception being more important than what really happened in creating political conflict?

The attack on Danby

By 1678 there was little doubt that Danby was Charles II's pre-eminent minister. His power also appeared to be on a much securer basis than Clarendon's had been before 1667. Danby had supported his influence by:

▨ working with Charles's mistresses, especially Portsmouth

▨ appreciating the key influence of the position of treasurer

▨ using the King's patronage through his position as treasurer to construct a 'court' party.

In constructing a 'court' party, Danby encouraged the formation of a 'country' party and the emergence of division. His power naturally provoked opposition, particularly through his dominance of patronage.

> The threat which his patronage system seemed to pose to the independence and integrity of Parliament revitalized fears of 'arbitrary government' as he tried to damp down fears of 'popery'. There had earlier been attacks on sale of office or the 'corrupt' use of crown patronage, but these had been driven mainly by resentment that Parliamentarians had been rewarded at the expense of Cavaliers. Now, however, fears were expressed that Danby was reducing Parliament to a mere rubber-stamp for the king's will. Fears for the survival of the ancient constitution gave added depth to the divisions created by Danby's abrasive and adversarial approach to politics.

3   *J. Miller, **After the Civil Wars: English Politics and Government in the Reign of Charles II** (2000)*

Montagu, who had been ambassador in Paris, sought revenge for his removal when it was revealed he had conducted an affair with one of Charles's former mistresses and her daughter. Elected to the 1678 Parliament in December, he presented evidence of Danby's knowledge of Charles's continuing relations with Louis XIV, despite securing money from Parliament for an army to be used against France as part of a pro-Dutch policy. Danby, against the policy he wanted to follow, had acted on direct instructions from Charles in writing to Montagu to get money from Louis XIV. In response to the attempt to impeach Danby and, more importantly, the knowledge of his own duplicity in foreign affairs Charles prorogued Parliament at the end of December before dissolving the Cavalier Parliament on 24 January 1679.

Given Charles's direction of policy, particularly his insistence on a pro-French line, his subsequent protection of Danby was motivated by self-preservation. Charles dismissed Danby in March 1679 but needed to avoid any trial which would make clear his own role in strengthening the relationship with France. Charles suppressed a trial by pardoning Danby. The Commons pursued Charles's minister through means of an **attainder**.

As the attainder process was nearing completion, Danby surrendered to the Lords and was committed to the Tower where he spent the next five years.

The attack on Danby should be seen in the context of the apparent move towards arbitrary government which was to feed into the Exclusion Crisis. The fear of popery and arbitrary government was heightened by Charles's rule in Scotland and Ireland.

Scotland

In Scotland, Charles had effectively allowed Lauderdale to centralise government in his name. The focus in the Exclusion debates of May 1679

Key terms

Attainder: a medieval method that allowed anyone who was seen as a threat to the state to be removed by Parliament without the need of a formal trial.

Activity

Group discussion

To what extent was the greatest obstacle to Danby's success Charles II, rather than factional opposition, in the years 1673 to 1678?

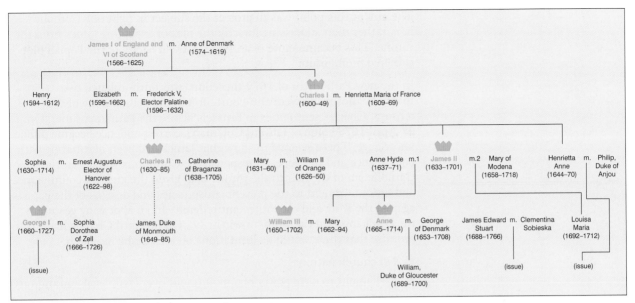

Fig. 2 *The House of Stuart and the line of succession, 1603–1714*

on Scotland is clear from the attempt to get Charles to remove Lauderdale. The dissolution of Parliament prevented further attacks on Lauderdale but Charles decided to remove him anyway. In his place James Duke of York returned from temporary exile and took up effective control of Scotland in two stints, November 1679 to February 1680 and October 1680 to March 1682. In Scotland James continued the strengthening of the power of the Crown. In doing so he made Exclusionists even more concerned at what might happen when James became king. James's time in Scotland allowed him to build up support that was to be crucial in strengthening his position when he did succeed his brother.

Ireland

The fear of the growth of the influence of Catholics in Ireland, where they were the majority of the population, added to the concern at what might happen when James came to the throne. In 1680 Shaftesbury informed the Privy Council of plans for another Catholic rising with French assistance. There seems little of substance in this report of rebellion but it fed on widely held beliefs about the threat from Ireland as well as its potential as a launching pad for a French invasion. The archbishop of Armagh, Oliver Plunkett, was executed for supposed contacts with the French.

1679 Parliament – the First Exclusion Parliament (6 March–27 May)

In England, the Popish plot continued to accelerate the Exclusion Crisis. Edward Coleman, James's ex-secretary, with three others was executed. Five Catholic peers were set to be impeached. This heightened fear of Catholicism meant that the new Parliament, which met on 6 March 1679, was a very different body from the Cavalier Parliament.

Parliament took measures to try to secure freedom and rights in the event of a Catholic succession. It granted £200,000 to disband the army and secured a Habeas Corpus Amendment Act (May 1679). This reinforced the Common Law right whereby, with the exception of treason or felony, the cause of imprisonment had to be stated and a case brought to trial, normally within three days. It also made illegal the practice of moving prisoners from one prison to another, or imprisoning 'beyond the seas' to avoid **habeas corpus**.

Key terms

Habeas corpus ('You have the body'): a writ to bring a person before a court or judge to ensure that they are legally held prisoner.

The aim at this point was to protect the subject in light of a Catholic heir, rather than addressing directly the idea of excluding James from the throne. This became more of an issue as the hysteria of the Popish plot gathered momentum.

In the new Parliament of 1679 the 'court' was outnumbered two to one by those who were anti-court. To try and defuse some of the tension, Charles sent James to Brussels before the Parliament met. On 27 April 1678 some of Edward Coleman's correspondence became public knowledge. These seemed to show that James had been negotiating with both France and the Pope. In response the Commons voted that the Catholicism of the heir to the throne had 'given the greatest countenance and encouragement to the present conspiracies and designs of the papists against the King and the Protestant religion'. In an appeasing gesture the Lords inserted the word 'unwittingly'. On 30 April Charles had to promise that there would be limitations on a Catholic monarch:

■ No church patronage.
■ Parliament to have power of appointment over civil, legal and military offices.

Such measures appeased some like Halifax but those more committed like Shaftesbury moved to pushing for James's exclusion. Miller (2000) has argued that the 'debates on the dangers from a popish successor showed that fear of future tyranny and retribution led logically to the demand for exclusion; but having threatened James's birthright, the threat of retribution became greater. Having embarked on exclusion, it became a matter of self-preservation to go through with it'.

On 11 May one MP called for James's impeachment on charges of high treason. This was followed by the reading of an Exclusion Bill on 15 May. On 21 May, the Exclusion Bill passed its second reading 207 to 128. These numbers, from a total of 509 MPs, indicate that many made a conscious decision not to vote, suggesting that there was a possible group for the King to exploit. At this point, Charles intervened by proroguing Parliament on 27 May.

Scottish rising: Bothwell Bridge

In May 1679 some Covenanters dragged Archbishop Sharp from his coach and stabbed him to death in front of his daughter while they sang psalms. After troops trying to suppress a Conventicle at Drumclog were defeated 6,000 Presbyterians rose in the Western Lowlands in revolt. Their Declaration called for armed defence of Protestantism.

This was not a unified movement and in particular had little support from the Scottish elite. A force under Charles's eldest illegitimate son, James Scot, Duke of Monmouth, defeated the rebellion on 22 June at Bothwell Bridge. Charles followed up this victory by issuing a Third Letter of Indulgence. This legalised Conventicles in private houses.

Charles responds

There were, however, negative aspects for Charles from Monmouth's victory over the Scots. Monmouth had been working with Shaftesbury for the Duke of York's exclusion. Monmouth was a Protestant and appeared a possible candidate for the throne, despite his illegitimacy. Charles, wary of Monmouth's return to London in triumph, dissolved the first Exclusion Parliament in July 1679. Charles then pushed harder with negotiations with both the French and Dutch for funds in order to avoid the Parliament he had said would be summoned in October.

Activity

Revision exercise

What were the stages of Exclusion in the Parliament of 1679?

In late August Charles became seriously ill. Charles's illness made calls for exclusion more heated and as a result he temporarily exiled Monmouth to the Netherlands in September 1679 and the Duke of York was sent as Charles's representative to re-establish order in Scotland.

Key profile

James, Duke of Monmouth

Although not the sharpest, Monmouth was rapidly promoted by his father to become, by 1678, Captain-General of all the English land forces. Protestant and popular with the crowds, his involvement with Whigs saw him removed from office in 1679. Implicated in the Rye House Plot he was forced into exile. Here he plotted the failed rising that led to his execution.

Here James led Charles's new policy of repression against nonconformity. One group, known as the Cameronians, were defeated at Aird's Moss in July, but the 1680s essentially witnessed a guerrilla war between Scottish nonconformists and the English crown.

In England Charles remodelled his Privy Council. In April 1679 Charles had included some of his leading opponents into his Privy Council: Shaftesbury, Halifax, Essex and Russell as an attempt to appease them but the appointments were in reality worthless as being in the Privy Council did not necessarily mean influence with the King. Now Shaftesbury was removed, while Halifax removed himself from court and Essex resigned his post as head of the Treasury Commission. These men were replaced by younger advisors:

- The Earl of Sunderland.
- Sidney Godolphin.
- Clarendon's son, Laurence Hyde.

Key profiles

Robert Spencer, second Earl of Sunderland, 1641–1702

Sunderland's initial support of Exclusion in November 1680 led to his dismissal. He was reinstated in January 1683 and became central to Charles's construction of further links with France. Sunderland remained as a principal adviser to James II until just before the revolution, converting to Catholicism. When James resorted to pro-Anglican policies Sunderland supported him but became a scapegoat and James dismissed Sunderland in October, egged on by his catholic advisers. Sunderland went to the Netherlands, only being able to return to England in 1690. Within two years Sunderland was again playing the role of leading adviser to the Crown.

Sidney Godolphin, first earl of Godolphin, 1645–1712

Supported Exclusion. Promoted to first Lord of the Treasury in 1684 briefly after the fall of Laurence Hyde, but lost this on the accession of James II. Godolphin supported the votes in the Convention Parliament, calling for the establishment of a regency during James's life. William III, however, recognised Godolphin's financial talents and appointed him to the treasury Commission in 1689.

Exploring the detail

The Killing Time was a term used by 18th century Scottish historian Robert Wodrow to describe the extra-judicial field executions authorised by the Scottish Privy Council against Covenanters in the years 1680–8.

■ **Key profile**

Laurence Hyde, first Earl of Rochester, 1642–1711

Supported limitations rather than Exclusion but was increasingly in favour of the Duke of York from 1682. He became Lord Treasurer under James II but lost favour because of his ardent Anglicanism, eventually being dismissed in 1687. Rochester sought an accommodation between James and William, being a chief advocate of a regency in the Convention.

■ **Activity**

Revision exercise

In what ways did Charles II respond to Exclusion?

At the same time as Charles remodelled his Privy Council, there were purges of county commissions of peace which put local power in hands of loyalists. Charles also knew that he had a small standing army that he could turn to, if necessary. Charles also announced the prorogation of the Parliament that had not even met yet. This meant that politics shifted even more out of the parliamentary arena into print and the street.

Petitions, pamphlets, processions, plots and prosecutions – non-parliamentary pressure

Petitions

In response to Charles's prorogation of Parliament, Shaftesbury's group organised a petitioning campaign calling for a meeting of Parliament without any more prorogations and the defence of Protestantism. In London, tables were actually set up with pens and ink to promote the petition. The London petition had 16,000 signatures and there were also numerous county petitions. Charles, however, ignored them claiming that they had no validity.

Pamphlets

During 1679 to 1681, 200 Exclusionist pamphlets were produced. Their focus was:

■ personal attacks on James

■ the consequences of the imposition of Catholicism, including massacres

■ justifications for Exclusion.

As part of the reimposition of monarchy a Licensing Act had reintroduced censorship in 1662. That this lapsed in 1679 allowed more freedom for the production of pamphlets.

Processions

The usual November processions in London focused on anti-Catholicism, including pope-burning processions. These were also recorded in pamphlets. These should not be seen, however, as signs of disorder but part of normal political life.

Fig. 3 *Contemporary broadsheet with depiction of Sir William Stafford and the Popish plot*

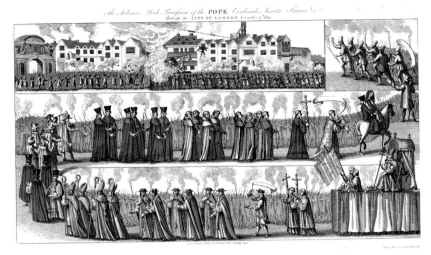

Fig. 4 *A pope burning procession. Every year 17 November, Elizabeth I's accession day, traditionally saw anti-Catholic demonstrations*

Plots

The key plot was Oates' Popish plot but others came forward with conspiracy theories which had long been part of anti-Catholicism. As a result of a fabricated plot by one Dugdale, the Catholic Viscount Stafford was executed.

Oates, as a result of his lies, was responsible for the death of 35 men. By 1683 the Plot was collapsing. Oates was arrested in Amsterdam in 1684 as a result of accusing the Duke of York of being a traitor. Oates was convicted of perjury and sentenced to be imprisoned for life. Oates was in fact released after the 1688 revolution.

Prosecutions

In June 1680 charges were brought before the Middlesex Grand Jury in an attempt to prosecute James as a recusant. This was stopped by Lord Chief Justice Scroggs as Charles had the jury dissolved before it could make a judgement. There was also an attempt to prosecute Charles's French mistress, Louise de Kerouaille, the Duchess of Portsmouth, as a prostitute and a Catholic French agent.

The response of the Tories

Alongside petitions and pamphlets there were more detailed printed forms of arguments for and against Exclusion. The most significant was the publication for the first time in 1680 of Robert Filmer's work of 1628–31, *Patriarcha*. This was done by Archbishop Sancroft in support of the Tory cause.

Filmer claimed that absolute monarchy was ordained by the law of nature. This was set at the Creation in Adam's rights as husband, father, property owner and king. Filmer also argued that medieval English history showed that parliament was subordinate to the Crown. It should be noted that Tory arguments for absolutism recognised that a monarch had to respect the laws and the interests of their subjects or they would become a tyrant.

Filmer's key text was supported by numerous others:

Did you know?

Another part of Oates' sentence was to be put in the pillory and pelted with eggs and rubbish. This was to happen five times a year for the rest of his life.

Activity

Group activity

Produce a piece of Whig propaganda in any of the following forms: pamphlet, petition, poem or playing card.

Cross-reference

For more on Filmer, see Chapter 8.

Author	Title	Date
John Nalson	Common Interest of King and People	1678
William Falkner	Christian Loyalty	1679
George Hickes	Discourse of the Sovereign Power	1682
Thomas Goddard	Plato's Demon	1684
William Sherlock	The Case of Resistance	1684
Edmund Bohun	Defence of Sir Robert Filmer	1684

Perhaps of more note, certainly with more readers, was the range of other Tory propaganda produced as part of the Exclusion Crisis. There was a range of Tory newspapers, the most influential being L'Estrange's *Observator*, which came out initially two days a week and then three times a week between 1681 and 1687. Other written forms such as pamphlets, broadsides, prints, poems and even playing cards were also produced to strengthen the Tory cause.

It was L'Estrange, however, who was probably pre-eminent in publicising the Tory argument. There were 64,000 copies of L'Estrange's tracts in circulation in 1679.

There was a reaction in Charles's favour by moderates in 1680 to 1681 against Whig petitioning, their apparent radicalism and memories of civil war. The Abhorrence Movement of 1682 produced addresses stating abhorrence at Shaftesbury's alleged Protestant Association. Known as 'abhorrers' they stated their abhorrence of the perceived radicalism of the Exclusionists. They stood for divine right, prerogative, patriarchalism and passive obedience. Harris (2005) has written of a 'core' Tory ideology in their response to the Whigs. The Tories 'developed a range of arguments to show that they were committed to the defence of the true Protestant religion, the rule of law, and the protection of people's lives, liberties and estates – arguments which were a more significant dimension to their ideological platform than their pronouncements about divine-right monarchy, and which run the risk of being obscured if we choose simply to represent the Tories as Filmerian absolutists'.

Alongside these written forms the Tories made use of the pulpit as well as the playhouse. There was a government controlled newspaper, the London Gazette, and Charles II produced a Declaration in April 1681 attacking the Whigs.

The Response of Whigs

John Locke started work on his *Two Treatises of Government*. At the time Locke was in the household of Shaftesbury and it is therefore very likely that they discussed the manuscript. Locke focused on:

- contractual theory of government
- equality of man
- popular sovereignty
- the law of nature
- right of resistance.

Although Locke's work and his connection to Shaftesbury were significant, the fact that the *Two Treatises* was not actually printed until after the 1688 Revolution meant that others at the time were more significant:

Did you know?
Censorship

Charles II sought to repress what he thought might pose a threat. In 1681 performances of Shakespeare's Richard II were banned as its focus was the deposition of a king.

Fig. 5 *John Locke, philosopher whose work was printed in support of the Whigs*

Henry Neville	Plato Redivivus	1681
John Sadler	Rights of the Kingdom	1649 and 1682
William Petyt	Antient Right of the Commons of England Asserted	1680
William Atwood	Jani Anglorum Facies Nova	1680
John Somers	Brief History of the Succession	1680

The republican Neville in *Plato Redivivus* argued that in response to the Exclusion Crisis limitations should be imposed on the monarch in effect making their position analogous with a Venetian Doge under whom a Senate wielded power.

The second Exclusion Parliament of 1680

In the summer of 1680 Shaftesbury went on the offensive, playing upon fear of an Irish Catholic rebellion. Charles used seven prorogations to delay the opening of the next Parliament until October 1680, a year after it should have opened. Parliament finally met on 21 October 1680. Another Exclusion Bill passed through its three readings in the Commons and was with the Lords by 15 November. Charles intervened by attending sessions in the Lords and the Marquis of Halifax spoke repeatedly in favour of a compromise of limitations on a Catholic successor. Halifax was the personification of a Trimmer, those who saw themselves as moderates between the extremes of Whigs and Tories. In 1684 Halifax produced a *Character of a Trimmer*. The Lords rejected the Exclusion bill, 63 to 30.

In response the Commons sought to use its financial muscle, offering £600,000 for Exclusion, and then reinforced this by a stated refusal to grant any money until Exclusion was granted. Charles dissolved Parliament on 18 January 1681. Charles declared that the next Parliament for March 1682 would sit in Oxford, a loyalist area, rather than London.

Charles could resist the financial pressure of Parliament if he secured finance from Louis XIV. In a treaty of March 1681 he secured £40,000 immediately and £115,000 annually for three years. For his part he had to break his alliance with Spain and promised not to call another parliament for three years. The French money was the background for Charles's harsher line with the Oxford Parliament which met in March.

The Oxford Parliament of 1681

In the Oxford Parliament Charles offered that William and Mary would be regents for James. The Commons planned a new Exclusion bill with Shaftesbury openly calling for Monmouth to be the next monarch. On 26 March the Commons decided, with only 20 dissenting voices, that another Exclusion bill should be introduced. With his French money secured on 28 March Charles dissolved the Oxford Parliament.

Charles followed the dissolution with propaganda outlining his moderate stance; in particular he released in April a *Declaration Touching the Reasons that Moved Him to Dissolve the Two Last Parliaments*. This was ordered to be read from every pulpit. His strong stance and the public mood meant he defeated Exclusion.

Activity

Revision exercise

What were the stages of Exclusion in the Parliament of 1680?

Continuing crisis

Although the threat of Exclusion was removed Charles failed to get a settlement with Parliament and was in practice reliant on Louis XIV. Zook (1999) has argued that the Exclusion Crisis must be looked at beyond the traditional end dates of either the dissolution of 1681 or the failure of the Rye House Plot of 1683. For her 'the Whig exclusion movement became increasingly more exclusive, more determined, and more radical in the years that followed'. She has labelled those who continued this struggle 'Whig radicals', distinguishing them from 'Whig exclusionists' by their willingness to resort to force.

Why Exclusion failed

Limits of the Whig argument

The Whig argument was limited by the fact that they were part of the elite. Most Whigs refused to argue what was logical from their position, that the Commons' authority was supreme as the representative of the people. The Commons voted three times for Exclusion and were only opposed by the Lords and king. The King had sat in the Lords during their debate to influence them. The Whigs agreed Charles had the authority to do this and resorted to trying to put pressure on him by the threat of popular revolt, but this made them appear more radical and strengthened the Tories' claim that '41 is here again'.

'1641 is here again'

There was a resurgence of loyalism in 1680–1. The cries of 'forty-one all over again' that have been emphasised by Scott (2000) were, according to Zook (1999), essentially Tory propaganda. Scott saw the crisis as 'a repeat screening of the crisis of the reign of Charles I', whereas Knights (1994) and Zook see the memory of 1641 being used by the Tories. Exclusion could be portrayed as pretexts for men who actually wanted to establish another republic.

Scotland

The situation in Scotland meant that there was not a repeat of 1641. Only a section of the Scottish elite were alienated. Scottish rebellion was crushed. Charles II maintained control over Parliament whereas in 1641 defeat by the Scots had made Charles I need to keep his English Parliament in sitting.

Harris (2005) has stated that 'York's support for the Episcopalian establishment in Scotland did much to reassure the English bishops that they had no cause to fear for their Church when the Duke eventually succeeded to the throne'. Through the support built up in Scotland and by the Crown's ability to manipulate a Scottish Parliament through a steering committee known as the Lords of the Articles, a Succession Act was passed in August 1681. This guaranteed that no matter James's religion if he was next in line when Charles died he would be king. This raised the prospect that if the English Parliament excluded James he would still be king of Scotland. Would this spark renewed 'British wars'?

Charles's financial position

Charles had secured, just three days before the Oxford Parliament met, 5 million livres over the next three years as part of another secret treaty with Louis XIV. For this money Charles had to agree not to call a Parliament in support of Spain against France. On top of this Charles had increased revenue from Customs Duties. This was, ironically, partly as a result of the initiative of Shaftesbury when he was Chancellor of the Exchequer in 1671. Shaftesbury brought the collection of customs duties back under crown control ending the system of customs farming. French money meant Charles could dissolve Parliament.

Support of the Lords and the Church

A fundamental problem for the Exclusionists was that Exclusion would never pass the Lords. For example in November 1680 the Lords voted by a majority of 40 (70 to 30) against it. Charles could rely upon a block of support in the Lords from the bishops. In relation to this Mullett (1993) has argued that 'the support of the Church was to prove indispensible to the Crown in weathering the storms of 1679–81 and in rebuilding its authority thereafter'.

Wider support

From studies of the *London Crowd* by Harris (1987) and of *Public Opinion* by Knights (1994) it is now clear that there was genuine popular support for the Toryism. This was strengthened by the propaganda produced. Harris (2005) has commented that 'the government's ability to claim that the people were on its side and that it was in tune with public opinion was crucial to the success of the Tory Reaction'. There were demonstrations of popular support, particularly on 29 May, the anniversary of the Restoration and Charles's birthday. Part of Charles's strategy was to wait for public opinion to rally to him.

Prerogative powers of prorogation and dissolution

Charles was resolute where he was normally weak. For Mullett (1993) the 'judicious use of these powers of prorogation and dissolution, more than any other single 'constitutional' factor, allowed Charles II to weather and eventually to survive the storm of Exclusion'.

Radicalism of Exclusion

The radicalism of the Exclusion Bill should not be forgotten. It was a Test Act singling out James. The Bill actually called for James to be subjected to the death of a traitor – by hanging, drawing and quartering – if he tried to take the Crown. The same punishment was reserved for those who supported him, in print, by preaching or other means.

Charles gambled in putting forward William and Mary as regents for James, for if the Whigs had accepted this he would have been limiting the power of monarchy as well as alienating James. That the Whigs did not accept this option made Shaftesbury and Exclusionists look more radical.

Exclusion was also seen as radical because it could be argued that it was unlawful and unnecessary. It was unlawful in that it was trying to change the divine succession. This also had implications for property rights which were the basis of the power of the ruling elite. It was unnecessary in that the Test Acts and parliament's financial muscle could be argued as limits on any monarch. Furthermore, if Parliament resisted the Crown, what was to stop the people resisting those who claimed to rule for them?

Prorogation and dissolution
Line of succession
Leadership of the church
More control over local government
Whig leaders removed
Persecution
Propaganda
Financial position healthy
An army of 10,000

Fig. 6 *Charles's growing power*

Activity

Class discussion

Try to place the factors given here in order of importance, beginning with the most important.

The Exclusionists could also be seen as radical because even if the Lords passed a Bill the royal assent could be refused by Charles. What would then happen? Such thoughts were linked to the general fear of another civil war. If James won a civil war he would then be free to impose Catholicism and absolutism.

Limits of Whig support

There were limits to Shaftesbury's political support and to the coherence of the Whigs and Shaftesbury's control or influence of them. The voting figures in the Commons also indicate that there was a body of moderates who did not vote for Exclusion, or indeed others who could be described as Trimmers. Only a minority of MPs voted for Exclusion. In May 1679 there were 509 MPs. Out of these only 335 voted at all, let alone in favour of Exclusion. There was clearly potential for Charles to get support from the MPs who did not vote.

Even the influence of the Whig crowd could be seen as limited. It was certainly less of a real threat than in 1641. Miller (2000) has referred to demonstrations as more of 'theatre' than a real threat. The Whigs faced the problem of naming a successor if it wasn't to be James. Mary was married to the Dutch William and Monmouth was regarded as mentally weak. There was tension within the Whig opposition, between those who supported a legal or extra-legal strategy, between those who felt a solution could be achieved through legislation or the law courts and those who resorted to plotting.

Persecution

Persecution and repression was also used by Charles against his opponents, backed by those who had rallied to the Tory agenda. For Harris (2005) the 'defeat of the Whigs was the result of both policy and police: exploitation of the media to convince moderates, waverers or unsure loyalists to pledge their allegiance to the Crown and the succession and to allow themselves to stand up and be counted was backed up by a rigorous campaign to suppress all forms of political and religious opposition, to remove Whigs and nonconformists from positions of power at the central and local levels, and to intimidate the sizeable number of people who still sympathised with the Whig agenda into political silence or acquiescence'.

Was Exclusion needed?

Charles was only three years older than James, so there was the real prospect that James would die before Charles anyway. Even if he didn't die, until 1688, James had no male heir. After James's death the throne could pass to either of his protestant daughters, Mary or Anne.

It was the coming together of these factors after 1681 that transformed Charles II's position.

Different historical interpretations of the Exclusion Crisis

For Miller (1983) the 'exclusion campaign was the logical culmination of the Commons' growing distrust of both James and Charles'. Some do not see 1679–81 or even 1660 as a turning point. Finlayson (2001) stresses that the fear of Catholicism and absolutism which was at the heart of the Exclusion Crisis and was central in the period before the civil war of 1642 and in this sense the Restoration did not resolve one of the fundamental problems of early Stuart Britain. In a similar vein Hutton (2004) has argued that 'the events of 1640–63 had changed an enormous amount but settled nothing, because the basic issues which caused the turbulence of those years all remained unsettled'.

These tensions were:

- between the executive and legislature
- between Church and Dissenter
- between court and country
- created by the multiple-kingdom dimension.

Added to these tensions Hutton (2004) identifies four novel post-1660 features that created political insecurity:

- A fear of a repetition of the 1640s.
- The stabilising and fall of agriculture prices made the elite more dependent on office.
- The numbers of Dissenters.
- The external threat.

This external threat compromised three aspects:

- Scottish nobility and Irish Catholics more prepared to support the Crown because of what they saw as the negative impact of the 1640s and 1650s when they had opposed it.
- The rise of France.
- James as a Catholic. In 1580 half of the population of Europe was Protestant. By 1680 this was down to one-fifth – essentially all through conversion of monarchs. Harris has argued that Whigs linked the international situation with Exclusion.

Harris (2005) has stressed the multiple-kingdom dimension of the crisis:

> It was a crisis that stemmed from the problems of managing a troubled multiple-kingdom inheritance where the political and religious tensions that existed within each kingdom cut deep into society, and where any initiatives taken to try to deal with the problems that these tensions generated were likely to cause further difficulties. Thus when the crisis came in 1679–81 it was about much more than what might happen, in the future, should York inherit the crown. It was about the failings of the Restoration polity; it was about Charles II's style of government in all three of his kingdoms; it was about the threat of popery and arbitrary government in the present.

4   *T. Harris, **Restoration: Charles II and his Kingdoms** (2005)*

Spurr (2001) has also set the Exclusion Crisis in a broader context:

> This was not a narrow crisis about exclusion, but more a controversy over the succession problem and the political and constitutional implications of all the various expedients offered to solve it. It was not, in truth, merely a succession crisis either, but rather a collapse of political confidence. This collapse can be traced to anxieties about the whole range of Charles II's misgovernment, his toadying to France, the corruption of parliament, the creation of standing armies, the abuse of law, and the persecution of dissenters, and to even wider concerns about public and private interest.

5   *J. Spurr, **England in the 1670s** (2001)*

Scott (2000) saw exclusion as a minor issue, with the main issue being the threat of arbitrary government. Scott stressed the similarities between 1679–81 and 1640–2 – these periods shared the following:

■ Extent of royal prerogative.
■ Regularity of parliament.
■ Nature of the established church.
■ Threat of popery.

Miller (2000) has also seen the similarities with 1640–42, including distrust of the monarch and his family in the context of popish conspiracies. No matter the differences between the two periods, as Miller argues, in 1679–81 'contemporaries did not have the benefit of hindsight: their perceptions were coloured by memories of civil war, when ideological divisions had led to pressure on individuals to declare themselves and ultimately to bloodshed. There seemed every possibility that this would happen again'.

Knights (1994) has seen the crisis in the context of a series of interrelated crises:

■ The question of the succession.
■ The nature of government and the threat of absolutism.
■ The relationship between crown and people.

Smith (1998), like Scott (2000), has set the Exclusion Crisis in the context of that of 1640–2 and the nature of the Restoration Settlement:

> The Restoration Settlement not only restored the pre-war constitution but also pre-war fears about the growth of 'popery and arbitrary government'. It consciously revived the early Stuart constitution complete with all its grey areas and stress points surrounding the nature of monarchy and the relationship between Crown and Parliament. The inherent ambiguities of these constitutional arrangements were compounded by a Church settlement that institutionalized a bitter division between Anglicans and dissenters. The Whig/Tory divergence grew out of long-standing tensions and uncertainties about the nature of Church and State that had been left unresolved at the Restoration Settlement. The two 'parties' embodied contrasting attitudes not only to the issue of exclusion, but to the whole nature of Charles's kingship and the threat of 'popery and arbitrary government'. The King's tactical victory in the Exclusion Crisis prevented those issues from being resolved in 1681. Instead, the sources of instability persisted, until at the end of the decade an even greater crisis exploded that would finally necessitate the fundamental overhaul of this polity.

> **6**   *D.L. Smith, **The Double Crown: A History of the Modern British Isles, 1603–1707** (1998)*

■ Charles's growing absolutism

For Harris (2005) 'Such was the nature of the royal recovery in the final years of Charles II's reign that when James II came to the throne, in 1685, he enjoyed the strongest position of any English monarch certainly since the accession of the Stuarts in 1603 and arguably since the accession of Henry VIII in 1509'. This strengthening of the regime was accomplished in a number of ways.

Charles's exploitation of the prerogative

From 1676 Charles II appointed judges 'during the King's pleasure' rather than while 'they shall do good' and from this point he removed 11 judges. In 1684 Charles did not call a Parliament which he should have done under the Triennial Act.

Local government was also manipulated. In the summer of 1681, many Whigs were purged from the commissions of peace and lieutenancies. Town charters were also used as a means to limit the influence of the Whigs and dissenters in their traditional urban strongholds. In December 1681, Charles had demanded a new charter for the City of London giving him the power, which he finally secured in 1683, to appoint the Lord Mayor, sheriffs and all other major office-holders. The inability of London to defend its charter led others to not defend theirs and this increased the influence of Tories in urban areas. Between 1681 and 1685 51 new charters were issued and 47 prepared when Charles died. By these means Tories sought to control local government, have more influence over parliamentary elections and restrict dissent. For Mullet (1993) 'English municipal government had been brought within the parameters of Tory absolutism'. Linked to this the judiciary became dominated by Tories.

Weiser in *Charles II and the Politics of Access* (2003) has argued that political concerns, not personality, brought Charles II to initially favour open access as a means to aid the reunification of the nation. When his political agenda changed so did the politics of access. It became more limited and Charles used it as a political tool to galvanise supporters and dishearten opponents.

Arrests and executions

In July 1681, Shaftesbury was arrested on charges of treason. He was released in November when two London Whig sheriffs assembled a Whig-minded grand jury. Shaftesbury went to Amsterdam in November 1682 and died in 1683.

Amid rumours that Monmouth was planning a rising, he was arrested while in the north-west of England. According to studies by Ashcraft and Greaves there was a radical underground headed by powerful members of the Whig elite. The Rye House Plot which emerged in June 1683 enabled Charles to remove his other leading opponents. The Plot involved former Cromwellians planning to assassinate Charles and James at Rye House as they returned to London from Newmarket races. Essex, Russell and Sidney were imprisoned after being falsely implicated. On 13 July Essex was found with his throat cut. Russell and Sidney were executed.

Persecution of dissent

Persecution of dissent became harsher, with the Quakers especially suffering. At least 400 Quakers were to die in prison. In marked contrast Catholics were treated very leniently, fuelling more doubts about Charles's own religion. In 1679 70 per cent of those convicted of recusancy in Middlesex were Catholics. In 1681 only six per cent were convicted. Hutton (1989) referred to Charles as 'the most savage persecutor' of all English monarchs. For Harris (2005) 'People were exploited, brutalized, persecuted, hounded to death by a regime that felt desperately insecure after two decades of civil war and republican rule'.

> ### Exploring the detail
>
> Algernon Sidney's *Discourses Concerning Government*.
>
> This argued that:
>
> - People had a duty, not just a right, to disobey bad laws, depose or even kill a tyrant.
> - From this it argued that Charles II should be brought to trial because he 'despises the law'.
> - If Charles was not brought to trial 'extrajudicial' methods should be used.
>
> The Rye House Plot increased support for the Crown which was reinforced by continued propaganda.

In this period the powers of the Crown were extended through:

- prorogation and dissolution
- line of succession
- leadership of the Church
- more control over local government
- Whig leaders removed
- persecution
- propaganda
- healthy finance position
- an army of 10,000.

 Activity

Revision exercise

Construct a chart noting the position of Charles II and monarchy in 1662 and 1685 in relation to the areas indicated.

	1662	1685
Parliament		
Religion		
Finance		

Yet although the powers of the Crown had increased Harris has referred to the Crown consequently being a 'prisoner of party' circumscribed by the Tory-Anglican agenda.

The context for Charles's defeat of Exclusion and his growing absolutism was a contradictory failing of the regime and an increasing stress on its power. Hutton (2004) has commented on the final years of Charles II's reign that 'without Parliaments the regime could neither legislate nor raise war taxation, so that England was paralysed both as a legislature and as a military power'.

Summary questions

1 Why did Danby provoke opposition?

2 What was the most important reason for the failure of Exclusion?

3 To what extent was Charles II in a stronger position after 1681 more because of the failure of the Whigs rather than his own actions?

The Glorious Revolution of 1688–9

Fig. 1 *The Protestant William at the Battle of the Boyne, Ireland (1690) where he defeated supporters of the deposed Roman Catholic James II. Illustration by John Leech (1817–74)*

The Battle of Boyne (1690) in Ireland saw the immediate end of James II's hopes of reclaiming the throne.

James II, his personality and aims

Personality

James II was naturally authoritarian. For Mullett (1993) while James was 'dignified, soldierly and regal' he was also 'humourless, arrogant, obstinate, sometimes cruel, hectoring, brusque and unintelligent'. For Smith (1998) he was a 'conviction politician'. James was inflexible and, like his father Charles I, regarded all opposition as treason. He believed, as his mother did, that his father's problem was that he was weak and concessions had been a mistake. What made James's position much weaker was his open Catholicism.

Aims

Speck in *Reluctant Revolutionaries* (1988) argued that James sought to establish absolutism. In contrast Smith (1998) has argued that James 'did not systematically try to establish an absolutist State'. There is little debate, however, that James was driven by his Catholicism. He did not understand English anti-Catholicism. His ultimate aim was to improve the position of Catholics and everything else can be seen as subservient or a means to achieve his religious goals. He wanted the repeal of the penal laws against Catholics, but also dissenters and part of this would entail the repeal of Test and Corporation Acts. James was a determined Catholic. There had been a special mission by bishops to James in a failed attempt to re-convert him. Miller (1983) has stressed that James was an aging man in a hurry. James felt a need to protect his infant son, and thus needed to secure the position of the Crown and Catholicism. Miller therefore concludes that 'to achieve these objectives James had to extend his prerogative in ways which were dubiously legal, which, given his subjects' preconceptions, were bound to provoke fears of absolutism'. Hutton (2004) has argued that not only did James want to give Catholics toleration, he wanted to give them power and it was this that created the real political difficulties.

Hutton's argument is based on the fact that toleration was offered by:

- leading Tory politicians
- two-thirds of JPs and deputy-lieutenants in 1686
- William of Orange in 1687.

They accepted that penal laws should no longer be enforced. That James refused to accept this indicates that he aimed for more than toleration. Thus, according to Hutton, James had to:

> ... ensure the highest possible number of conversions to Rome before his demise; he set about trying to hand over large parts of the established structure of authority to Catholics, as fast as possible. The policy soon proved to be impossible to effect with the consent of any existing national body, and so he set out to achieve it not only with the maximum speed but the maximum crudity of means.

1

R. Hutton, Debates in Stuart History (2004)

Activity

Thinking point

Write a paragraph outlining why James was unlikely to succeed in his aims.

In trying to do so, James would encounter the deep anti-Catholicism of the English. London crowds actually shouted 'A Pope, A Pope' at James. As the Exclusion Crisis had shown the link in the public mind between Catholicism and absolutism was entrenched. One thing that Whigs, Tories and Dissenters had in common was a hatred of Catholicism. It was not only that James was a Catholic, but that as a Catholic he posed the real threat of wiping out Protestantism and in the process establishing absolutism.

Ministers

Most prominent in James II's Privy Council were:

- Halifax – Lord President
- Hyde, Earl of Rochester (brother-in-law) – Lord Treasurer
- Godolphin and Sunderland – former Exclusionists.

James's declarations at the start of his reign were designed to ease fears about his Catholicism and the threat of absolutism. He claimed he would 'never depart from the just rights and prerogative of the Crown'. His fundamental problem was, despite the strength of his position in 1685, the Tory reaction was based on the symbiosis of Crown and Church. James failed to recognise that this Tory loyalty to an essentially intolerant Church of England overrode their loyalty to a monarch who wanted to radically alter the religious settlement. James, like his father Charles I, by dogmatically sticking to his policies forced subjects who wanted to be loyal into opposition. Some, however, immediately declared their opposition.

Monmouth's rebellion

In response to James securing the throne, Monmouth had plotted a rebellion in the west of England. This only raised a force of at most 4,000 farmers, tradesmen and cloth workers.

Monmouth's *Declaration*, written by the radical Whig Robert Ferguson, was radical as an appeal to those lower down the social scale. It included calls for:

- annual parliaments
- repeal of laws against nonconformity.

The rebels were crushed by the standing army of 8,000 from Charles's reign at Sedgemoor at the start of July 1685. Monmouth was executed on 15 July.

In nine days Judge Jefferies sentenced 250 to death and 800 were transported to West Indies as slaves in what became known as 'the Bloody Assizes'. Some courtiers received bribes from some of those transported to secure them against execution. Many others died in jail. Mullett (1993) has stressed that such retribution was not out of the ordinary:

> The numbers selected for capital punishment [...] suggest the traditional government policy of teaching the lower orders in a given region a post-revolt punitive lesson of deterrence. Further, the fact that noble and officer-corps participants were reprieved confirms the impression that the mass killings were designed to protect the regime in future by reinstilling the lesson that the lower classes had a duty only to obey, never to rebel.

2   M. Mullett, *James II and English Politics, 1678–1688* (1993)

There was a similar brutal response to a Scottish rebellion. 177 were to be transported to New Jersey and in traditional Campbell lands there were summary executions and destruction of houses and land.

Reasons for the failure of the 1685 rebellions:

- Military weakness and tactical errors.
- Lack of coordination of risings.
- Limited support for the leader Argyll.
- Rapid government response.
- Lack of support from moderate Presbyterians.
- Limited support for Monmouth, in numbers and particularly the lack of gentry support in London.

The 1685 Parliament

Charles II's purges and the Tory Reaction meant that James's first Parliament (May 1685) was a Tory one with only 57 Whigs out of a total of 532 MPs. In the context of Monmouth's rising and its Tory makeup, Parliament voted James substantial funds so that he had an income of about £2 million a year during his reign. Parliament also voted for James to extend his army to 20,000 troops by December 1685. James however used his dispensing power to appoint almost 90 Catholic army officers. Parliament protested against this, indicating that there were limits to Tory support.

Did you know?
The execution of Monmouth

It took the executioner five attempts with the axe to sever Monmouth's head. The executioner was a hangman and had not used an axe before. He was also drunk. His first swing of the axe had missed Monmouth's neck and sliced open his shoulder. The next two blows only managed to loosen an ear and nick Monmouth's neck. At this point reports suggest that Monmouth raised his head. The executioner resorted to finishing his task with a hacksaw.

Did you know?
Executions

Of the 29 sentenced to die at Dorchester on 7 September, the executioners could only manage to hang, draw and quarter 13 in a day. The last woman executed for treason was as a result of the retribution that took place after Monmouth's rebellion. Elizabeth Gaunt had harboured a Monmouth rebel. For this she was taken to London and burned at the stake. It was normal for the victim to be shown some mercy first by being strangled. Gaunt was not and was left to burn alive.

There was concern over James's promotion of Catholics as army officers as they might have given him the potential of a force loyal solely to him, a personal guard. The issue led to a constitutional clash in November as parliament argued only they could exempt them from the Test Acts to allow them to serve in the army. In response James prorogued Parliament which had been sitting for less than two weeks and in doing so lost the grant of £700,000.

Godden vs. Hales, June 1686

This was a test case of James's dispensing power focused on Edward Hales, a Catholic who had served in the army. After testing the opinions of the judges before the trial James had six removed. The judgement was 11 of 12 judges in James's favour. James made use of this dispensing power from this court judgement that 'There is no law whatsoever but may be dispensed with by the supreme lawgiver [the King] … the laws of England are the king's laws'. In July 1686 four Catholics were appointed to the Privy Council.

James's actions were not, however, supported by Tory-Anglicans across the country who prevented the mass and did little to prevent anti-Catholic riots. James issued a Declaration to Preachers forbidding attacks on the Catholic Church by ministers. In response to Compton, the Bishop of London, refusing to suspend an anti-catholic London clergyman from preaching in July 1686 James set up the Commission for Ecclesiastical Causes under Sunderland and 'absolutist lawyers' Jeffreys and Herbert to enforce his control. This body removed Compton. According to Mullett (1993) 'By the summer of 1686 the King could be seen as defending the Church of Rome by conducting a campaign of aggression against the Church of England'. James also removed his Lord Treasurer Rochester when he declared he would never become a Catholic. He was replaced by the Catholic Lord Belasyse in January 1687 as head of a Treasury Commission.

Fig. 2 *Charles I, with his second son, James, Duke of York, in 1647. Painted by Peter Lely (1618–80)*

Multiple-kingdom dimension

Ireland

In January 1687 James appointed an Old English Catholic as his Lord Deputy, Richard Talbot, the Earl of Tyrconnell. The aim was to re-establish the power of the Old English Catholics. James appointed Catholic army officers in Ireland, making Tyrconnell lieutenant general of the Irish Army. Tyrconnell swiftly remodelled the army so that by September 1686 67 per cent of the troops and 40 per cent of the officers were Catholic. James also remodelled the judiciary to favour Catholic judges and similarly remodelled corporations to favour Catholics. This meant Catholic control of corporations, the bench and any future Irish Parliament. There was even an attempt to alter the land settlement that had further undermined the position of Catholics during the Interregnum. Tyrconnell sought to improve the land ownership of Catholics by getting Protestants to give up half of their land.

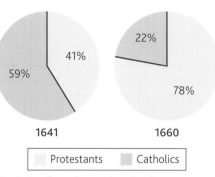

Fig. 3 *Land transference in Ireland*

James's policy of supporting and promoting Catholicisation destroyed the balance of forces in Ireland and made the situation even more fragile than was the norm.

Scotland

Argyll's rising of spring 1685 in the southwest Highlands failed and as elsewhere James appointed Catholics.

■ **Key profile**

Archibald Campbell, ninth Earl of Argyll

Son of the Covenanter leader who had been executed by Charles II in 1661. The ninth Earl, then imprisoned and sentenced to death, had the sentence rescinded and restored to his estates in 1663. Appointed to Scottish Privy Council in 1664 and remained loyal. Supported the 1681 Succession Act. Turning point was the Scottish Test Act of 1681. Charged with treason and sentenced to death after he wrote of his objections. Escaped from Edinburgh Castle and went into exile. Estates confiscated.

When the Scottish Parliament rejected James's proposal for toleration for Catholics, James proceeded through his prerogative. In February 1687 James proclaimed freedom of private worship for Catholics and Quakers, but not Presbyterians. James's policy in Scotland created:

- division of the Scottish elite
- opposition out of a loyal parliament
- the alienation of some in the Privy Council
- disaffection of many churchmen
- increase in anti-popery.

Declaration of Indulgence

In 1686, James shifted from Tory-Anglicans to build up support with Catholics and Dissenters – a political act to get toleration of Catholicism. By the June 1687 Declaration of Indulgence there was complete toleration and right to office for Catholics. Presbyterian conventiclers received the right of private worship and a relaxation of penal laws.

As well as being shaped by political considerations James's actions were also shaped by personal contacts with Dissenters such as the Quaker William Penn.

■ A closer look

William Penn, 1644–1718, Quaker leader and founder of Pennsylvania

Attended his first Quaker meeting in Cork in 1667. Taking over the family estates to become a man of substance promoted his influence in Quaker ranks as someone who could further their cause and he became friendly with George Fox. Penn then began to promote Quakerism and Dissent in a series of pamphlets. Penn also developed connections at court, notably Sunderland, Godolphin and Laurence Hyde. Involved in colonial affairs since the 1670s, Penn received a royal charter for Pennsylvania in 1681 and emigrated in 1682. Government in Pennsylvania was to be on inclusive political participation regardless of religion.

Penn returned to England in 1684 and was cultivated by James II who sent him as an envoy to the Hague in 1686. Here he found that while William and Mary would not repeal the Test Act they were willing to grant toleration. In 1687 Penn was involved in the writing of the Declaration of Indulgence. Penn became a spokesman for James II's policies with regard to toleration. News of William's plans to invade saw James retreat on his policies and this undermined Penn's influence. Under William he was imprisoned and his right to govern Pennsylvania revoked. Penn recovered his freedom and the governorship of Pennsylvania, the state recognising his influence with Quakers and in the colony but he never recovered the sway that he held briefly under James II.

The Declaration can also be seen in the context of Louis XIV's persecution of Huguenots. The Edict of Nantes had secured religious freedom for the 1 million Protestant Huguenots. Louis XIV revoked this and there was increased persecution of French dissenters. At least 1,500 were made galley slaves and between 50,000 to 80,000 fled to England. James's Declaration can be linked to economic considerations. Mullett (1993) has written of James being 'committed to fostering a national commercial progress in which thrifty, enterprising and diligent Dissenters might play a key part: hence his moves to encourage the immigration of foreign skilled workers'. Miller (2000) has gone further, seeing James's abandonment of the Anglicans and his adoption of the Nonconformists in the context of his accompanying shift in economic policy away from favouring the landed gentry and agriculture to the middling classes, the towns, trade and money.

James's attitude to Dissenters was different to his approach to Catholics. For example he was not willing to allow Dissenters into the universities or serve as army officers. In November 1686 he established a Licensing Office from which Dissenters could buy certificates of dispensation for immunity from the penal laws. The 4 April 1687 Declaration of Indulgence suspended the Test and Corporation Acts and penal laws against Catholics and Dissenters.

Some Dissenters were convinced by James's actions but many simply did not trust a Catholic. Halifax played upon their scepticism in his *Letter to a Dissenter* (1687).

■ Exploring the detail

Halifax's *Letter to a Dissenter*

A mark of the impact of Halifax's pamphlet was its sharp increase in price. On the first day of its release it sold at 3d. The next day it was being sold at 6d. The pamphlet soon rose to a price of 5 shillings. By October it had gone through six editions and sold 24,000 copies.

Many Dissenters believed that they had more in common with conformists than Catholics. James tried to get William of Orange to make a statement of his support for his Declaration of Indulgence of 1688. William refused to do this and stated his support for the Test Act. In February 1687, the Dutch emissary Dykvelt had secret contact with Nottingham, Shrewsbury, Halifax and Bishop Compton. A pamphlet, *A Letter written by Mijn Heer Fagel* of early 1688 stated Mary's opposition to the repeal of the Test Acts. Both Mary and William were willing, however, to support toleration, even for Catholics. Thus Dissenters knew that they did not need to support James over repeal.

James's attempt to impose Catholics on the universities of Cambridge and Oxford provoked further concern as Fellowships were regarded as a form of property and James's removal of the Fellows of Magdalen, Oxford was seen as a direct attack on this fundamental right.

Parliament

James secured a seven to five judgement on whether the dispensing power could exempt individuals from the Test Act. James then replaced four judges. In his short time as king James removed more judges than any other 17th century monarch. When James could not secure a judgement that he could suspend a statute he used the power anyway. In all of this he had some support from some Tories, Whigs, nonconformists and opportunists.

Fig. 4 *Louis XIV (1638–1715), King of France from 1643. Known as The Sun King* (Le Roi Soleil)

On 2 July 1687, James dissolved Parliament and tried to ensure the next would repeal the Test and penal laws. James was attempting to reduce parliament to a rubber stamp with which he hoped to change law to his advantage. With regard to this Jones (1980) has argued that it could have been a success, whereas Miller (1978) and Speck (1989) believe it would not have been a success.

James had the Lord Lieutenants ask JPs and Deputy Lieutenants three questions:

If elected would they:

- repeal the penal and test laws?
- help elect people who would support repeal?
- support the Declaration of Indulgence?

Mullett (1993) has argued that 'the polling process in itself awoke national debate, and thereby opposition'. Similarly James's summer tour of 1687 to build up support was counterproductive. He went to the south west, Wales and Midlands, but his Catholicism was all too apparent in his actions of promoting Catholics and visiting Catholic sites.

With only a third responding positively to James's three queries (mainly Catholics and Dissenters), purges of local government were increased and many replaced with those seen as reliable. This was an attack on the traditional ruling elite's dominance of their local area. They resented being replaced by less prominent men, whether Catholic or nonconformist.

By this stage James's ruling circle was wholly Catholic, including a Jesuit priest. This did not provoke resistance, however. The elite, on the whole, remained wedded to the concept of passivity. This gave James confidence of

Activity

Group discussion

From the perspective of the Dissenters list the advantages of James's policies. Why would there be some concern among the Dissenters about James's intentions?

■ Activity

Thinking point

Was James II's position in the summer of 1687 still viable? Construct a chart indicating the positive and negative elements of James's position by the summer of 1687.

■ Key dates

1685–8: opposition to James II

1685

May Argyll's rebellion in Scotland fails

July Monmouth's rebellion crushed

November Parliamentary protests at use of dispensing power

1687

February Dykvelt the Dutch emissary in contact with James's opponents

April Resistance of fellows of Magdalen College, Oxford

1688

May Archbishop Sancroft and six bishops petition that the suspending power was illegal

June Acquittal of Sancroft and six bishops

June 'Immortal Seven' invite William of Orange to England

September William's invasion plan sanctioned by states of Holland

September William's Declaration of reasons for appearing in arms in the kingdom of England

■ Activity

Group discussion

How did the case against the seven bishops strengthen and weaken James's position?

success with his next Parliament. For Miller (1983) 'James's regime could be challenged only by a professional army from outside the British Isles'. Yet James's actions meant that if there was such a challenge the English elite were alienated enough to not support him. According to Harris (2005):

> … in his efforts to help Catholics, James undoubtedly did exceed his legal powers. In the process, he managed to alienate broad cross-sections of the population: clerical and lay; upper, middling and lower sorts in both town and countryside; those at the centre of power and those remote from it. Most significantly, James succeeded in alienating the Tory-Anglican interest, which had backed the crown so wholeheartedly during the final years of his brother's reign but which now proved determined to uphold the rule of law against what they perceived to be the illegal actions of an arbitrary monarch.

3   *T. Harris,* **Revolution: Charles II and His Kingdoms** *(2005)*

■ Political and religious opposition to James II and the crisis of 1688–9

James announced that his next parliament, due in November, would enact his reissued Declaration of Indulgence of April 1688. James ordered that this was to be announced from all Anglican pulpits in late May and early June 1688. This led to a direct petition from Archbishop Sancroft and six bishops that as the Declaration was based on a power that Parliament regarded as illegal, there should be no statement from the pulpit. These men were not radicals and should have been James's natural supporters. All they wanted was for churchmen not to read the Declaration but James forced them into opposition and martyrs by committing them to the Tower and putting the seven of them on trial.

The judges divided over the question of the legality of the suspending power. Two judges who argued against the royal suspending power were dismissed. The jury acquitted the churchmen. This was a constitutional judgement against the King's suspending and dispensing powers; only parliament could repeal statutes. The case raised the question as to whether passive disobedience could work if James was going to use the courts in such a way.

THE SEVEN BISHOPS RETURNING FROM THE TOWER.
"*Engelands Godsdienst hersteld,*" 1689.

Fig. 5 *The seven bishops depicted as heroes*

A closer look

'Whig radicals'

Melinda Zook (1999) has argued that the whole of the 1680s should be seen as part of the Exclusion Crisis and that the influence of 'radical Whigs' should not be overlooked. In relation to the revolution of 1688 she has written:

> In the course of their years of struggle, radical Whigs formulated an ideology worthy of justifying their aims and activities, one that not only played upon long established fears of popery but also promoted an alternative political settlement for the country. After all, if radicals meant to meddle with the royal succession, they had to show proper cause. They consequently framed their political principles in the very English story of the ancient constitution, and through it propagated an ideology that vindicated the people's right to alter the succession. Radical Whigs also asserted that government was man-made, a historical construction particular to the nation that conceived it. They believed that government was contracted between the people and their chosen leader. They believed in the supremacy of the law, and most important for their movement, they believed in the people's right of resistance.

Zook, with regard to Whig culture and the violent struggle of the 1680s, has argued that in:

> '1688, radical Whig ideology was best expressed by Robert Ferguson, known as 'the Plotter', in his Brief Justification of the Descent of the Prince of Orange, arguably the true manifesto of the Glorious Revolution. The ever pragmatic Ferguson knitted together several strands of Whig argumentation developed in the course of the 1680s. The end result was a secular, contraction theory of government, which resonated with political sentiments, opinions, ideas, and visions already in circulation and familiar to the public. Radical Whig ideology not only justified the conspiracies of Whig radicals in the decade before 1688, but also fed what I see as a broader 'revolution culture'. This culture, in turn, made up of the ideas and adventures of these Whig desperadoes – set forth in tracts, weeklies, newsletters, manifestos, dying speeches, crude broadsides, and satirical songs – helped create the atmosphere that made the Glorious Revolution of 1688–9 possible'.

Key dates

1688

5 November	William lands at Torbay
19–23 November	William advances from Exeter
8 December	Hungerford meeting between William and commissioners of James
11 December	James brought to London after a failed attempt to reach the continent
18 December	William enters London
23 December	James escapes to France
24–26 December	Assembly of Peers and William's irregular assembly calls on William to call a Convention and take over government
28–29 December	William agrees to call a Convention

William's opposition

The trigger for heightened opposition and a different stand from William of Orange was the fact that on 10 June 1688 James's wife, Mary of Modena, gave birth to a son. James was already 54, but now there was the prospect of his being succeeded by another Catholic rather than his Protestant sister Mary. As the Tories were committed to the idea of a legitimate succession some now had to question the legitimacy of James's son. It was James's obvious willingness to use the courts to his own ends and the birth of his son that made some now decide that action was needed.

The threat of another attack by Louis XIV in the summer of 1688 and the birth of James's son pushed William into action. His wife would no longer be the next monarch of England, depriving him of probable

Did you know?

James's son, James Francis Edward, lived until 1766. His son, Charles Edward, born in 1720, lived until 1788. By 1788 the English crown had passed from William and Mary to James's daughter Anne, and then the Hanoverians – George I, George II, George III and George IV, who reigned until 1830.

■ **Exploring the detail**

William's position in the Dutch Republic

The Dutch Republic was made up of seven provinces. Holland was the richest and most influential province. The Republic had a decentralised government with each province having self-government and major towns in each province also having a lot of influence. The House of Orange was looked to as the most traditionally powerful family for leadership in times of crisis and war. The provinces and towns were concerned that William III was trying to make himself absolute.

■ Activity

Thinking point

Write a report for William of Orange outlining the reasons why he should invade England, including James II's domestic position and William's European concerns.

■ **Did you know?**

When William I launched his invasion of England in 1066 he brought 7,000 troops with him. For the aborted operation 'Sealion' in 1940, the intended German invasion of Britain, Hitler had a theoretical invasion force of at least 125,000 men.

English support against Louis XIV. William sent an emissary, Zuylestein, to congratulate James on the birth but Zuylestein's real task was to meet opposition figures and get William an invitation to invade.

On 30 June 1688, five Whigs (the Earls of Shrewsbury and Devonshire, Viscount Lumley, Edward Russell and the author of the invitation Henry Sydney) and two Tories (Danby and Compton the Bishop of London) who became known as the 'Immortal Seven' wrote to William. They invited him to invade England assuring him that the majority of the population were 'generally dissatisfied with the present conduct of the government, in relation to their religion, liberties and properties'. The aim of his invasion would be to secure a 'free Parliament' and investigate the legitimacy of James's son.

The European context

William regarded an invasion of England as beneficial to Dutch strategic and economic interests. The Dutch were under increasing pressure from Louis XIV's expansion of France's north-eastern border. In the first part of the 1680s opposition from Amsterdam and Holland's other major towns had limited what William could do. James had been unwilling to act against Louis XIV. In the summer of 1686 William had formed an alliance with the Holy Roman Empire, Spain, Sweden and the Electors of the German states of Bavaria, Saxony and the Palatinate. If England could be brought in to this League of Augsburg there was the prospect that France could be encircled. In 1687 the Turkish threat was halted so Austria could turn west and pose another threat to France.

William actually seemed concerned in the spring of 1688 that Louis's next assault on the Dutch Republic might be supported by James. The Revocation of the Edict of Nantes changed Dutch views about the seriousness of the threat Louis XIV posed. There was mistreatment of Dutch merchants in France, a flood of Huguenot refugees and new French tariffs on Dutch trade that turned opinion much more against France. In September 1688 Louis actually seized the Dutch wine fleet. By this stage, in economic terms, the Dutch had little to lose by going to war with France.

Invasion

James was spending £530,000 a year on the military as opposed to Charles's £200,000 and therefore William of Orange was taking a risk with an invasion. Against the risks William saw England's military as a vital part of his European strategy. From early July William was preparing his force:

- 463 ships.
- 5,000 horses.
- 15,000 men.

William also managed to keep James and Louis unsure of his actual intentions. Louis stated that if William invaded England he would attack the Dutch Republic. By September, however, Louis believed that it was too late for William to attempt an invasion of England and on 14 September committed his forces to an attack on the Rhenish Palatinate. On 29 September the States of Holland supported William's plan to invade in a secret resolution. On 30 September William issued a Declaration of reasons for appearing in arms in the kingdom of England. William did not state any intention of taking the throne. To do so would have been politically dangerous and it is likely William wanted to see what would happen once in England. His initial aim was to secure Dutch interests through intervention in English politics; a remodelling of Parliament and Council to ensure England supported the Dutch republic against Louis XIV.

Fig. 6 *The Dutch Republic*

Faced by the prospect of an invasion, James sought to compromise with his opponents in England. According to Harris (2006) even before the invasion there 'was an Anglican revolution in the autumn of 1688' which 'preceded the ultimate William revolution'. James met with Archbishop Sancroft and eight other bishops and as a result James:

- dissolved the Commission for Ecclesiastical Causes
- promised that the Church of England would be 'secured according to the Act of Uniformity'
- reinstated the Fellows of Magdalen, Oxford
- allowed London and some other corporations to regain their charters
- removed Sunderland from his Council.

Harris (2006) has argued that if the Tory-Anglican interest had carried out their programme in full there would have been 'an Anglican revolution'. It was too late. Harris stresses that James 'came undone because he failed to realise the extent to which the strength of the monarchy was based on [the] alliance between the Crown and the Tory-Anglican interest'.

Throughout October the wind did not allow William to set sail, but an easterly 'Protestant wind' allowed him to finally sail on 1 November. The same wind confined James's navy to port. On 5 November William landed at Torbay and by 9 November he had occupied Exeter. From here he called for a free Parliament. Some areas such as Cheshire, Nottinghamshire and Yorkshire were secured for William by peers who were sympathetic. Generally, however, the bulk of the population did not want to get involved, reinforcing the fact that if this was a revolution it was very much a revolution from above. The lack of support for James was a comment on how unpopular he was. For Harris (1990) 'that William did not need to engage the King's army in major battle [...] does not detract from the fact that what happened was a foreign conquest'. 25,000 were to die in the war in Ireland between William and James. It was a 'foreign conquest' with, however, the acquiescence of key elements of the British elite.

As with the vagaries of the weather and the threat of Louis it was also not preordained that William would be successful if he managed to land in England. The strength of James's position was:

■ control of London

■ a standing army of 53,000

■ reluctance to depose James, even among his leading critics.

Against this, once William did land James's weaknesses came to the fore. James's nerve effectively collapsed. He marched west and reached Salisbury on 19th November but failed to really act. His army also suffered from desertion, including officers such as John Churchill.

■ Key profile

John Churchill, 1650–1722

Churchill led the forces to crush Monmouth's rebellion. He supported William of Orange in disgust at James's promotion of Catholicism. Monmouth planned to use part of the army for William of Orange and in November 1688 he deserted William with 400 officers and men. Under William he was created Earl of Marlborough and continued to hold important posts in the army.

Fig. 7 *William III*

As William moved towards London James retreated to the capital. Here Rochester persuaded him to summon a free Parliament. This was to meet on 15 January 1689. James sent Halifax at a head of a delegation to meet with William.

At this 8 December meeting William, although demanding the dismissal of Catholics from military and civil positions, made no claim to the throne. Again, however, James played into William's hands by abandoning London. On 9 December he sent his wife and son to France and on 11 December he left London, deliberately dropping the Great Seal of England into the Thames. This allowed many who would have been reluctant to go over to William a way to claim they had no choice as James had 'withdrawn himself'. On 11 December 1688 bishops and peers, led by Sancroft and Rochester, met at the Guildhall and stated that as James had flown they were going to 'apply' to William. On 11, 12 and 13 December, London experienced three nights of anti-Catholic riots.

James returned to London on 16 December after being caught on Faversham beach by a group of fishermen who thought he was a Jesuit. In his absence Rochester and the Bishop of Ely had begun to organise an Assembly of Peers to run the country.

On 18 December, William arrived in London. James tried to resume government but then retreated to Kent. He was deliberately left lightly guarded and took the opportunity to flee to France on 23 December, playing into William's hands. Fearful for his son and determined not to betray his religion he took the opportunity to flee. On 23 December William called for advice from an irregular assembly of:

■ all surviving MPs from Charles's Parliaments, but not James's

■ the Lord Mayor and Court of Aldermen of the City, fifty representatives of the Common Council of London from the government of London.

This assembly of about 400 was predominantly, without MPs from James's parliaments, a Whig institution likely to favour William.

On 24 December, the Assembly of Peers invited William to take over government and this call was repeated by William's irregular assembly on 26 December. They also called for elections to establish a Convention that would preserve 'our religion, rights, laws, liberty and property'. Furthermore the Convention would aim to put these things on 'sure and legal foundations that they may not be in danger of being again subverted'. On 29 December writs were issued for elections. For Smith (1998), 'in essence a Dutch coup had taken place'.

The 'revolution' of 1689 and the position and power of monarchy

The 'Glorious Revolution'

William had his own forces as an occupying army in London, where they remained until May 1690. James's army had also gone over to William. On 22 January 1689 the Convention met. This was an Assembly that had 319 Whigs and 232 Tories. There was division over the succession. Whigs, who accepted a contractual theory of kingship, argued that as James had 'broken the fundamental laws of the constitution' he had forfeited the throne. In contrast Tories argued that James was only 'incapacitated' and that William and Mary should only be regents or Mary should rule with William as only consort.

There was, however, a moderate consensus between Whigs and Tories that secured a middle ground and compromised conservative settlement, what Morrill (1993) has referred to as 'a centrist compromise and constitutional blur'. Smith (1998) has similarly seen it as 'a pragmatic compromise that sought to re-establish political stability by consciously appealing to as wide a range of opinion as possible. In general it achieved this aim very successfully and only the two extreme ends of the ideological spectrum were left alienated'. This compromise can be seen from the Commons' statement of 28 January to which only three Tory MPs were opposed:

> King James II, having endeavoured to subvert the constitution of the kingdom, by breaking the original contract between king and people; and by the advice of Jesuits and other wicked persons having violated the fundamental laws; and having withdrawn himself out of this kingdom; has abdicated the government; and that the throne is thereby vacant.

4

Tory objections to this statement in the Lords led to demonstrating crowds outside Parliament. On 3 February William, in a secret meeting with peers, warned them that he 'would go back to Holland' unless he were made king. There were two provisos:

- His wife, Mary, would share the title of monarch, although without the power.
- If Mary died and William married again, any children from this second marriage would be behind Anne in the line of succession.

Activity

Group discussion

What other approaches could James have adopted to the crisis he faced? Did James II throw away the Crown?

Activity

Class debate

Who was the most unfit to be king: Charles I or James II?

Key dates

1689

January–August	First session of Cavalier Parliament
	James declared to have 'abdicated' with the throne left 'vacant'
	Declaration of Rights constructed
13 February	Throne offered to William and Mary with Declaration of Rights read to them
14 February	Proclamation of William and Mary as King and Queen
20 March	William granted a revenue of £1.2 million a year
28 March	Mutiny Act declares standing army in peacetime illegal unless agreed by Parliament
April	William and Mary crowned king and queen of England and Ireland
May	Scottish throne accepted by William and Mary
24 May	Toleration Act
July	Prelacy abolished in Scotland
October–January 1690	Declaration of Rights enacted as Bill of Rights

■ **Key profile**

Queen Anne, 1665–1714, Queen 1702–14

Fourth child and second daughter of James II and Anne Hyde, but only her and her elder sister, Mary II, survived into adulthood. Charles II made sure she and Mary were brought up Anglicans. She married Prince George of Denmark (1653–1708) in 1683. Anne was, according to her biographer Edward Gregg, 'the major perpetrator, and perhaps the originator, of the calumny that her stepmother's pregnancy was false'. James had married the 15 year old Catholic Mary of Modena in 1673 and Anne had never been close to her step-mother. She supported the takeover by William of Orange and her sister Mary. Anne produced 18 children, only five of whom were born alive. One son, the Duke of Gloucester, lived until he was eleven, dying in 1700.

■ **Key terms**

de facto: a monarch or government in possession of power. Many in the 1650s would still have regarded Charles II's exiled court as the *de jure* government.

de jure: a monarch or government recognised as the legal, legitimate ruler or government.

■ **Exploring the detail**

The Bill of Rights, 1689:

- No Catholic was to inherit the throne.
- No king could marry a Catholic.
- No standing army.
- No ecclesiastical commissions.
- Suspending and dispensing powers of the monarch declared unconstitutional.
- Parliament had to consent to all taxation.

■ **Exploring the detail**

The Toleration Act of 1689:

- Freedom of worship for all Protestants.
- Dissenters were still deprived of civil and political rights by the Test and Corporation Acts.

On 6 February this was accepted by the Lords and confirmed by the Commons on 8 February. A Declaration of Rights, produced by a parliamentary committee of 16 Whigs and 6 Tories, was not made a condition of giving William the throne. This Declaration stated that Catholics were never to inherit the Crown.

The Declaration was very much a compromise document that was left deliberately ambiguous in terms of the constitutional implications of James's removal. There was no statement that James had been resisted, deposed or that he had broken a contract. Similarly William and Mary were not referred to as 'rightful' or 'lawful heirs'. This meant that those who wished to regard William and Mary as **de facto** monarchs or monarchs by conquest could recognise them as rulers without denying that James was **de jure** king.

On 13 February, there was a formal ceremony offering the Crown to William and Mary at which the Declaration was read out after. On 11 April at William and Mary's coronation there was a different coronation oath from that sworn by previous monarchs indicating their different position and that of Parliament:

- **Previous:** 'Confirm to the people of England the laws and customs to them granted by the Kings of England'.
- **William and Mary:** 'To govern the people of this kingdom of England, and the dominions thereunto belonging, according to the statutes in Parliament agreed on, and the laws and customs of the same'.

In December 1689 a watered down version of the Declaration of Rights was passed as the Bill of Rights.

In March 1689, a Mutiny Act prevented the creation of any standing army without the consent of Parliament. In May 1689 the Toleration Act exempted Dissenters from penal laws if they took an oath of allegiance and declared against transubstantiation (Catholic belief that during the Mass the bread and wine are transformed into Christ's body and blood). They still, however, could not hold public office because of the Test and Corporation Acts. This was much less tolerant to Dissenters than the Calvinist William would have wanted. Dissenters could worship freely in licensed meeting houses which had to keep their doors open. It did address some of the issues left from the 1650s and not dealt with in 1662.

The financial revolution

On 20 March a revenue of £1.2 million a year was settled on the Crown. It was specified that half be used for civil government and the other half for war. The Crown immediately went into debt. For Miller (1983) 'the failure to grant William an adequate revenue in 1689–90 was deliberate. The destruction of all hope of an independent royal revenue transformed the Crown's relationship with parliament. Now the Commons, if they chose, could force their wishes on the King by withholding supply.

In practice, the picture was more complex, but the fact remains that the great constitutional change brought about by the Revolution owed far more to the impact of the financial settlement (compounded by the war) than to the change of ruler or the Bill of Rights'. Smith (1998) also emphasises the constitutional significance of the financial settlement: 'the long term significance of the financial settlement was immense: in a period of almost incessant war, it imposed a genuine restraint on the Crown and secured for Parliament a permanent role in government in a way that the Bill of Rights never could'.

Others have also seen revolution not so much in the political changes of 1688–9 but significant changes that this brought through war and financial revolution. Scott (2000) has argued that 1688 broke the mould of Stuart politics for good and allowed real state building. It was this, the transformation of the state to fight the wars of the next century, that transformed Britain into a world power.

Multiple-kingdoms

Scotland

On 14 March 1689 William summoned the Convention of Estates. This body, with the Scottish Jacobites, supporters of James, refusing to attend, voted that James had forfeited the throne. This vote was then reinforced a week later in the Claim of Right which stated that as James had forfeited the throne it was vacant. In this sense events in Scotland were more revolutionary. In the absence of Tories, the Convention had proceeded on a contractual theory of kingship that had been deliberately avoided in England to accommodate Tories. The Revolution in Scotland was also more revolutionary than that in England in terms of religion, with William agreeing to the abolition of prelacy.

On 11 May, William and Mary accepted the Scottish throne. In the summer of 1689 he faced Jacobite rebellion from the Highlands and although these forces were defeated at Cromdale in May 1690 it was clear to William that he would need the Presbyterians for support in Scotland. As a result the Scottish Parliament secured the following:

- Repeal of the 1669 Act asserting the royal supremacy over the Church.
- Abolition of the Lords of the Articles.
- Act establishing Presbyterian Church government.
- Act abolishing lay patronage. Kirk sessions were to present ministers.

These measures were followed by the purging of over 600 ministers in the next seven years, a further mark of the supreme position of the Presbyterians in post-revolutionary Scotland. Royal favour had returned to more radical Protestants in the Lowlands and thus consolidated influence of Presbyterianism. Catholics and Gaelic clan allegiance to the Stuarts in the long run saw their destruction.

Key dates

1689

March James lands at Kinsale, Ireland

April Londonderry besieged by James's forces

May–July James convenes a Parliament in Dublin

July Victory for Jacobite forces in the Scottish Highlands at Killiecrankie

30 July Siege of Londonderry broken by Williamite forces

1690

May Defeat of Scottish Jacobites at Cromdale

June William arrives in Ireland

1 July Battle of the Boyne – crushing defeat for James

4 July James leaves Ireland for France

Ireland

Ireland was the centre of Jacobite resistance and therefore posed a threat to William as part of the international war he was engaged in. By March 1689 the Catholics under Tyrconnell controlled all of Ireland apart from Ulster. Then James landed with 3,000 French troops. With the war going badly William landed in Ireland in June 1690. In total William could call on about 36,000 troops to face James's 25,000. On 1 July William defeated James at the Battle of the Boyne. James fled to France where he died in 1701. Protestant control was imposed on Ireland.

Harris (2006) has also set the events of 1688 in their British context. William's invasion 'precipitated three very different revolutions in the three kingdoms':

- **England:** Mostly conservative – but implications wide-ranging.
- **Scotland:** More radical – overturned the Restoration settlement in church and state.
- **Ireland:** Attempted Catholic revolution and counter-revolution by William.

These three revolutions led to a fourth revolution; a revolution in the relationship between the three kingdoms: Scotland lost its independence in 1707 and Ireland became a colony with the Declaratory Act in 1720.

The position and powers of monarchy after 1688

As a result of the revolution, and particularly the financial revolution, the monarchy became more dependent on Parliament. For Speck (1989) 'In 1689 parliament was finally transformed from an event into an institution'. William's wars against France reinforced this dependence. In the period after 1688 the following developments changed the position and powers of monarchy:

- Crown income becomes national income raised and managed by Parliament.
- Crown needs parliamentary support.
- Parliament begins to oversee foreign policy.
- Crown accepted the need to have regular parliaments.
- Crown had to accept ministers who could get them parliamentary support.

Learning outcomes

From this section you will have gained an understanding of continuing political division and the emergence of Tories and Whigs in the context of the Exclusion Crisis. This will also have led to an understanding of how Charles defeated Exclusion and as a result emerged with the monarchy strengthened. You will also have considered the personality and aims of James II, gaining an understanding of why James's policies provoked opposition and from this the nature of this opposition. You should also be able to explain the different elements of William's motivation in intervening in British affairs in 1688. You will also have gained an understanding of the nature of the Glorious Revolution and the revolution settlement. In the context of these you will also have considered the position and powers of monarchy as a result of 1688.

Activity

Thinking points

Why did James's policies provoke opposition? How revolutionary was the Glorious Revolution? Why were the powers of the monarch more limited as a result of 1688–9?

 Examination-style questions

1. To what extent was the Exclusion crisis of 1678–83 political rather than religious?

To answer this question the essay needs to address both the political and religious aspects of the 1678–83 crisis. Looking at Charles's actions it is possible to judge this as a political crisis to which he reacted politically. By focusing on Charles's actions you should discuss the following:

- Admission of opponents to the Privy Council.

- The exile of James.

- Danby's dismissal.

- Refusal to interfere with the Popish plot trials.

- Resistance to Shaftesbury and the use of Charles's prerogative powers.

In making a judgement there should be stress on the link between the two factors in the crisis to produce a stronger answer. Politics and religion cannot be separated in the 17th century. Although the Exclusion Crisis might have manifested itself in a political form it was derived from religious concerns. Some assessment of the level of the crisis would also be useful.

2. How important was the issue of multiple-kingdoms, the interrelation between England, Scotland and Ireland, in the political unrest of the years 1649 to 1689?

In the examination there will be the opportunity to respond to a question covering a broad theme over a substantial period of years. To answer this specific question the essay needs to cover the period 1649 to 1689. As this is a 40-year period, treatment of these years is not expected to be extensive. It is therefore important to select good illustrative examples. Constructing a chart or plan listing examples of when events in Ireland and Scotland had a significant impact on English affairs across the period 1649–89 will help to structure the essay clearly. Split the years 1649 to 1689 into easily manageable periods structured around what can be regarded as turning points. For example:

1649–60

1660–78

1678–85

1685–9

Give relevant examples for each of these periods, focusing on factors that caused political unrest in these years. When these are framed by an introduction and conclusion, you have the structure of an essay.

You also need to give some explanation of why there was a multiple-kingdom issue in this period. This essentially derived from the Stuarts being monarchs of all three kingdoms. Your arguments can be supported by reference to the role of religion across all England, Scotland and Ireland, particularly the differences between the kingdoms and the consequent political impact of these differences.

Conclusion

The years 1642 to 1689 were witness to some of the greatest events in British history – a civil war, regicide, the deposition of the monarch and his replacement by the Dutch William of Orange as King William III. While each of these three major events of the period had their own individual short-term causes they, and the Stuart Age itself, were linked together as the crisis of the state. This crisis was derived from, and triggered by, reactions to a fear of Catholicism and absolutism. The way in which these three transformations were triggered, developed and finally resolved after 1689, saw the emergence of a remodelled fiscal-military state that was the basis of Britain's position in the world in the next century.

Fig. 1 *The death warrant of Charles I showing the signatures of the regicides: Bradshaw (first), Cromwell (third), Ireton (ninth), Harrison (sixteenth)*

The years 1642 to 1689 were a dynamic period. They laid the foundations for the gradual emergence of a modern British state, as what had been a minor European power now stood on the verge of becoming a world power. From the period 1642 to 1689, there emerged what were to be features of the next 200 to 300 years of political life, such as the formation of Britain itself, formalised in 1707 by the Union of England and Scotland. The period also saw the development of Tories and Whigs as political bodies, which were to be the dominant political groupings until early 20th century. This was, however, a process that took place over time rather than an abrupt shift into the modern world.

Within the elements of continuity and change across these 47 years, the English Revolution of 1649 stands out. In 1660 the execution of the remaining regicides was part of a process of the re-imposition of monarchy. Yet the Restoration may have enabled a returning monarch to illustrate his power, but the Crown's authority after 1649 could never be the same as it was before the regicide. As Smith (1999) has argued:

> When the monarch was restored in 1660, a systematic attempt was made to turn the clock back, but the memories of the traumas of the 1640s and 1650s could never be erased. They left a legacy of fear and division, especially in religious matters, that could not be allayed and that shaped the nature of Restoration politics both inside Parliaments and more widely. This legacy contributed to the downfall of James II and the Revolution of 1688–9.

1   *D.L. Smith, **The Stuart Parliaments, 1603–1689** (1999)*

Although there was a Restoration, none of the underlying tensions, the crises of state, were actually resolved. The problems were:

- the limited finances of the Crown
- the limited adminstration available to the Crown
- the inability to conduct war on the European stage
- ruling three kingdoms
- the religious differences between Catholics and Protestants within the three kingdoms
- the differences between Protestants within the three kingdoms.

Under the pressures of war, the English state had been transformed between 1642 and 1660 into a nation capable of waging war successfully. The Restoration merely interrupted this process. A key element of continuity and change across the 17th century and over the 47 years of this study was the creation of a modern, powerful state, a process that was beginning before the mid-century revolution. While the Restoration may have interrupted the process, it was not halted, and Britain continued to transform itself.

One of the constant forces through our period of study was a continuing fear of Catholicism and absolutism. These were crucial underlying themes that made the Stuart monarchy potentially unstable and were fundamental to the crisis of state of 1642 to 1689. British society experienced a deep-seated fear of the Catholic religion uniting with royal power in one single, dominating force. These two fears, coupled with the problematic nature of the finances of the state and the inherently ambiguous constitutional relationship between Crown and Parliament were not resolved by the Restoration settlement and were thus also still issues in 1688.

Regarding the Revolution, the single greatest moment of change in our period, historians are still debating both its events and meaning. They question exactly when the English Revolution occured, suggesting dates such as 1641, 1647–9 or 1640–60. They have debated what kind of revolution it was. Some argued that it was a revolution whereby the gentry gained more influenced. More recently others have argued that it was a failed revolution for the true revolutionaries, groups like the Levellers. Even the term 'British' has provoked debate given the nature of the relationship between the three kingdoms of England, Scotland and Ireland.

Alongside turbulent moments of change, there were also continuities. Harris, who in a series of works has examined the Restoration period, has highlighted the continuities that persisted over the 47 years covered by this study. For Harris (1991) the 'year 1660 should not be seen as marking too much of a watershed' and 'if we look at the struggles which emerged in the 1670s and 1680s we find there were more continuities than is usually recognised'. For Harris the following continuities can be seen:

- **A continuity of personnel:** Across the period the monarchy remained the central institution.

- **A continuity of concern over the security of Protestantism:** Across the period there was a concern about whether Protestantism would survive.

- **A continuity of concern over the threat of Catholicism:** Across the period there were concerns about the threat of Catholicism from Europe and Ireland as well as internally.

- **A continuity of division between Protestants:** Across the period there were large numbers of Protestants who did not agree with the established Church of England.

Fig. 2 *Anthony van Dyck's Charles I on horseback*

In addition to the overarching fear of Catholicism, what tied these 47 years together was the impact of war on both government and society. War was fundamental to the crisis of state, but also transformed the state. At the start of the Stuart Age in 1603, England was a minor European power. With regard to the 1620s, Conrad Russell argued that the English state was on the verge of 'functional breakdown'. Charles I's attempts to intervene in the European Thirty Years War during the 1620s proved disastrous, and England remained essentially insignificant in European power politics until 1651. The civil wars of 1642–1651 addressed this crisis of state.

Under Cromwell, England was courted by the main European powers, reflecting changed perceptions of the power that Cromwell could, potentially, unleash. With the Restoration, however, Charles II was humiliated by the Dutch in the 1660s and became, in effect, a client of the French monarch Louis XIV in the 1670s. After 1689, William of Orange's involvement in European conflicts transformed England into Britain and into a world power through the emergence of a fiscal-military state, and in doing so resolved the crisis of state. To fight the war, William worked with parliament to secure finance and also had to develop an efficient and larger administration. Both of these inter-linked developments saw the emergence of something more closely recognisable as a modern state.

This transformation of the state through war was tied, as we have seen, to the fear of Catholicism and absolutism. Scott (2000) argued that 'England's 17th-century wars, whether civil (1640s) or international

(1624–9, 1665–7, 1689–1713), were ideological. These were wars against popery and arbitrary government'. Furthermore:

> … the modern English state was a product of, as well as a structure for ending, its religious wars. Those same beliefs and fears which in circumstances of military and political weakness resulted in state paralysis (1620s and 1670s) were equally responsible in other contexts for the construction of the state. The transformation of the English into the British state in the 1650s, and more decisively in the early eighteenth century, was again a product of these ideological, and particularly religious, concerns.

2   *J. Scott, England's Troubles: Seventeenth-Century Political Instability in European Context (2000)*

Yet this transformation of the British state only happened after 1690, because the impact of the revolutions of 1649 and 1688–9 changed the fundamental relationship of the state, that between Parliament and Crown. Increasingly after 1689 Crown and Parliament worked more together in order to finance and organised Britain's role as a European and world power.

The key feature of the 47 years studied in this book was that Britain was in a process of both transformation and continuity. The British monarchy's crisis of state was resolved when it was finally transformed into a world power with a relatively settled relationship between Crown and Parliament. The reality of this resolution is more than 300 years of relatively stable political relations in Britain from the Glorious Revolution to the present day.

Glossary

A

Absolutism: a monarch with unlimited powers, specifically to make law and raise taxes without the need for Parliament's agreement.

Adjutators: men and junior officers who took a leading role in the politicisation and political life of the army.

Ancient constitution: a system that had evolved over time. Part of this constitution were documents like the Magna Carta, but the working of the constitution depended upon trust between Crown and Parliament and the balance of the prerogative and privilege.

Antinomianism: a belief that those destined to achieve salvation could not sin and as a result had been freed from normal moral law.

Arbitrary government: phrase used predominantly from the early 1670s onwards in reaction to the fear that Charles II was becoming absolutist.

Attainder: a medieval method that allowed anyone who was seen as a threat to the state to be removed by Parliament without the need of a formal trial.

B

Baroque: highly ornate and extravagant in style and, in the case of Louis XIV and Charles II, designed to give prestige to their courts and impress other powers.

C

Catholicism: branch of the Christian church headed by the Pope. In the eyes of many English at the time, linked with absolutism and threat of both symbolised by the power of Spain and after 1660 increasingly with the threat of Louis XIV's France.

Cavalier: derogatory term for those who fought for Charles I in the civil war and also applied to the Cavalier

Parliament, Charles II first elected parliament that was a conservative reaction to the Interregnum.

Commonwealth: term for the republic of the Rump Parliament (1649–53 and 1659). Commonwealthsmen was a term used for and by republicans like Arthur Haselrig.

Comprehension: the aim of broadening the established Church of England to allow a greater range of non-conformists to conform to and come within the Church of England.

Conformity: term for agreeing to the set practices and order of the Church of England imposed by the monarch as Supreme Governor and the bishops appointed by the monarch.

Conspiracy theory: a belief, in any period, that the explanation for events or actions is more sinister than the official explanation.

Conservatism: general term for those who stood for tradition and order in politics, religion and society. A relative term for during the years of revolution those who had been considered radical before 1642 could be considered conservative in the context of the emergence of Levellers or Ranters.

Constitution: the rules by which a state is governed. Before 1653 and after 1660 there was no 'written constitution' and England was said to be governed by the 'ancient constitution', a system that had evolved over time. Part of this constitution were documents like the Magna Carta of 1215 but the working of the constitution depended upon trust between Crown and Parliament and the balance of the prerogative and privilege. In 1653 *The Instrument of Government* was Britain's first written constitution.

Coup: an attempt to overthrow the set order or remove key leadership figures from power. In the context of this period this can be applied

to the interventions by the New Model Army to end or disrupt sittings of Parliament, most notably in 1648, 1653 and 1659.

Crown patronage: the power of a monarch or leading crown ministers to bestow jobs or offices as a means to bind the recipient as a loyal client.

Crypto-Catholics: Catholics who kept their Catholicism as secret or 'closet' to maintain their political roles or position at court.

D

De facto: a monarch or government in possession of power. Many in the 1650s would still have regarded Charles II's exiled court as the *de jure* government.

De jure: a monarch or government recognised as the legal, legitimate ruler or government.

Dissent: post-Restoration non-conformists who dissented from, did not agree with, the established Church of England.

Dissolution: term used in relation to the prerogative right of a monarch to dissolve, end the sitting, of Parliament.

Divine right: belief that the monarch was God's representative on earth and therefore a key justification for the prerogative.

E

Early modern: the period in British history c.1485–1750.

Episcopacy: church run by bishops. The Church of England had the monarch as Supreme Governor and then the Archbishop of Canterbury and Archbishop of York. There were bishops underneath these to administer the discipline of the Church.

Exclusion: term for the attempts to exclude or prevent James, Duke of York from succeeding to the throne when Charles II died.

F

Feudal/feudalism: a system introduced into England by the Normans after the conquest of 1066.

Fiscal-military state: a state financially organised for war with a supporting administration.

Freethinkers: those who were outside the Church of England and did not believe in the literal truth of the Bible. They believed that the world could be understood through examining nature.

G

Gentry: section of society below the aristocracy who formed the bulk of the political nation being represented in parliament and controlling local government alongside the aristocracy. There were different degrees of gentry status, all based on landed wealth.

Great Chain of Being: contemporary phrase for the idea of the ordered society in the 17th century set in place by God and where everyone was tied to each other and accepted their place.

H

Habeas corpus: a writ to bring a person before a court or judge to ensure that they are legally held prisoner.

I

Indemnity: insurance against prosecution and in this period particularly applying to the concerns of soldiers in 1647 as well as those who might be excepted from punishment at the Restoration.

Independency: a broad term which embraced the Independent sects who had rejected the concept of a state church for gathered churches of fellow believers.

Interregnum: the years 1649 to 1660, when England was 'in-between kings'.

K

Kingship: the offer of the Crown to Cromwell in 1657.

L

Latitudinarianism: a belief that reason and personal judgement are more useful than church doctrine.

Long 18th century: the term used by some historians who, with regard to the periodisation of History, believe that the period 1688–1832 merits study as a whole because of themes that run through it.

M

Militia: England did not have a standing professional army. Each county had a militia which in times of need was to be formed into the basis of an army.

Millenarianism: belief in the end of the world as foretold in the Bible and specifically the Books of Daniel and Revelation. The end of the world was marked by the second coming of Christ and the establishment of his kingdom. A belief that was common but groups like the Fifth Monarchists believed that the end of the world was imminent.

N

Natural law: a law that is set by nature and therefore has validity everywhere above human laws. Associated with natural rights that limited the power of monarchy.

O

Ordinances: by the terms of the *Instrument of Government* Cromwell and the Council of State could legislate by Ordinance between the sittings of Parliaments. Between 24 December 1653 and 2 September 1654 Cromwell and the Council brought in 83 ordinances. The majority of Ordinances dealt with finance, making the tax collecting system more efficient.

P

Personal Monarchy: the power of the Crown in this period was theoretically absolute and this was supported by the concept of the Divine Right of Kings. In such a framework the monarch was government and expected to actively rule. Therefore their personality and aims shaped policy and thus it was a system of Personal Monarchy.

Political Nation: the section of society, the gentry and the aristocracy who had power in early modern Britain through local government, parliament and, fundamentally, land as the key source of wealth.

Politicisation: process by which the soldiers and officers of the New Model Army saw the solution to their material grievances after the end of the first civil war through direct involvement in politics. Part of this politicisation also came from their religious belief that they were God's instrument.

Popery: derogatory term for Catholicism derived from the Pope being head of the Catholic Church. Anti-popery was a key component of English Protestantism in the 17th century.

Predestination: at its most radical this was the belief that salvation was already decided by God and was not dependent on leading a good life.

Prerogative: the power of the Crown in theory derived from God as divine right. From divine right the powers of the Crown were referred to as the prerogative.

Presbyterianism: Presbyterians were those who supported a church with a government of equal presbyters, or elders, often appointed by the congregation, rather than others systems such as episcopacy (bishops).

Privy Council: the King's selected advisers who met in private to shape the monarch's wishes into policy and oversee its implementation.

Protestantism: churches separated from Catholicism by reformation. The Protestant Church of England had become established under Henry VIII and Elizabeth I.

Providence: belief in God's direction of earthly affairs. Key figures like Oliver Cromwell saw God's hand in his life and this belief in providence shaped how they made political decisions and lived their life.

Puritanism: a more radical form of Protestant who saw themselves as the 'godly' and sometimes referred to as 'the hotter sort of Protestant'. They sought a further reformation of the English Church to remove the vestiges of Catholicism that remained from the Reformation.

R

Recognition: at the start of the Protectorate some republican MPs questioned the legitimacy of the *Instrument of Government*. In response Cromwell declared 'four fundamentals'.

Recruiter MPs: the recruitment of MPs to replace those that were with the King to maintain numbers in the Commons.

Regicide: the execution of the monarch. The regicides were those 59 men who signed the death warrant of Charles I, although the act of regicide was supported by others, notably in the New Model Army and those of more radical religious views.

Republicanism: nominally support for rule without a monarch. There were in the period different interpretations of republicanism. For example one model was the position of the Stadholder in the United Provinces or the Venetian model of an aristocratic oligarchy (rule by a few).

Revolution: another term which had various meanings applied to it in the 17th century. Most notably revolution may be applied to the events of 1647–9 and 1688–9 in the sense of an overturning of the established political, religious and social order. In this sense some historians would therefore label the whole of the period 1640–60 as an English Revolution because of the relative radicalism of the period.

Restoration: the reimposition of the monarchy in 1660 with the return of Charles Stuart, Charles I's eldest son, as Charles II. In 1660 some used the term Revolution for what we term Restoration in the sense of a revolution, a cyclical return to the previous norm.

Rump Parliament: name derived from the nature of the body as a result of Pride's Purge of 6 December 1648, which removed MPs to enable the trial of Charles I.

S

Stuart Age: the period 1603–1714 during which the Stuarts were monarchs of England, Scotland and Ireland.

Suspending power: prerogative to suspend operation of any law. Used by Charles and James to suspend penal laws against Catholics.

Succession: England was ruled by a hereditary monarchy, apart from the Interregnum, which saw the line of succession, who should be the next monarch, pass to the eldest son. In the absence of a son it would then pass to daughters or whoever had the strongest family claim. Thus Charles II was Charles I's eldest son, born in 1630. His next eldest child was Mary who had been born in 1631. As Charles II did not have a legitimate heir the line of succession was, however, not Mary but the next eldest son James who had been born in 1633 and in 1685 did succeed to become James II.

U

Universal monarchy: the concept of one monarchy having world power, or striving for world power. In the 16th century the English saw this threat coming from Spain. In the 1660s some Anglican Royalists saw the threat coming from Dutch republicanism with its commercial and colonial success. The military success of France under Louis XIV made the French the latest pretender to universal dominion.

Bibliography

For student use

Anderson, A. (1999) *Stuart Britain, 1603–1714*, Hodder.
Coward, B. (1997) *Stuart England, 1603–1714*, Longman
Smith, D. L. (1998) *A History of the Modern British Isles, 1603–1707*, Blackwell
Wilkinson, R. (1999) *Britain 1603–1714*, Hodder

For student reference

Coward, B. (1994) *The Stuart Age, 1603–1714*, Longman
Kishlansky, M. (1996) *A Monarchy Transformed: Britain 1603–1714*, Penguin
Morrill, J. (2000) *Stuart Britain: A Very Short Introduction*, Oxford University Press

For teachers and extension

Barnard, T. (1997) *The English Republic 1649–1660*, Longman
Bliss, R. M. (1985) *Restoration England 1660–1688*, Routledge
Cruikshanks, E. (2000) *The Glorious Revolution*, Macmillan
Doran, S. and C. Durston (2002) *Princes, Pastors and People: The Church and Religion in England, 1529–1689*, Macmillan
Harris, T. (1993) *Politics Under the Later Stuarts: Party Conflict in a Divided Society, 1660–1715*, Longman
Harris, T. (2006) *Restoration: Charles II and His Kingdoms, 1660–1685*, Penguin
Harris, T. (2007) *Revolution: The Great Crisis of the British Monarchy, 1685–1720*, Penguin
Hutton, R. (1985) *The Restoration: A Political and Religious History of England and Wales 1658–1667*, Oxford
Hutton, R. (1989) *Charles II*, Oxford
Knights, M. (1994) *Politics and Opinion in Crisis, 1678–1681*, Cambridge University Press
Miller, J. (1988) *The Glorious Revolution*, Longman
Miller, J. (1989) *James II*, Methuen
Miller, J. (1991) *Charles II*, Weidenfeld and Nicolson
Miller, J. (1997) *The Restoration and the England of Charles II*, Longman
Miller, J. (2000) *After the Civil Wars: English Politics and Government in the Reign of Charles II*, Longman
Seaward, P. (1991) *The Restoration, 1660–1668*, Macmillan
Scott, J. (2000) *England's Troubles: Seventeenth-Century English Political Instability in European Context*, Cambridge University Press
Smith, D. L. (1999) *The Stuart Parliaments 1603–1689*, Arnold
Spurr, J. (1991) *The Restoration Church of England, 1646–1689*, Yale
Woolrych, A. (1986) *Commonwealth to Protectorate*, Oxford University Press
Worden, B. (1974) *The Rump Parliament*, Cambridge University Press

Acknowledgements

The author and publisher would like to thank the following for permission to reproduce material:

Source texts:

p2 Kishlansky, M. *A Monarchy Transformed: Britain 1603–1714*, Penguin, 1996. Reprinted with permission of Penguin Books UK. p2 Morrill, J. *The Tudors and Stuarts*, Oxford University Press, 1992. p14 *Calendar of State Papers Domestic 1644–1645*. p15 Young, M. *Charles I*, Palgrave Macmillan, 1997. Reprinted with permission. p17 Ashton, R. *Counter-Revolution: The Second Civil War and its Origins, 1646–8*, Yale University Press, 1994. Reprinted with permission of Yale University Press. p21 Winstanley, G. *The Law of Freedom in a Platform*, 1652. p22 Thomas Rainsborough at the Putney Debates of 1647. p27 (top) Oliver Cromwell to Robert Jenner and John Ashe, 20 November 1648. p27 (bottom) Declaration of the army, 1 August 1650. p28 The Declaration of Many Thousands of the City of Canterbury, or County of Kent 5 January 1648. p29 Kishlansky, M. *A Monarchy Transformed: Britain 1603–1714*, Penguin, 1996. p30 *The Remonstrance*, 1648. p32 *The Charge Against the King*, 1648. p33 Scott, D. *Politics and War in the Three Stuart Kingdoms, 1637–49*, Palgrave Macmillan, 2004. Reprinted with permission of Palgrave Macmillan. p36 Woolrych, A. *Commonwealth to Protectorate*, Clarendon Press, 1986. Reprinted with permission of The Estate of A. Woolrych. p38 Coppe, A. *A Fiery Flying Roll*, 1650. p39 (top) Manning, B. *1649: The Crisis of the English Revolution*, Bookmarks, 1992. Reprinted with permission of the publishers. p39 (middle) Coward, B. *Stuart England 1603–1714*, Longman, 1997. Reprinted with permission of Pearson Education Ltd. p39 (bottom) Morrill, J. *Revolution and Restoration: England in the 1650s*, Collins and Brown, 1992. Reprinted with kind permission of the author. p42 Cromwell's Declaration to the Irish Catholic clergy, January 1650. p46 Barnard, T. *The English Republic*, Longman, 1982. Reprinted with permission of Pearson Education Ltd. p47 Brenner, R. *Merchants and Revolution: Commercial Change, Political Conflict and London's Overseas Traders 1550–1653*, Cambridge University Press, 1993. Reprinted with permission of Cambridge University Press. p53 extract from Lambert's *Instrument*. p59 Hutton, R. *The British Republic 1649–1660*, Palgrave Macmillan, 1990. Reprinted with permission of Palgrave Macmillan. p59 (bottom) Barnard, T. *The English Republic 1649–60*, Longman, 1982. p60 Cromwell, April 1657. p66 (top) Captain William Bradford to Oliver Cromwell, 4 March 1657. p66 (middle) Officer's Petition of 1657 to Cromwell. p70 Bell, M. 'Freedom to Form: the Development of Baptist Movements during the English Revolution' in Durston, C. and J. Maltby (eds.), *Religion in Revolutionary England*, Manchester University Press, 2006. Reprinted with permission of Manchester University Press. p73 McGregor, J. F. 'Seekers and Ranters' in McGregor, J. F. and B. Reay (eds.), *Radical Religion in the English Revolution*, Oxford University Press, 1984. Reprinted with permission of Oxford University Press. p76 *Instrument of Government*, 1653. p78 *The Saints Guide*, 1653. p81 Smith, D. L. 'Oliver Cromwell: A Great Parliamentarian?' in *Cromwelliana*, 1995. Reprinted with kind permission of the author. p88 Capp, B. *Cromwell's Navy: The Fleet and the English Revolution 1648–1660*, 1992. p101 Harris, T. *Politics Under the Later Stuarts: Party Conflict in a Divided Society 1660–1715*, Longman, 1993. Reprinted with permission of Pearson Education Ltd. p108 Speech of the Speaker of the Lords, August 1660. p111 Seaward, P. *The Cavalier Parliament and the Reconstruction of the Old Regime, 1661–1667*, Cambridge University Press, 1989. Reprinted with permission of Cambridge University Press. p113 Harris, T. *Restoration: Charles II and His Kingdoms*, Penguin, 2005. Reprinted with permission of Penguin Books UK. p115 Harris, T. *Restoration: Charles II and His Kingdoms*, Penguin, 2005. Reprinted with permission of Penguin Books UK. p129 Miller, J. *After the Civil Wars: English Politics and Government in the Reign of Charles II*, Longman, 2000. Reprinted by permission of Pearson Education Ltd. p140 Knights, M. *Representation and Misrepresentation in Later Stuart Britain*, Oxford University Press, 2006. Reprinted with permission of Oxford University Press. p142 Miller, J. *After the Civil Wars: English Politics and Government in the Reign of Charles II*, Longman, 2000. Reprinted by permission of Pearson Education Ltd. p153 (middle) Harris, T. *Restoration: Charles II and His Kingdoms*, Penguin, 2005. Reprinted with permission of Penguin Books UK. p153 (bottom) Spurr, J. *England in the 1670s*, Blackwell Publishing, 2001. p154 Smith, D. L. *The Double Crown: A History of the Modern British Isles, 1603–1707*, Blackwell Publishing, 1998. Reprinted with permission. p158 Hutton, R. *Debates in Stuart History*, Palgrave Macmillan, 2004. Reprinted with permission of Palgrave Macmillan. p159 Mullett, M. *James II and English Politics, 1678–1688*, Routledge, 1993. Reprinted by permission of Taylor & Francis Books UK. p164 Harris, T. *Revolution: Charles II and His Kingdoms*, Penguin, 2005. Reprinted with permission of Penguin Books UK. p175 Smith, D. L. *The Stuart Parliaments, 1603–1689*, Hodder Arnold, 1999. Reprinted with permission of Edward Arnold (Publishers) Ltd. p177 Scott, J. *England's Troubles: Seventeenth-Century Political Instability in European Context*, Cambridge University Press, 2000. Reprinted with permission of Cambridge University Press.

Photographs courtesy of:

Ann Ronan Picture Library 29, 30, 44, 69, 84, 88, 90, 112, 118, 119, 140, 146, 147; Bridgeman Art Library 9, 15, 32, 78, 80; Edimedia Archive 4, 34, 97, 102, 135, 148, 157, 160, 163, 164, 168, 176; Literature Archive [The] 20, 40 (top), 40 (middle), 43, 45, 55, 57; Photo12 52, 104, 117 (top), 117 (bottom); Public Domain 16, 23, 50, 53, 107, 111 (bottom); Sante Archive [The] 111 (top); Topfoto 25, 47; World History Archive 2, 11, 12, 13 (top), 13 (bottom), 19, 22, 33, 37, 42, 54, 61, 73, 103, 129, 174.

Cover photograph: courtesy of Geoff Buxton/The Sealed Knot

Photo research by Unique Dimension, www.uniquedimension.com

The publishers have made every effort to trace the copyright holders, but if they have inadvertently overlooked any, they will be pleased to make the necessary arrangements at the first opportunity.

Index